P9-EDJ-515

The Art and Science of Portraiture

The Art and Science
of Portraiture

Sara Lawrence-Lightfoot
Jessica Hoffmann Davis

Jossey-Bass Publishers
San Francisco

Substantial discounts on bulk quantities of Jossey-Bass books
are available to corporations, professional associations, and
other organizations. For details and discount information, contact the special sales department at Jossey-Bass Inc., Publishers
(415) 433–1740; Fax (800) 605–2665.

For sales outside the United States, please contact your local
Simon & Schuster International office.

Jossey-Bass Web address: http://www.josseybass.com

Manufactured in the United States of America on acid-free,
recycled paper that contains a minimum of
20 percent post-consumer waste.

Library of Congress Cataloging-in-Publication Data
Lawrence-Lightfoot, Sara, date.
The art and science of portraiture / Sara Lawrence-Lightfoot,
Jessica Hoffmann Davis. — 1st ed.
p. cm.
Includes bibliographical references and index.
ISBN 0-7879-1064-3 (cloth)
1. Social sciences—Research.   2. Social sciences—Methodology.
3. Portraits—Social aspects.   4. Art and society.   5. Art and
science.   I. Davis, Jessica Hoffmann, date.   II. Title.
H62.L33 1997
300′.72—dc21   97-4902

FIRST EDITION

HB Printing   10 9 8 7 6 5 4 3 2 1

CONTENTS

THE AUTHORS

Sara Lawrence-Lightfoot, a sociologist, is a professor of education at Harvard University. She did her undergraduate work in psychology at Swarthmore College (1962–66), studied child development and teaching at Bank Street College of Education (1966–67), and did her doctoral work in sociology of education at Harvard (1968–72). Since joining the Harvard faculty in 1972, she has been interested in studying the schools as social systems, the patterns and structures of classroom life, the relationships between adult developmental themes and teachers' work, and socialization within families, communities, and schools.

Lawrence-Lightfoot is a prolific author of articles, monographs, and chapters. She has written five books, including *Worlds Apart: Relationships Between Families and Schools* (1978), *Beyond Bias: Perspectives on Classrooms* (1979) (with Jean Carew), and *The Good High School: Portraits of Character and Culture* (1983), which received the 1984 Outstanding Book Award from the American Educational Research Association. Her book *Balm in Gilead: Journey of a Healer* (1988) won the 1988 Christopher Award, given for "literary merit and humanitarian achievement." Lawrence-Lightfoot's most recent book is *I've Known Rivers: Lives of Loss and Liberation* (1994).

In addition to her teaching, research, and writing, she sits on numerous professional committees and boards of directors, including the National Academy of Education, the *Boston Globe,* and the John D. and Catherine T. MacArthur Foundation. Lawrence-Lightfoot has been a fellow at the Bunting Institute at

Radcliffe College and at the Center for Advanced Study in the Behavioral Sciences at Stanford University. In 1984, she was the recipient of the prestigious MacArthur Prize Award, and in 1993 she was awarded Harvard's George Ledlie Prize, which is given for research that makes the "most valuable contribution to science" and that "benefits mankind." Lawrence-Lightfoot has been the recipient of over a dozen honorary doctoral degrees from colleges and universities in the United States and Canada. In 1993, the Sara Lawrence-Lightfoot Chair, an endowed professorship established at Swarthmore College, was named in her honor.

Jessica Hoffmann Davis is a lecturer on education and the founding director of the Arts in Education Concentration at the Harvard Graduate School of Education. She is a cognitive developmental psychologist whose research addresses the gift, fragility, and promise of artistic capacities throughout the life span. As a principal investigator at Harvard Project Zero, Davis has just completed two broad-based multiyear national research initiatives addressing arts learning beyond school walls. In Project Co-Arts, she led an investigation of educational effectiveness in urban community art centers, and in Project MUSE (Museums Uniting with Schools in Education), an exploration of teaching and learning in and through art museums. Her research is informed by her experience both as a teacher and practitioner in the visual arts.

Davis received both her master's and doctor of education degrees from Harvard University, and her bachelor of arts degree in English from Simmons College after three years of classical education at St. John's College. She has served as an at-risk youth task force advisor to the President's Committee on the Arts and Humanities and a co-director of the arts and humanities children's initiative of the American Academy of Arts and Sciences. Davis has published numerous articles, monographs, and book chapters on the subject of artistic development and education. She has a persistent belief that arts learning should be part of every child's daily life at school.

ACKNOWLEDGMENTS

The idea for this volume was spawned one morning over breakfast at beautiful Squam Lake. For years our partners had patiently listened to (and occasionally participated in) the "portraiture" talk between us. In an act of keen insight and strategic self-defense, Irving Hamer suggested that we write a book together that might echo and refine the long and vigorous conversations that had punctuated our times together. It was a challenge that we ultimately could not resist. We thank Irving Hamer for his inspiration and provocation; and we thank Will Davis for his generous and gentle forbearance.

For the last dozen years Sara Lawrence-Lightfoot has taught a graduate seminar on the methodology of portraiture that has clarified her thinking, honed her discipline, and engaged her imagination. She is indebted to all of her students, whose critique and challenge have helped her develop her tools, her perspective, and her authority. In adapting the methods of portraiture for use by an ensemble of researchers, Jessica Hoffmann Davis has been supported by the fine work and rigorous inquiry of her colleagues and students. She is ever grateful for the courage and perseverance of the original Co-Arts team and for the enthusiasm and talents of portraitists who followed their lead. She celebrates with appreciation the glittering gifts of her primary research assistant, Elisabeth Soep.

We greatly appreciate the efforts of two associates who were part of our collaboration from the beginning. David Greene, our research assistant, brought his sophisticated knowledge of research rituals and design, his energetic detective work, and his deft professionalism to our project. Wendy Elisabeth Angus, Sara's wondrous assistant, offered her great technical skills, her discerning mind, and her generosity of spirit. We are also indebted to our editor, Lesley Iura, for her perceptive and sage counsel. Throughout this volume we use excerpted illustrations from three of our earlier works: *The Good High School, Safe Havens,* and *I've Known Rivers*, revisiting the portraits of people and institutions whose lives and cultures were recorded in them. We are doubly thankful to the "subjects" of these earlier portraits for their courage and candor in telling their stories and sharing their perspectives. The work of Project Co-Arts was made possible by the Nathan Cummings, Geraldine R. Dodge, and Ford Foundations as well as the Andy Warhol Foundation for the Visual Arts and the Alexander Julian Foundation for Aesthetic Understanding.

Finally, we would like to thank the Spencer Foundation for its generous support of our work and for its genuine interest in the development and articulation of diverse and pioneering methodologies that capture the complex dimensions of teaching, learning, and development.

Cambridge, Massachusetts   Sara Lawrence-Lightfoot
May 1997   Jessica Hoffmann Davis

For
Irving Hamer and Will Davis,
whose voices, insights, witness,
and love
turn our duet into
a rich and colorful
quartet.

INTRODUCTION:
THE FRAME

Sara Lawrence-Lightfoot

This volume draws the contours of *social science portraiture,* a genre of inquiry and representation that seeks to join science and art. Portraiture is a method of qualitative research that blurs the boundaries of aesthetics and empiricism in an effort to capture the complexity, dynamics, and subtlety of human experience and organizational life. Portraitists seek to record and interpret the perspectives and experience of the people they are studying, documenting their voices and their visions—their authority, knowledge, and wisdom. The drawing of the portrait is placed in social and cultural context and shaped through dialogue between the portraitist and the subject, each one negotiating the discourse and shaping the evolving image. The relationship between the two is rich with meaning and resonance and becomes the arena for navigating the empirical, aesthetic, and ethical dimensions of authentic and compelling narrative.

In the pages of this volume we illuminate the origins, purposes, and features of portraiture, placing it within the larger discourse on social science inquiry and mapping it onto the broader terrain of qualitative research. We delineate the processes, methods, and strategies of research design, data collection, and analysis, underscoring the structure and the improvisation, the order and the creativity. We also chart the development of the portrait and the shaping of the narrative, blending literary principles, artistic resonance, and scientific rigor. *The Art and Science of Portraiture,* then, is a book about boundary crossing. In defining concepts and describing the methods of portraiture, we navigate borders that typically separate disciplines, purposes, and audiences in the social sciences—bridging aesthetics and empiricism, appealing to intellect and emotion, seeking to inform and inspire, and joining the endeavors of documentation, interpretation, and intervention.*

Our collaboration as coauthors of this work is itself a conversation across boundaries. Lawrence-Lightfoot, a sociologist, ethnographer, and biographer, invented portraiture as described here and has used it to document the culture of schools, the life stories of individuals, and the relationships among families, communities, and schools. Davis, a cognitive psychologist, is an authority on the development of artistry and herself a student of the visual arts; she has used portraiture to study community art centers and adapted the methods for use by a group of researchers. In this volume, we highlight the contrasts in our perspectives by using two voices: the voices of a sociologist and a psychologist, an organizational and cultural analyst and a human developmentalist, an innovator and an adaptor, a writer of narrative and a creator of visual expression.

The opening chapters define the frameworks, experiences, and perspectives that each of us brings to this work. In Chapter One, Lawrence-Lightfoot speaks about the autobiographical and intellectual roots of portraiture, declaring its uniqueness in the realm of social science inquiry while drawing on historical antecedents that reach as far back as the eighteenth century. She also explores the voice of portraiture as counterpoint to the dominant chorus of social scientists whose methods and goals have been greatly influenced by the positivist paradigm, whose focus has largely centered on the identification and documentation of social problems, and whose audiences have been mostly limited to the academy. Portraiture, on the other hand, is framed by the phenomenological lens; it seeks to illuminate the complex dimensions of *goodness* and is designed to capture the attention of a broad and eclectic audience.

In Chapter Two, Davis traces her predilection for and experience with portraiture and considers the aesthetic aspects of the methodology in terms of a cognitive approach to artistic production and perception. She looks specifically at the generative boundary crossing between the visual arts and empirical portraiture, underscoring the similar sources of illumination, expression, and impact. In addition, Davis examines the equally important and enduring boundary that is usually drawn between the innocent beauty and expression found in children's art and the sophisticated, premeditated renderings of adult profes-

---

* As women writing together about a research genre that we have created and pioneered, we take the liberty throughout this book of referring to portraitists and researchers using portraiture in the feminine gender. Of course, we encourage men and welcome them into the field, and we honor their work, but it simplifies the task of writing to use one set of pronouns.

sional artists. She quotes Picasso's poignant statement, which becomes the ironic litany for this volume: "I painted all my life like Raphael so that one day I could paint again like a child."

The opening chapters, then, convey our histories, our values, and our orientations, revealing the contrasts between our perspectives and the richness of our collaboration. Chapters Three through Seven examine the five essential features of portraiture: Context, Voice, Relationship, Emergent Themes, and Aesthetic Whole. In exploring the conceptual themes and methods of each feature, we continue to speak in two voices. In the first section of each chapter, "Illumination," Lawrence-Lightfoot examines the feature's dimensions and function, offering a conceptual understanding of its origins and expression, comparing it to the ways the concepts are used in other research realms, and underscoring key strategies for interpreting the feature in the process of data collection, analysis, and narrative development.

In the section that follows, "Implementation," Davis describes practical structures, schemata, and methods for engaging the *process* of portraiture (collecting and interpreting data) and rendering the *product* (the portrait). She emphasizes the ongoing dialectic between process and product that is emblematic of portraiture. She focuses, in particular, on describing the ways in which the methods of portraiture are altered and recreated to respond to and embrace the differences among a group of researchers. When portraiture becomes a collaborative (rather than an individual) endeavor—when researchers use a group voice—different challenges and opportunities arise that require the development of rigorous structures and unison processes.

Finally, each chapter concludes with a brief "Artistic Refrain" written by Davis and illustrated with the drawings of children and professional artists. The drawings echo themes from the earlier conceptual and methodological discussions. Comparing these child and adult images helps us understand the convergence and the contrasts between the work of visual artists and narrative portraitists. We discover the rigor and discipline of creating art and the creativity and improvisation that enrich the research of portraitists.

Picasso's portrait *"Girl Before a Mirror,"* which graces the cover of this volume, captures many of the aesthetic and empirical themes that thread their way through our book. The girl looks in the mirror and does not see her likeness. Instead, she comes face to face with a more penetrating image—one that is both revelatory and disturbing. She does not see the literal portrayal that she expects, the smiling prettiness that she anticipates. Rather she perceives, in the refracted forms and surprising colors, a deeper, more authentic reflection of who she is. She sees, and reaches out to, her essence. In *The Art and Science of Portraiture,* through documentation, interpretation, analysis, and narrative, we raise the mirror, hoping—with accuracy and discipline—to capture the mystery and artistry that turn image into essence.

The Art and Science of Portraiture

Tête de Jeune Fille 4th state
16 March 1949

CHAPTER ONE

A VIEW OF THE WHOLE

Origins and Purposes

Sara Lawrence-Lightfoot

*A primary function of art and thought is to liberate
the individual from the tyranny of culture.*
—Lionel Trilling 多制·暴汉

For as far back as I can recall, I have been drawn to the liberating and transcendent power of art—the music that makes my heart sing, the poetry that soothes my soul, the dance that releases my rage, the novel that takes me to distant lands and brings me home, and the painting that offers me a new angle of vision. And for most of my adult life, I have had a deep respect for the rigor and discipline of science. I have admired the rules of design and the rituals of methodology, and have been engaged by the process of intellectual debate informed by evidence and argumentation. I have been both challenged by, and devoted to, the search for authenticity and authority, for resonance and truth. "Portraiture" has become the bridge that has brought these two worlds together for me, allowing for both contrast and coexistence, counterpoint and harmony in my scholarship and writing, and allowing me to see clearly the art in the development of science and the science in the making of art.

For more than a dozen years I have been laboring over the development and refinement of "portraiture," the term I use for a method of inquiry and documentation in the social sciences. With it, I seek to combine systematic, empirical description with aesthetic expression, blending art and science, humanistic sensibilities and scientific rigor. The portraits are designed to capture the richness, complexity, and dimensionality of human experience in social and cultural context, conveying the perspectives of the people who are negotiating those experiences. The portraits are shaped through dialogue between the portraitist and the subject, each one participating in the drawing of the image. The encounter between the two is rich with meaning and resonance and is crucial to the success and authenticity of the rendered piece.

My story of invention begins with this central encounter, experienced first as the subject of a portrait (actually many portraits rendered in various materials—pastels, oils, stained glass, clay). It is a story that can only be told in retrospect because it seemed to evolve as much out of intuition, autobiography, and serendipity as it did from purposeful intention. In *The Good High School* (1983), I describe two inspirational and provocative encounters—the first when I was a child of eight, the second when I was in my mid-twenties. The former was a swift sketch in pastels as I sat in my mother's rock garden, and the latter a laborious, carefully crafted oil painting that took several weeks to complete in an artist's studio. Despite the great differences in these experiences, I learned many of the same lessons about the power of the medium, about the relationship between artist and subject, and about the perspective of the person whose image and essence is being captured. These were my first methodological lessons.

I learned, for example, that these portraits did not capture me as I saw myself; that they were not like looking in the mirror at my reflection. Instead they seemed to capture my essence—qualities of character and history some of which I was unaware of, some of which I resisted mightily, some of which felt deeply familiar. But the translation of image was anything but literal. It was probing, layered, and interpretive. In addition to portraying my image, the piece expressed the perspective of the artist and was shaped by the evolving relationship between the artist and me. I also recognized that in searching for the essence, in moving beyond the surface image, the artist was both generous and tough, both skeptical and receptive. I was never treated or seen as object, but always as a person of strength and vulnerability, beauty and imperfection, mystery and openness. The artist needed to be vigilant in capturing the image, but always watchful of my feelings, perspective, and experience. I learned, as well, that the portraits expressed a haunting paradox, of a moment in time and of timelessness. In the portrait of the young woman, for example, I could see myself at twenty-five, but I could also see my ancestors and the children in my future. Time seemed to move through this still and silent portrait of a woman, rendering the piece—now twenty-five years later—both anachronistic and contemporary. It is still a vital document of who I am (and who I may become), even if it no longer looks like me.

More than a decade later, when I was searching for a form of inquiry that might capture the complexity and aesthetic of human experience, I had the benefit of those early experiences as an artist's subject from which to develop my methodological tools. In trying to create what I called "life drawings" of high schools and trace the connections between individual personality and organizational culture, I felt the echoes of being on the other side of the artist's palette. I wanted to develop a document, a text that came as close as possible to painting with words. I wanted to create a narrative that bridged the realms of science and art, merging the systematic and careful description of good ethnography with the evocative resonance of fine literature. I wanted the written pieces to convey the authority, wisdom, and perspective of the subjects, but I wanted them to feel—as I had felt—that the portrait did not look like them, but somehow managed to reveal their essence. I wanted them to experience the portraits as both familiar and exotic, so that in reading them they would be introduced to a perspective that they had not considered before. And finally, I wanted the subjects to feel *seen* as I had felt seen—fully attended to, recognized, appreciated, respected, scrutinized. I wanted them to feel both the discovery and the generosity of the process, as well as the penetrating and careful investigation. Inevitably, I knew these would be documents of inquiry *and* intervention, hopefully leading toward new understandings and insights, as well as instigating change.

But beyond the echoes of my early experience as an artist's subject, which got interpreted into my stance toward inquiry, I was also influenced—however subliminally—by a long arc of work, reaching back two centuries, that joined art and science. So when I speak about my invention of portraiture, I am not claiming that this form of inquiry and representation is all mine, or all new. There is a long and rich history of dialogue and collaboration between artists and scholars, between novelists and philosophers. As a matter of fact, the intersection of fiction and social science has occurred since at least the eighteenth century, when these two approaches to the study of life began to emerge from similar impulses and express common themes. Philosophers turned from closed systems of thought—where they sought the purity and elegance of rationality and logic—to discerning observations of the world around them, which often recorded the messy chaos and illogic of reality. Writers of fiction, as Samuel Johnson remarked in 1750, turned to "that experience which can never be attained by solitary diligence, but must arise from general converse and accurate observation of the living world" (Williams, 1970, p. 143).

Novelists and philosophers began to read each other; Rousseau and Diderot wrote both novels and treatises. Their motivations became intertwined, their purposes fused. Novelists and social scientists began to strive for a closeness to life, seeking to capture the texture and nuance of human experience. But both artists and scientists recognized the limits of their media, their inability to capture and present the total reality. Their purpose, then, became not complete and full representation, but rather the selection of some aspect of—or angle on—reality that would transform our vision of the whole. Both artists and scientists hoped that their choice of views, their shaping of perspective, would allow their readers to experience the whole differently.

We hear echoes of this integration of art and science in the history of clinical work as well, in work whose purpose it has been to intervene, to help, and to heal. In his wonderful book, *The Man Who Mistook His Wife for a Hat* (1985), neurologist Oliver Sacks extols the combining of narrative and science in the "richly human clinical tales" (p. viii) that dominated neurological medicine and reached their peak during the nineteenth century. This clinical storytelling—the "intersection of fact and fable" (p. ix)—declined as neurological science became increasingly routinized, codified, and impersonal. The efforts to increase the rigor and the *science* led to caricatures and distortions in seeing, hearing, and healing the patient, in defining the doctor-patient relationship, and in identifying points of intervention and sources of strength leading to the patient's recovery. Sacks's book, therefore, is an earnest and intelligent effort to recapture the marriage of science and art, "to harken back to an ancient tradition . . . of the first medical historian, Hippocrates, and to that universal and prehistorical tradition by which patients have always told their stories to doctors" (p. viii). Sacks feels "compelled to speak of tales . . . the scientific and romantic cry out in such realms to come together" (p. ix).

Closer to the traditions and rituals of social science we also find a lively and rich history of resisting the tyranny that Lionel Trilling refers to, by embracing the intersection of aesthetics and empiricism. At the turn of the century, William James—whose family and writings spanned both realms—spoke about the younger generation's resistance to the reign of logic and abstraction and their determination (and I think his) to discover forms of representation that would capture the fluidity and complexity of the living world.

> It is difficult not to notice a curious unrest in the philosophic atmosphere of the time, a loosening of old landmarks, a softening of oppositions, a mutual borrowing from one another on the part of systems anciently closed, and an interest in new suggestions, however vague, as if the one thing sure were the inadequacy of the extant school-solutions. The dissatisfaction with these seems due for the most part to feeling that they are too abstract and academic. Life is confused and superabundant and what the younger generation appears to crave is more of the temperament of life in its philosophy, even tho it were at some cost of logical rigor of formal purity [1904, p. 52].

Thirty years later, John Dewey echoed James's admiration of boundary crossing and improvisation, the desire to push beyond the narrow cannons and abstractions of science in order to represent reality. Focused on life in schools, Dewey's classic *Art as Experience* (1934/1958) underscored the need not only to capture the cognitive, social, and affective dimensions of educational encounters, but also to find frameworks and strategies for representing the aesthetics of teaching and learning. If we wanted education to be artful—beautiful not merely pretty, creative not merely competent, discovery not merely mimicry— then, suggested Dewey, we would have to find ways of envisioning and recording the experience that would not distort its texture and richness. This would require joining aesthetic and empirical approaches, merging rigor and improvisation, and appreciating both the details and the gestalt. Dewey referred to the arts—to music, poetry, drama, and painting—to illustrate his views regarding the representation of social reality.

The reciprocal interpretation of parts and whole, which we
have seen to constitute a work of art, is effected when all the
constituents of the work, whether picture, drama, poem, or
building, stand in rhythmic connection with all other members
of the same kind—line with line, color with color, space with
space, illuminative with light and shade in a painting—and all
of these distinctive factors reinforce one another as variations
that build up an integrated complex experience.

But . . . there is a tendency to limit rhythm to some one
phase of an art product, for instance, to tempo in music, lines
in painting, meter in poetry, to flattened or smooth curves in
sculpture. Such limitation always tends in the direction of what
Bosanquet called 'easy beauty' and when carried through
logically, whether in theory or practice, results in some matter
being left without form and some form being arbitrarily
imposed upon matter [1934/1958, p. 171].

More recent scholars have cultivated this fertile ground and merged the
realms of art and science in an effort to represent the nuance and complexity
of the whole, in an effort to speak about things that resist reductionism and
abstraction, in an effort to challenge the tyranny of the academy, and in an
effort to build bridges between theory and practice, research and action. In
his wide-ranging eclecticism, W.E.B. DuBois was the quintessential boundary-
crosser. More than any other social scientist I can think of, in his work and in
his life, DuBois captured the interdisciplinary as he moved from social philosophy to empirical sociology to autobiography to political essays to poetry
and literature to social activism. He invented a way of being, a point of view,
a style of work that quite naturally, dynamically, organically integrated science, art, history, and activism. In his biography of DuBois, Arnold Rampersod spoke about his extraordinary integration of science and art as being
shaped and illuminated by his powerful imagination. Rampersod sketched
DuBois' paradigm:

For DuBois, Imagination meant above all the vision of Unity.
Because he was born into a divided world, where Race was
set apart from Race—be they Anglo-Saxon, African, Celtic—
the vision of Racial Unity became the first tableau projected
by Imagination. But racial unity was only an insistence of the
will to harmony generated by his free mind. DuBois declined
to see a separation between Science and Art, believing that such
a distinction violated the integrity of intelligence, which could
set no wall between one fundamental form of knowledge and
another, since all belonged to the world of nature, of Truth. . . .

> He devoted himself to a knowledge of this world equal to the
> power of his mind to imagine a better one. Science—social
> science, historical science, the daily observation of persons,
> places, events—became the mast to which the sail of the
> imaginary was lashed [1976, pp. 65–66].

Anthropologist Clifford Geertz (1973) also speaks about imagination as being a crucial ingredient in the drawing of cultures. He links imagination and interpretation in his depiction of what he calls "thick description" (p. 6), "the researcher's constructions of other people's constructions of what they are up to" (p. 9). But in addition to his emphasis on the interpretation at the heart of thick description, Geertz underscores the "creative," the imaginative "tableau." He claims that anthropological writings are "fictions" (p. 15), something made, something fashioned, and he likens his ethnographic work to the task of painting a likeness. "The line between the mode of representation and substantive content is as undrawable in cultural analysis as it is in painting" (p. 16). We must then, Geertz says, admit (maybe even celebrate) the fact that the "researcher's imagination" is a fundamental aspect of cultural depiction. "It is not against a body of uninterpreted data . . . that we must measure the cogency of our explications," he writes, "but against the power of scientific imagination to bring us in touch with the lives of strangers" (p. 16). But in admitting the centrality of interpretation, imagination, and creativity, we must not be misled. These "humanistic" dimensions must always be in close communion with rigorous and systematic attention to the details of social reality and human experience. Behavior, interaction, encounter, and gesture must be attended to with exactness, and retained, "because it is through the flow of behavior—or more precisely of social action—that cultural forms find articulation" (p. 17).

It was against this colorful historic canvas—from Rousseau to James to Dewey to DuBois to Geertz—that I began to draw the artistic and scientific forms that overlapped to shape my version of social science portraiture. I was not only inspired by this long legacy, but also by my resistance to many of the dominant canons and preoccupations of social science. I was concerned, for example, about the general tendency of social scientists to focus their investigations on pathology and disease rather than on health and resilience. This general propensity is magnified in the research on education and schooling, where investigators have been much more vigilant in documenting failure than they have been in describing examples of success.

To some extent the focus on pathology is understandable, maybe even laudable. Certainly some investigators have identified things that do not work, or work poorly, as a prelude to trying to figure out ways of fixing what is broken. In this case, social scientists have regarded their investigations as providing the evidence for better-informed and strategic social action. But the relentless scrutiny of failure has many unfortunate and distorting results. First, we begin to get a view of our social world that magnifies what is wrong and neglects evidence of promise and potential. Second, this focus on failure can often lead to a kind of cynicism and inaction. If things are really this bad and there is no hope for change, then why try to do anything about it? Third, the documentation of pathology often bleeds into a blaming of the victim. Rather than a complicated analysis of the coexistence of strengths and vulnerabilities (usually evident in any person, institution, or society), the locus of blame tends to rest on the shoulders of those most victimized and least powerful in defining their identity or shaping their fate. Fourth, the focus on pathology seems to encourage facile inquiry. It is, after all, much easier to identify a disease and count its victims than it is to characterize and document health. The former requires focused methodologies that have been well used and developed, the latter invites a more complicated and eclectic set of research tools and some pathbreaking paradigms.

Portraiture resists this tradition-laden effort to document failure. It is an intentionally generous and eclectic process that begins by searching for what is good and healthy and assumes that the expression of goodness will always be laced with imperfections. The researcher who asks first "what is good here?" is likely to absorb a very different reality than the one who is on a mission to discover the sources of failure. But it is also important to say that portraits are not designed to be documents of idealization or celebration. In examining the dimensionality and complexity of goodness there will, of course, be ample evidence of vulnerability and weakness. In fact, the counterpoint and contradictions of strength and vulnerability, virtue and evil (and how people, cultures, and organizations negotiate those extremes in an effort to establish the precarious balance between them) are central to the expression of goodness.

Not only do portraits seek to capture the origins and expression of goodness, they are also concerned with documenting how the *subjects* or actors in the setting define goodness. The portraitist does not impose her definition of "good" on the inquiry, or assume that there is a singular definition shared by all (this is not the case of the expert researcher defining the criteria of success or effectiveness and using that as the standard of judgment). Rather the portraitist believes that there are myriad ways in which goodness can be expressed and tries to identify and document the actors' perspectives.

In addition to my concern for developing a methodological stance that might record the complex evidence of goodness, I also wanted to reshape the relationship between researcher and audience. More specifically, I was concerned with broadening the audience for my work, with communicating beyond the walls of the academy. Academicians tend to speak to one another in a language that is often opaque and esoteric. Rarely do the analyses and texts we produce invite dialogue with people in the "real world." Instead, academic documents—even those that focus on issues of broad public concern—

are read by a small audience of people in the same disciplinary field, who often share similar conceptual frameworks and rhetoric. The formulaic structure of the written pieces—research question, data collection and analysis, interpretation, policy implications—is meant to inform, not inspire.

With its focus on narrative, with its use of metaphor and symbol, portraiture intends to address wider, more eclectic audiences. The attempt is to move beyond academy's inner circle, to speak in a language that is not coded or exclusive, and to develop texts that will seduce the readers into thinking more deeply about issues that concern them. Portraitists write to inform and inspire readers. In Clifford Geertz's terminology, portraits are designed to "deepen the conversation" (1973, p. 29).

In a penetrating essay reviewing the purposes and values of portraiture, Joseph Featherstone (1989) links the private, intimate storytelling at its center with the public discourse that it hopes to influence. He connects the voices of the storytellers, the narrator, and the audience, and draws the continuum between "analysis and solidarity." The power of portraiture, he claims, lies in its explicitly humanistic impulse. It embraces both analytic rigor (a perspective that is distant, discerning, and skeptical) and community building (acts of intimacy and connection). Featherstone calls this "a people's scholarship"—a scholarship in which "scientific facts gathered in the field give voice to a people's experience."

> There is much more to this business of creating portraits and telling stories. It is a quest for something missing from a good deal of popular scholarship in education and other realms . . . we hear the sound of a human voice making sense of other voices, especially those not often heard, voices of women and of people of color. We trace the line of a story set in a historical context, placing the actors in a long-running moral and political drama. The text itself enacts the writer's deepest moral and political values, the eclecticism of method and material. What if this kind of work were to become more prevalent? What are the implications of a kind of scholarship in education that combines the distancing power of analysis with another kind of power, the deep gesture of solidarity. . . . Surely analysis and solidarity could stand as two poles of scholarship. Much research has neglected the second, studying teachers, for example, as though they were fruit flies. . . . It is in the quest of the power that comes from looking beyond the isolation at the little difference there is between humans, and the supreme importance of that difference. It searches for the energizing shock of sympathy and of human community [pp. 375–376].

But deepening the conversation and broadening the audience are not only acts of analysis and solidarity. They are also inevitably acts of intervention. In the process of creating portraits, we enter people's lives, build relationships, engage in discourse, make an imprint . . . and leave. We engage in acts (implicit and explicit) of social transformation, we create opportunities for dialogue, we pursue the silences, and in the process, we face ethical dilemmas and a great moral responsibility. This is provocative work that can disturb the natural rhythms of social reality and encounter. This is exciting work that can instigate positive and productive change. Again, Featherstone appreciates the benign, generous impact of portraiture, even as he recognizes the huge, ethical responsibilities weighing on the portraitist.

> The telling of stories can be a profound form of scholarship moving serious study close to the frontiers of art in the capacity to express complex truth and moral context in intelligible ways. . . . *The Good High School* utilizes portraiture to argue against today's top-down reformers. It reminds us that the creation of a learning community is an essential feature of successful schools. Community, in this context, suggests the power of the local actors on the scene to create conversations and find shared meanings, the significance of the voices of teachers, and the crucial importance of local context, as well as the commitment of a scholar to truth and solidarity. The methodologies are inseparable from the vision. Historians have used narrative as a way in which to make sense of lives and institutions over time, but over the years they have grown abashed about its lack of scientific rigor. Now, as we look for ways to explore context and describe the thick textures of lives over time in institutions with a history, we want to reckon with the author's own stance and commitment to the people being written about. Storytelling takes on a fresh importance [Featherstone, 1989, p. 377].

The portrait, then, creates a narrative that is at once complex, provocative, and inviting, that attempts to be holistic, revealing the dynamic interaction of values, personality, structure, and history. And the narrative documents human behavior and experience in context. In fact, the portraitist insists that the only way to interpret people's actions, perspectives, and talk is to see them in context. Of course, this approach contrasts greatly with traditional perspectives in social science, which mimic the positivist paradigms of mathematics and physics. The positivist sees context as potentially distorting, a source of distraction and confusion. To reliably document human experience, positivists want to see it clearly, purely, abstracted from the setting. The laboratory experiment, for example, is the prototype of this approach; the investigator creates conditions that permit analysis of the phenomena under study separate from the messiness and complexity of the natural environment. Portraitists—like their cousins in anthropology—start with a counter proposition. Rather than viewing context as a source of distortion, they see it as a resource for understanding. The narrative, then, is always embedded in a particular context, including physical settings, cultural rituals, norms, and values, and historical periods. The context is rich in cues about how the actors or subjects negotiate and understand their experience.

But the portraitist is interested not only in producing complex, subtle description in context but also in searching for the central story, developing a convincing and authentic narrative. This requires careful, systematic, and detailed description developed through watching, listening to, and interacting with the actors over a sustained period of time, the tracing and interpretation of emergent themes, and the piecing together of these themes into an aesthetic whole. The process of creating a whole often feels like weaving a tapestry or piecing together a quilt. Looking for points of thematic convergence is like searching for the patterns of texture and color in a weaving. In creating the text, the portraitist is alert to the aesthetic principles of composition and form, rhythm, sequence, and metaphor. The portraitist's standard, then, is one of *authenticity*, capturing the essence and resonance of the actors' experience and perspective through the details of action and thought revealed in context.

This process of creating the narrative requires a difficult (sometimes paradoxical) vigilance to empirical description *and* aesthetic expression. It is a careful deliberative process and a highly creative one. The data must be scrutinized carefully, searching for the story line that emerges from the material. However, there is never a single story—many could be told. So the portraitist is active in selecting the themes that will be used to tell the story, strategic in deciding on points of focus and emphasis, and creative in defining the sequence and rhythm of the narrative. What gets left out is often as important as what gets included; the blank spaces and the silences also shape the form of the story. For the portraitist, then, there is a crucial dynamic between documenting and creating the narrative, between receiving and shaping, reflecting and imposing, mirroring and improvising. The effort to reach coherence must flow organically both from the data and from the interpretive witness of the portraitist.

In her exquisite autobiographical account, *One Writer's Beginnings* (1983), Eudora Welty makes a subtle but crucial distinction between listening *to* a story and listening *for* a story (p. 14). The former is a more passive, receptive stance in which one waits to absorb the information and does little to give it shape and form. The latter is a much more active, engaged position in which one searches for the story, seeks it out, is central in its creation. This does not mean that one directs the drama or constructs the scenes. It *does* mean that one participates in identifying and selecting the story, and helps to shape the story's coherence and aesthetic. Welty's distinction identifies one of the key contrasts between ethnography and portraiture. Ethnographers listen *to* a story while portraitists listen *for* a story.

The identity, character, and history of the researcher are obviously critical to the manner of listening, selecting, interpreting, and composing the story. Portraiture admits the central and creative role of the *self* of the portraitist. It is, of course, true that all researchers—whether working within the quantitative or qualitative methodological paradigms—are selective in defining and shaping the data they collect and the interpretations that flow from their findings. Even the most scrupulously "objective" investigations reveal the hand of the researcher in shaping the inquiry. From deciding what is important to study to selecting the central questions to defining the nature and size of the sample to developing the methodological strategies, the predisposition and perspective of the researcher is crucial, and this perspective reflects not only a theoretical, disciplinary, and methodological stance, but also personal values, tastes, and style. The shaping hand of the investigator is counterbalanced by the skepticism and scrutiny that is the signature of good research. Through rigorous procedures and methodological tools the researcher tries to rid the work of personal bias that might distort or obscure the reality of the subject matter. So at the center of all research, the investigator needs to manage the tension between personal predisposition (more or less explicitly recognized and expressed) and rigorous skepticism.

With portraiture, the person of the researcher—even when vigorously controlled—is more evident and more visible than in any other research form. She is seen not only in defining the focus and field of the inquiry, but also in navigating the relationships with the subjects, in witnessing and interpreting the action, in tracing the emergent themes, and in creating the narrative. At each one of these stages, the self of the portraitist emerges as an instrument of inquiry, an eye on perspective-taking, an ear that discerns nuances, and a voice that speaks and offers insights. Indeed, the voice of the portraitist often helps us identify her place in the inquiry. Even though the identity and voice of the portraitist is larger and more explicit in this form of inquiry, the efforts to balance personal predisposition with disciplined skepticism and critique are central to the portrait's success. One might even say that *because* the self of the portraitist is so essential to the development of the work she must be that much more vigilant about identifying other sources of challenge to her perspective. The counterintuitive must always be present even as the portraitist takes full advantage of the intuitive.

In summary, portraiture is a method framed by the traditions and values of the phenomenological paradigm, sharing many of the techniques, standards, and goals of ethnography. But it pushes against the constraints of those traditions and practices in its explicit effort to combine empirical and aesthetic description, in its focus on the convergence of narrative and analysis, in its goal of speaking to broader audiences beyond the academy (thus linking inquiry to public discourse and social transformation), in its standard of authenticity rather than reliability and validity (the traditional standards of quantitative and qualitative inquiry), and in its explicit recognition of the use of the self as the primary research instrument for documenting and interpreting the perspectives and experiences of the people and the cultures being studied.

Not only is the portraitist interested in developing a narrative that is both convincing and authentic, she is also interested in recording the subtle details of human experience. She wants to capture the specifics, the nuance, the detailed description of a thing, a gesture, a voice, an attitude as a way of illuminating more universal patterns. A persistent irony—recognized and celebrated by novelists, poets, playwrights—is that as one moves closer to the unique characteristics of a person or a place, one discovers the universal. Again Eudora Welty (1983) offers a wonderful insight gained from her experience as a storyteller. She says forcefully: "What discoveries I have made in the process of writing stories, all begin with the particular, never the general." Clifford Geertz (1973) puts it another way when he refers to the paradoxical experience of theory development, the emergence of concepts from the gathering of specific detail. Geertz (1973) says, "Small facts are the grist for the social theory mill" (p. 23). The scientist and the artist are both claiming that *in the particular resides the general.*

In this paradox we discover a very different way of thinking about generalization. It is not the classical conception typically employed in social science, where the investigator uses codified methods for generalizing from specific findings to a universe, and where there is little interest in findings that reflect only the characteristics of the sample. Before generalizing, the parameters of the universe are clearly articulated, as is the selection of the sample in an effort to define the relationship between them, and to be able to point to statistically significant differences. By contrast, the portraitist seeks to document and illuminate the complexity and detail of a unique experience or place, hoping that the audience will see themselves reflected in it, trusting that the readers will feel identified. The portraitist is very interested in the single case because she believes that embedded in it the reader will discover resonant universal themes. The more specific, the more subtle the description, the more likely it is to evoke identification.

This is certainly the way a novelist works, drawing the scene, defining the relationships among characters, creating the action, and tracing the story. The writer hopes the reader will feel the familiarity of the experience even if the setting and the people are exotic. The novelist offers the reader the opportunity of crossing boundaries of experience and geography, of moving across cultures and family dramas, of traveling to new worlds. But readers will only take the adventure if they feel some sense of connection or identification with the story being told. Portraitists work to create this same kind of resonance and identification.

In trying to create this resonance, the portraitist describes the details of action and manifest behavior, what people are doing, how they are behaving, what they are saying. She wants to carefully and systematically document those phenomena that are visible, discernable, often countable. But the recording of these discrete behaviors will not alone produce the resonance. The portraitist is interested, as well, in how these actions and interactions are experienced, perceived, and negotiated by the people in the setting. In fact, that is the primary interest. The behavior may serve as an important cue, but the portraitist is especially concerned about the meanings people attach to those behaviors.

Since the publication of my book *The Good High School* (1983), where I used the methods of portraiture for the first time to examine the culture of six secondary schools, I have been working on the development and refinement of this methodology. For several years I have taught an advanced graduate seminar on the topic, trying to clarify and document the assumptions, values, and goals that shape this work as well as describe and codify the tools and techniques that are part of the process of data collection, interpretation, and analysis. In addition to using my teaching as a vehicle for methodological development, I have also refined and enlarged the methodology through my own research and writing.

In my most recent work, *I've Known Rivers* (1994), I explore the life stories of six women and men using the intensive, probing method of "human archeology"—a name I coined for this genre of portraiture as a way of trying to convey the depth and penetration of the inquiry, the richness of the layers of human experience, the search for ancestral and generational artifacts, and the painstaking, careful labor that the metaphorical dig requires. As I listen to the life stories of these individuals and participate in the "co-construction" of narrative, I employ the themes, goals, and techniques of portraiture. It is an eclectic, interdisciplinary approach, shaped by the lenses of history, anthropology, psychology, and sociology. I blend the curiosity and detective work of a biographer, the literary aesthetic of a novelist, and the systematic scrutiny of a researcher.

But *The Art and Science of Portraiture* is not a solo, it is a duet. There will be two voices in this volume, the second belonging to Jessica Hoffmann Davis. As a visual artist and a student of human development with expertise in the field of aesthetics, Davis has used portraiture extensively to study successful community art centers in city neighborhoods. Her *Safe Havens* (1993) includes rich and detailed portraits of six community art centers, tracing the structural, ideological, relational, and cultural themes that have made them resilient and creative organizations. Not only has Davis codified and transposed the methods of portraiture presented in *The Good High School* to accommodate the ecology of neighborhood art centers, she has also modified and extended the method to include what she calls "group voice"—portraiture done by an ensemble of researchers, with three or four people involved in the data collection, thematic analysis, and narrative development. In this work, Davis has also developed a process of documentation and evaluation that is explicitly activist and interventionist, and that can be used by practitioners in the field as a way of strengthening their programs and institutions and as a way of becoming more self-critical and thoughtful about their work. There is in Davis's work the purposeful attempt to link research and practice, and to profit from the combined scrutiny and wisdom of the portraitists and the actors.

This volume takes advantage of our experience in producing these three pieces of portraiture—*The Good High School, Safe Havens,* and *I've Known Rivers*—employing textual examples adapted from these works for illustration, charting the methodological themes that are common to all the works, as well as identifying the particular variations found in group voice and human archeology. In each of these works, we explore the connection between the phenomena under study and the chosen methodology—substance and technique are intentionally intertwined, one informing the other.

The Art and Science of Portraiture is enhanced by our collaboration, combining our disciplinary approaches (sociologist and human developmentalist, storyteller and visual artist), joining our rich range of experiences, including illustrative work in a variety of settings, and challenging the individualistic and idiosyncratic nature of this work, searching for the elements that are teachable, replicable, and discernable. In this highly personal and artistic genre, what are the dimensions and techniques that can serve as guidelines and standards for others seeking to do this work? We hope that this volume will serve as a handbook for social scientists from a range of disciplines (and their students) who are eager to learn more about the purposes, uses, and methods of portraiture, that it will be illuminating to humanists and other scholars of narrative who are part of a growing body of writers and thinkers engaged in interdisciplinary discourse. And that it will inform practitioners (immersed in education, social service, and social action) who seek to document, and reflect on, their work, analyze the impact of their interventions, and make better use of the frameworks and insights of social science. In keeping with the aesthetic and empirical purposes of portraiture, we hope that our book will both inform and inspire, that it will be both didactic and illustrative, and that it will underscore the importance of both strategy and insight in this work.

Tête de Jeune Fille 1st state
11 January 1949

CHAPTER TWO

PERSPECTIVE TAKING

Discovery and Development

Jessica Hoffmann Davis

I painted all my life like Raphael so that one day
I could paint again like a child.
—Pablo Picasso

W hen I first read the richly layered portraits that Sara Lawrence-Lightfoot produced in *The Good High School,* I was pleased and disarmed. Here was writing in which I recognized the thoroughness and rigor of exemplary social science inquiry. At the same time, however, the narrative portrayals demonstrated features I was not accustomed to encountering in the domain of research. The writer was inside—not outside—the work; the forbidden element of judgment was everywhere present, and the spirited writing had a rhythmic pace more reflective of works of art than of science.

I am not only referring here to works of art of the literary sort—those resonant stories that deliver a reality both apart from and at the heart of one's own. I am referring as well to works of art of a visual nature—those compelling images that are comprehended all at once in their entirety, even as their various details of presentation demand attention. Lawrence-Lightfoot's portraiture, it seemed to me, crossed the lines that traditionally separate science and art and forged a new territory in which artistic elements were intrinsic to both the process and the product of the research methodology.

The crossing of boundaries has always appealed to me. Where most children draw pictures only until they learn to write words, I have persisted as a maker of images straddling both regions of symbolization: language and visual art. Art in itself represents the breaking of many boundaries, including the perceptual boundaries between experience and representation, the temporal boundaries between past and present, and the cultural boundaries between individual and humankind.

Transporting my attachment to art into my work as a developmental psychologist, my focus has been on cognition, specifically as aesthetic development. By virtue of its interdisciplinary nature, cognitive psychology is also a boundary breaker, informed as it is by philosophy and linguistics as surely as by computer science. From a cognitive perspective, the production and perception of a work of art are viewed as processes of thought. And even that viewpoint challenges the traditional conceptual boundary of art as the exclusive realm of emotion.

My work in cognitive psychology has explored the crossing of yet another boundary, this one *within* the territory of art, comparing the drawings of very young children with those of professional artists. Although the boundaries created by experience and skill might seem too dense to cross, a consideration of the playful creations of young children in terms of the serious work of professional artists informs understanding on both sides of the divide.

The boundaries of value and expectation that generally separate our understanding of child and adult art are as tenacious and ingrained as those we set between art and science. We see art as arbitrary and fictive; science as precise and real. And as ready as we may be to consider science as a boon to art (say in the chemical compounds from which paints derive) or art as a boon to science (say in the importance of drawing skills for presenting scientific studies), we less frequently address the potential scientific rigor of artistic processes, and the potential artistry of science. It is this merging of potentials that underlies both the art and the science of the methodology of portraiture.

By the time I was encountering *I've Known Rivers,* I had literally been let into the portraiture process. As the manuscript was being written, I read evolving sections and responded through copious memos. I shared my experience as active reader making sense of the lives of the *Rivers* subjects, juxtaposed as they were with the voice of the storyteller. This was a powerful learning experience, and one that I was positioned to put to good to use. At the time that I was reading the developing text, I was working with a group of researchers attempting to adapt the individual process of portraiture to our group's research agenda and collective capabilities.

On one hand, I was on my own experiencing Lawrence-Lightfoot's expert, seamless process, and on the other, I was working with my colleagues to draft a pattern that we could all follow. I brought my ever more intimate understanding of portraiture to our efforts at channeling that fluid, individualistic process into a more fixed and replicable structure. Our aim was to apply the structure to the creation of portraits of the subjects of our research: exemplary community art centers in economically disadvantaged communities.

All the researchers on the Project Co-Arts team were visual artists. Where Lawrence-Lightfoot's entry into the process of portraiture stemmed from her experiences as the subject of a portrait made by others, ours derived from our experiences at making portraits ourselves. When we set out to write what we called *gesture drawings* of community art centers in order to refine our portraiture skills as we came to know the field, we had all encountered the actual experience of sketching gesture drawings from live models. For us, the artistic experience would not be a metaphor for the written experience; the written experience would be a new encounter with a familiar activity.

The artist and teacher Kimon Nicolaides identifies *gesture* as "the function of action, life, or expression," and writes of gesture drawings in his classic treatise *The Natural Way to Draw,* "They are like scribbling rather than like printing or writing carefully, as if one were trying to write very fast and were thinking more of the meaning than of the way the thing looks, paying no attention to penmanship or spelling, punctuation or grammar" (1941, p. 18).

As we developed guidelines for our own grammar or primer of portrait writing, we created about three dozen "gesture drawings"—brief narratives—of community art centers around the country. We wanted to develop our skills at capturing the essence of subjects as portraits do. Reviewing these written sketches, assessing our process in terms of the portraiture model, considering our collective needs and skills, and benefiting from periodic consultation with Lawrence-Lightfoot, we developed a version of the methodology that could be implemented by the group.

By the time our collection of portraits—*Safe Havens*—was complete, our adaptation of portraiture as a group process had reached the stage at which it could be reproduced by others. My experience with the methodology had come full cycle from my first encounter as a student of portraiture in 1989. Working in consultation with collaborating teachers and researchers, as well as with students interested in producing portraits of sites of arts learning, I have had the chance to learn more about portraiture from the experience of sharing it with others.

In contributing to this volume, I bring these relevant experiences into the fold: as a participant in and student of artistic production, recognizing portraiture's connections with making meaning through art, and as a methodologist looking within portraiture for the repetitive refrains that are the imprints of replicable structure. Our first chapter introduced, as context for the methodology, the historical and ideological precepts that situate portraiture within the domain of research. Here, we consider a different context, and address the theoretical precepts with which we situate the methodology in the domain of art. Understandably, our perspective embraces a cognitive approach and engages a comparison between child and adult art.

PORTRAITURE AS AN ARTISTIC PROCESS

Pablo Picasso is said to have made his statement about working all his life to paint like a child at an exhibit of children's art after the second world war. It is a statement that is often quoted and probed by champions and doubters of early artistry. Ensuing debates range from questioning whether Picasso ever really did paint like Raphael to asserting that of course he meant as his objective to recapture children's freewheeling approach to art—not literally to create works of art that look as if they had been made by children.

The artist Paul Klee, whose work is often thought literally to look like that of children, protested the comparison. Exalting the artist's well-directed expertise, Klee cautioned, "Don't translate my works to those of children. . . . They are worlds apart. . . . Never forget the child knows nothing of art . . . the artist on the contrary is concerned with the conscious formal compositions of his pictures, whose representational meaning comes about with intention" (Gardner, 1980, p. 8).

Intention is often cited as the crucial distinction. Children may make drawings that look like those of adult artists, but they do not *intend* to make their drawings look any way at all. Instead, children are said to create these artful images almost in spite of themselves. Intention is certainly a salient feature of the research methodology of portraiture. *Any* artful case study is not after the fact accidentally or incidentally a portrait. In applying the methodology, a researcher is consciously and carefully composing a portrait, "whose representational meaning comes about with intention."

Compare the following two nonobjective portrayals of the emotion Angry, collected in a study of the similarities and differences between the drawings of young children and adult artists (Davis, 1993b, 1996). The top drawing was created by a professional artist, the bottom one, by a five-year-old child (see pp. 26–27).

The two creators' processes of construction were as similar as their products. Five-year-old Sydney held her face in a severe frown as she drew, putting all her weight on the marker and relentlessly moving it round and round the paper. As the drawing progressed, Sydney frequently turned the paper, taking it in from different angles, and responding to these different views with additional dense tangles of lines. Looking at the drawing approvingly before she gave it to me, Sydney declared, "If I had time, you wouldn't see any of the paper showing through the lines." With one more aggressive turn of the marker, she added, "That's Angry."

Forty-five-year-old professional artist Lisa paused for a moment before she started to draw and then started muttering to herself about the policeman who had given her a ticket that week. As she spoke to herself of infuriating things, her face assumed a scowl—which she maintained until the completion of her drawing. Frowning and muttering, she turned the paper round and round, occasionally squinting an eye, but invariably adding to the drawing with each turn of the page.

Older children and nonartist adults more often draw literal portrayals of Angry, depicting an angry individual embroiled in the situation that has caused the anger. Sidney's and Lisa's portrayals are closer to gesture drawings, as Nicolaides has described them, which tell more of the "meaning than of the way the thing looks." The assumption of the emotion on the face of the artist—the physical emulation of the object of representation—is part of another lesson that Nicolaides gives his students: "You should feel that you are doing whatever the model is doing. If the model stoops or reaches, pushes or relaxes, you should feel that your own muscles likewise stoop or reach, push or relax. If you do not respond in like manner to what the model is doing, you cannot understand what you see. If you do not feel as the model feels, your drawing is only a map or a plan" (1941, p. 16).

A sure intention in the methodology of portraiture is capturing—from an outsider's purview—an insider's understanding of the scene. As if instructed by Nicolaides, portraitists try to feel as the subject feels and to represent that understanding in a portrayal that exceeds the level of literal depiction found in a map or a plan. Understanding the emotion of angry as the subject of their drawings, both five-year-old Sydney and adult artist Lisa behave like trained artists, deliberately feeling the emotion they are portraying as they produce very similar products.

Where then can the distinction be found? It has been suggested that properly matted and framed, a five-year-old's drawing could be hung on a gallery wall in a museum of modern art and remain unnoticed in the collection. Would that tour de force confirm the child's drawing as a genuine work of art? There are those who recognize "exhibition in an art museum" as the definitive criterion for art.

Philosopher Nelson Goodman eloquently explicates the Symbol Systems Approach—a particular cognitive perspective that recognizes the various "languages of art" such as drawing, music, and gesture, as systems of symbols. In his provocative essay *When Is Art?* (1978), Goodman dismisses the determination of *what* is and is not art as a most frustrating initiative. Pointing to the transient nature of symbolic objects, Goodman instead redirects his inquiry into the aspects objects display *when* they are functioning as art.

If the reader of a portrait of an urban school ignores the aesthetic aspects of the narrative and reads only to obtain the incorporated factual data, the portrait is not functioning as art. A psychologist who sees in five-year-old Sydney's drawing only an example of the scribbling stage of artistic development is not receptive to the drawing as a symbolic expression of emotion. Certain conditions need to be in place for objects to function as art, and when they are, aesthetic features become salient. Because they come and go, Goodman has labeled these conditions and features "symptoms" of the aesthetic.

Applying Goodman's directions to the considerations at hand, we need not wrestle over whether the five-year-old's drawing—or the adult's for that matter—is or is not art. It is not of importance whether research portraits deserve exhibition in a gallery of literary art. Instead, our consideration of portraiture as an artistic process, like our consideration of child and adult art, concerns the extent to which these entities demonstrate symptoms—to borrow Goodman's word—of the aesthetic.

Adult artist Lisa's drawing of Angry

Five-year-old Sydney's drawing of Angry

AESTHETIC ASPECTS OF THE WHOLE

The aesthetic aspects of the work of art are the elements through which the artist vests the work with meaning that goes beyond simple representation. In a work of art, the distinguishing aspect of these features is that they do more than refer away from themselves to the object of representation, their own properties have significance in themselves. In works of art, details such as the shape, width, or direction of a line (which can be of little importance in other settings) play a role in the viewer's comprehension of meaning.

As Goodman has explained, the properties of a line in an electrocardiogram are meaningless on their own (1976, p. 229). Whether the line is thick or thin, red or blue, is of no import. Instead, meaning is derived from the crucial points to which each rise and fall of the line refers. If the same line were in a painting describing a mountain range, each rise and fall would do more than indicate peaks and valleys. The breadth or thinness of the line, its color, and the shadows cast around it would communicate other crucial aspects, such as the mood evoked by the particular scene or by a more universal encounter with nature. When the physical properties of the line or symbol embody meaning on their own, they are considered by Goodman to be relatively *replete.*

In much writing in social science, the intention is to try and refer to meaning as precisely as do the points in the line of the electrocardiogram—away from the writing to the subject being described. In portraiture, the replete features of the text are a crucial element in the conveyance and determination of meaning.

Because the subject being described is embodied in the descriptive writing, readers must attend to the aesthetic features of the narrative. Therein they will find aspects of the subject not often included in more traditional research accounts, such as attitudes, feelings, colors, pace, and ambiance. In the implementation of the methodology of portraiture, as in the construction of a work of visual art, the significance of the details of presentation transport the portrayal beyond simple representation into the realm of expression.

Art historian Joshua Taylor's *Handbook for the Visual Arts,* a widely used reference for students of art appreciation, suggests: "To keep from confusing what we normally call the subject matter of a work—the identifiable objects, incidents, or suggested outside experiences that we recognize—with the more complete aspect, taking as it were, the part for the whole, it might be useful to adopt the term 'expressive content' to describe that unique fusion of subject matter and specific visual form that characterizes the particular work of art. 'Subject matter,' then, would be the objects and incidents represented; 'expressive content' would refer to the combined effect of subject matter and visual form" (1981, p. 51}.

Nelson Goodman recognizes expressive content or expression as the quality that a drawing metaphorically exemplifies. "Exemplification," Goodman indicates, "is possession plus reference" (1976, p. 53). In terms of Sydney's and Lisa's drawings, the end result of enhancing reference (to the emotion of anger) with possession (the containment of the emotion through the dense and frantic lines of the drawing) is that the exemplifying symbol serves as a sample of the property to which it refers. Sydney's and Lisa's drawings are in themselves examples of anger. As Sydney pointed out, "That's Angry!"

Rudolf Arnheim, eminent psychologist of art, explains this occurrence in his *Gestalt Theory of Expression:* "The phenomenon in question is actually present in the object of perception" (1966, p. 64). By virtue of their constitutive properties, Sydney and Lisa's drawings *are* angry drawings. But this exemplification of the depicted emotion is of course metaphoric. A drawing or a portrait cannot literally be angry.

In painting, the aesthetic aspects of production that can contribute to the expressive content include the use of line, shadow, color, texture, delineation, and placement of forms on the canvas, as well as the relationship that persists among these aspects, color to color, line to line, shadow to shadow, and form to form. Expressive content is achieved through thoughtful attention to each aesthetic aspect as well as to the relationships among them.

In the methodology of portraiture, the aesthetic aspects of production that can contribute to the expressive content include the use of keen descriptors that delineate, like line; dissonant refrains that provide nuance, like shadow; and complex details that evoke the impact of color and the intricacy of texture. The forms that are delineated convene into emergent themes and the interrelationship of these themes is woven through the connections of their content against the backdrop of their shared context.

RELATIONSHIP AND INTERPRETATION

At the heart of the aesthetic experience—a primary condition—is a conversation between two active meaning-makers, the producer and the perceiver of a work of art. This conversation results in a co-construction of meaning in which both parties play pivotal roles. Through the internal symbols or representations that are the vehicles of thought, the producer of art constructs a worldview. Through external symbols or representations—embodied in the work of art—the artist shares a worldview.

This sharing is realized when that worldview is reconstructed in terms of the internal symbols mediating the thought processes of the perceiver. The perceiver of art attends to the symbols the artist has produced—what they represent and how they are constructed—and from that perception, constructs his or her own understanding. Since each individual's understanding is uniquely constructed, the meaning of a work of art is negotiated and renegotiated repeatedly and variously as new perceivers encounter it.

To a certain extent, then, the aesthetic properties of a work exist because the perceiver attends to them. Perhaps of most importance, in a work of art, the perceiver attends to the aesthetic properties because the artist has intentionally drawn attention to them—rendered them significant. Nonetheless, individual perceivers will construct their various understandings according to their ability to read the aesthetic aspects that the artist has emphasized; their different readings of meaning are what are often called *interpretations.*

Interpretation as a cognitive activity involves recognizing, sorting, and organizing perceptions toward a cohesive construction of understanding. This activity of discerning the qualities of a subject that are necessary for understanding is a kind of active search for connections and coherence. Because interpretation is an activity so strongly identified with the arts, the methodology of portraiture as a process of interpretive description seems a priori akin to artistic activity.

However, because interpretation is so much a part of the construction and reconstruction of meaning, cognitivist Michael Parsons, who studies the development of aesthetic perception, places the activity of interpretation at the core of his discipline. As if he were evoking the methodology of portraiture, he represents this view in *Cognition as Interpretation:* "As important as anything else would be an acceptance of the fact that what we do, as psychologists and researchers, is also interpretive in character. If what we are finally interested in is the meanings children grasp, then we must ourselves interpret them as we study their artworks, choices, explanations. We must not continue to allow the dream of scientific objectivity to blind us to the fact that we as researchers are also making interpretations" (1992, p. 90).

Our view of the co-construction of symbolic meaning in art can be reframed in terms of interpretation and portraiture. In portraiture, the researcher—the artist—interprets the subject of the portrait internally by searching for coherence in what she observes and discovers. The researcher represents that interpretation through the construction of the portrait intentionally employing aesthetic aspects in order to convey meaning. The reader—the perceiver—makes sense of the subject that is portrayed through his or her active interpretation of the portrait. This new interpretation of the subject on the part of the reader or perceiver can be thought of as a kind of reinterpretation. With each reinterpretation, it is as if the portrait is being recreated.

Underlying this co-constructive structure is a series of relationships: the relationships between the artist-researcher and the subject, the artist-researcher and the work, the perceiver and the work, the perceiver and the subject of the work, and ultimately the perceiver and the producer—the two meaning-seekers interrelating through the interpretive work.

This series of relationships is demonstrated in Sydney's and Lisa's portrayals of Angry. The frowning mouth and angry muttering reflect the producer's relationship with the subject: anger. The scribbling of lines and repeated turning of the paper, assessing what to do next in response to each new view, demonstrate the relationship between the producer and the work. Through these actions with regard to subject and work, the artist is expanding understanding, developing interpretation.

As Nicolaides tells us, "A thing is factually the same from whatever point of view you see it, but seeing it from different points of view will illuminate the meaning of the forms and lines you have been looking at" (1941, p. 130). In the same breath with which Picasso explains that pictures don't change—that "first vision remains almost intact"—he points out, "A picture is not thought out and settled beforehand. While it is being done it changes as one's thoughts change" (Arnheim, 1962, p. 30).

Finally, in a perceiver's interpretation of those dark and swirling lines as the emotion of anger, the chain of relationships is completed. The perceiver, recognizing the emotion in the portrayal, is seeing the drawing as if he or she were in fact the artist, is relating to the artist as another interpreter of images, appraising the interpretation that is the drawing.

In the process of turning the paper and assessing the next move, the creator of the drawing is aware of that relationship; is repeatedly considering what the viewer will need to make sense of the portrayal, reading the text as if it were written by someone else. In the same way, the perceiver, identified with the artist, may consider his or her own interpretation as it is aligned with the drawing, "Ah yes, that is Angry. If I had done it the lines would be angled and not curved. But I understand this portrayal as unequivocally Angry."

THE IMPORTANCE OF CONTEXT

Throughout our considerations of aesthetic production and perception and the realm of interpretation as cognition, we cannot overestimate the importance of context. Without the larger frame of a modernist perspective on art, for example, we might not even be able to acknowledge the drawings of either Sydney or Lisa as representations, or the possibility of anger being the subject of a portrayal.

When comparing their drawings, we need to look beyond the parameters of the pages on which Sydney's and Lisa's apparently similar versions of Angry are drawn to the personal context in which the subject of these drawings was interpreted. On one point doubters and defenders of the artistry of children's art can be clear: the five-year-old and the forty-five-year-old understand a subject like Angry in terms of very different experiential contexts.

While both artist and child may be sifting through the nuances of particular experience for a quintessential expression of a more general feeling, their frames of reference, like their repertoires of artistic forms, necessarily differ greatly. Lisa is choosing the way in which she will represent Angry from many more alternatives than Sydney. As Taylor notes, "Works of art do not spring into being as isolated phenomena but are created as part of normal human activity, reflecting the judgments, the taste, the human evaluations of the artist who conceived them and often of the time of which they are a part" (1981, p. 139).

Context is an element that plays a role in the creation of a work of art on numerous levels. The *historical* context is evident in the modernist perspective thanks to which both Sydney and Lisa's apparent scribbles can be considered seriously as nonobjective art. The *personal* context in which the artist is creating includes, for example, the different experiential repertoires that Sydney and Lisa bring to their respective drawings. Finally, the *internal* context of the work is that in which the parts of the whole are perceived in terms of each other and the backdrop of the work.

Depending on the ground or backdrop of a painting that provides internal context for the subject, different aesthetic aspects of the work will be highlighted. Against a stark monochromatic ground, details of a form will be clearly discerned that might be harder to detect against an intricate linear backdrop. Consider, for example, the letter S written on a blank piece of paper. In that context, the contours of its form would be absolutely clear. But if you inserted the letter S somewhere between the lines in either Sydney's or Lisa's drawing, the entire form would be hard to detect.

In deciding on the ground for the work of art, the artist must decide which perceptual features need to be emphasized or deemphasized. As Arnheim points out, ". . . everything in this world presents itself in context and is modulated by that context. When the image of an object changes, the observer must know whether the change is due to the object itself or to the context or to both, otherwise he understands neither the object nor its surroundings" (1969, p. 37).

In portraiture, we find the same levels of context at play. The *historical* context can be seen as the variety of research frameworks from which portraiture derives and deviates, without which we would not be able to distinguish the artful qualities of the methodology. The *personal* context in which the researcher is creating a portrait is manifest in the experiential repertoire of the researcher; for example, whether he or she is familiar with the subject or has particular expertise, assumptions, or expectations that modulate the presentation of the subject.

The *internal* context of the portrait is manifest in contextual details (such as the subject's history, background, or location), which the researcher does or does not include and by virtue of which the subject is understood by the reader in one way or another. Clearly the context of a work of art or of a research portrait, inextricably tied to the content of the work and to the way in which that content will be understood, functions as a means of illumination. According to how it is directed, the context will shed more or less light on one or another of the aesthetic aspects of the whole.

BALANCING THE AESTHETIC WHOLE

The outer edges of the canvas on which the artist paints physically and psychologically frame an aesthetic space that is separate from the world at large. What occurs within the parameters of that frame is set off from everyday reality and evokes a response that is different from the response evoked by objects and events in the everyday world. Within the boundaries that frame the aesthetic space, the artist seeks to achieve a visual order through the interrelationship of the elements of the composition around the center of the work.

Arnheim defines composition as "the way in which works of art are put together of shapes, colors, or movements" (1988, p. 1). Since order is a necessary condition for human understanding, the arranging of these different elements into a coherent order is what makes the work intelligible. The commonly asserted goal of this compositional arrangement is *unity*—the unified integration of parts of the whole. The realization of that goal is achieved through balance.

Arnheim explains, "In a balanced composition, all factors of shape, direction, location, etc. are mutually determined by each other in such a way that no change seems possible, and the whole assumes the character of 'necessity' in all its parts" (1966, p. 76). Arnheim not only credits balance in composition with clarity in symbolic statement, but also indicates, "Under conditions of imbalance, the artistic statement becomes incomprehensible" (1974, p. 20).

Arnheim's explanation is evocative of a similar description by the Greek philosopher Aristotle in his classic treatise on poetry and fine art, *The Poetics.* Aristotle describes the balanced aesthetic whole as "the structural union of the parts being such that if any one of them is displaced or removed, the whole will be disjointed and disturbed. For a thing whose presence or absence makes no visible difference is not an organic part of the whole" (Aristotle, 1951 ed., p. 35).

The negotiation of balance in works of art and research portraits relies on the artist's or researcher's judgment—the manipulating of elements to find what is right, what works, and the equally important experience of deciding what doesn't fit and what needs to be reconsidered or excluded.

The eminent art historian Sir Ernst Gombrich likened the negotiation of the relationships between parts in the aesthetic whole of a painting to the simple act of arranging flowers:

> Anybody who has ever tried to arrange a bunch of flowers, to
> shuffle and shift the colours, to add a little here and take away
> there, has experienced this strange sensation of balancing forms
> and colours without being able to tell exactly what kind of
> harmony it is he is trying to achieve. We just feel a patch of
> red here may make all the difference, or this blue is all right
> by itself but it does not 'go' with the others, and suddenly a
> little stem of green leaves may seem to make it come 'right'. . . .
> When it is a matter of matching forms or arranging colors an
> artist must always be 'fussy' or rather fastidious to the extreme.
> He may see differences in shades and texture which we should
> hardly notice. Moreover, his task is infinitely more complex
> than any of those we may experience in ordinary life. He has
> not only to balance two or three colours, shapes or tastes, but
> to juggle with any number [1984, p. 14].

In portraiture, the boundaries of the narrative, set off as they are from the everyday reality of the reader and the subject, frame the relevant aesthetic space. It is within this narrative frame that the researcher is juggling "any number" of different kinds of data, discovering and providing coherence through emergent themes balanced around the center of the work.

Since the balance of the aesthetic whole is what makes the expressive content intelligible, composition may be regarded as the most important aesthetic agent of expression. Indeed, Gombrich points out, "All paintings must be interpretations but . . . not all interpretations are equally valid . . . all human communication is through symbols, through the medium of language, and the more articulate the language, the greater the chance for the message to get through" (1984, pp. 384–385).

The message expressed in a painting or a research portrait is the vision of the artist or researcher. As Nicolaides says, "Learning to draw is really a matter of learning to see" (1941, p. 5). Vision is made apparent by the hand of the artist constructing the painting and the voice of the researcher constructing the narrative. Hand and voice also make apparent the judgments that have been made in the balancing of the separate aesthetic aspects of the portrait into a cohesive aesthetic whole—an articulate, expressive statement commensurate with the vision achieved and intended for communication.

In the quest for balance, there is an ongoing dialectic for the artist between what he or she sees in the subject of the work of art and the actual reconciliation of that three-dimensional vision with the constraints of two-dimensional space. Similarly, for the portrait writer, there is an ongoing reconciliation between what has been seen in the multidimensional context of observation and interview and the final portrayal in narrative. The portrait writer, like the artist, is the negotiator in this scenario, and of central importance to the process. As Nicolaides explains to his students, "You, whether consciously or not, will draw what you see in the light of your experience with those and similar things on earth" (1941, p. 6).

The element of self is at play in all parts of the implementation of the methodology—forging relationships, determining context, searching for coherence, defining expression, and balancing a unified representation. Furthermore, self is imprinted on the lens through which the subject of the portrait is interpreted and thereby on the vision attained. Just as we see self guiding the artist's hand as it is imprinted on the artist's canvas, we hear self guiding voice as it is imprinted on the portrait. Through voice, self is heard explicitly in the context, language, and content of the portrait, and implicitly in the orchestration of the aesthetic whole. Indeed, another ingredient that the portraitist must measure is the amount of direct self-reference to be admitted to the whole.

Although voice resonates with past experiences, it is continuously redefined by the artist's or portraitist's immediate relationship with the current subject. That relationship, uniquely codefined by artist and theme, portraitist and subject, strikes new and different variations and tones with each new artistic endeavor.

TRANSFORMATION

Making and finding meaning through art is a transformative experience. Once we have encountered seeing and thinking in the aesthetic realm, our ability to think and see more generally is altered. Gombrich describes this experience:

> Here I think I can appeal to an experience most of us have had. We go to a picture gallery, and when we leave it after some time, the familiar scene outside, the road and the bustle, often look transformed and transfigured. Having seen so many pictures in terms of the world, we can now switch over and see the world in terms of pictures. For a brief moment, that is, we look at things a little with a painter's eye, or more technically speaking with a painter's mental set, scanning the motif for those aspects he can build up in paint on his canvas [1969, pp. 305–306].

Subjects of research portraits can report a similar transformation in their self-understandings. Once they have read their portraits, they may begin to see themselves and their actions with a portraitist's eye or mental set. They may even hold onto that vision of themselves and continue thereafter to think of their lives and works in terms of relationship, context, emergent themes, voice, and coalescing aesthetic whole.

This expanded vision allows the subject to continue to learn from the glass that is held to experience—from the telling of one's own story through another's voice, and from the clarity that can be gained from artistic perspective. How does that vision compare with those descriptive efforts that reach for apparently unambiguous statistics and avoid clearly nuanced interpretation? Aristotle distinguishes the more poetic documentation of events from historical accounts: "poetry tends to express the universal, history the particular" (Aristotle, 1951 ed., p. 35).

In portraiture, as in any work of art, the medium is an agent of discovery. Uniquely negotiated by the individual hand of the artist or voice of the researcher, aesthetic expressions of vision and understanding entitle perceivers or readers to new ways of seeing and thinking. After we have seen and understood Sydney's and Lisa's portrayals of Angry, we have a point of reference for future encounters with the emotion, and a new way of representing the emotion to ourselves and to others. As Gombrich points out:

> There is such a thing as a real visual discovery. . . . Whatever
> the initial resistance to impressionist paintings, when the first
> shock had worn off, people learned to read them. And having
> learned this language, they went into the fields and woods,
> or looked out of their window onto the Paris boulevards, and
> found to their delight that the visible world could after all be
> seen in terms of these bright patches and dabs of paint. The
> transposition worked. The impressionists had taught them,
> not, indeed, to see nature with an innocent eye, but to explore
> an unexpected alternative that turned out to fit certain experi-
> ences better than did any earlier paintings [1969, p. 324].

The alternative that portraiture provides raises a reflective glass to the stories that shape lives, pedagogy, and institutions. In so doing, portraiture illuminates and acknowledges the importance of these phenomena. The close observation that portrait writing requires unites the researcher to the subject—like the artist assuming the pose of the model—and affords a view of the parts of the whole that insiders know intimately.

The distance that portrait writing requires affords a view of the whole with which insiders may be less familiar. The portraitist works from the vantage point at which goodness can be apprehended—even as it is marked by mistakes and failure. Subjects struggling for success may not on their own have time for the luxury of recognition of achievement or the perspective of situating struggle within a larger construct.

The portraitist can deliver these views, and through structuring an aesthetic whole, can recognize and represent order in what insiders may perceive as disarray. There is much to discover in a portrait of an individual or institution that may have gone unnoticed internally—and, if the portrait is authentic, there is much to recognize in the portrayal that is at the heart of the insider's experience, surprisingly captured by an outsider's account.

While we speak of portraiture as an artistic process, we do not mean to suggest that it is a method reserved for those researchers who may also be artists. Experience has shown that a reframing of the purposes and skills of novice or expert researchers can result in the creation of successful portraits. Our hope is that this methodology's purposeful attempt to incorporate aspects of the artistic process into the genre of research will enable those who try portraiture to cross boundaries they have yet to explore.

Boundary crossing promises not just factual but also truthful representations that span the separated realms of artist and child, science and art, realism and poetry, imitation and imagination, fact and interpretation. Gombrich describes the artist's challenge in balancing the factual requirements of the subject with the interpretive inclinations of the artist in his description of the generational differences between nineteenth-century artist John Constable and his predecessor Thomas Gainsborough:

> Gainsborough, a man of the eighteenth century, finds the mere imitation of a real view unworthy of the artist who is concerned with the children of his brain, the language of the imagination. Constable is aware of the same difficulty, enhanced by the exacting demand of his literal-minded patron who wanted to have all the notable features of his beautiful estate faithfully recorded on the artist's canvas. The task for him is not an insult but a challenge. Steeped as he is in the love of nature that belongs to the contemporary of Wordsworth, he has forged himself a language that is both truthful and poetic, that makes it possible to fulfill the patron's demand for accuracy and his own urge for poetry [1969, p. 388].

In exploring the methodology of portraiture, researchers will find a similar challenge in realizing the field's "demand for accuracy" and the portraitist's "urge for poetry." It is in the resolution of this generative tension between the requirements of responsible research and the potential of artistic expression that the portraitist will successfully create an aesthetic whole—a portrait that tells the story faithfully, but in such a way that it holds interest for the general as well as the specialized reader. Portraiture strives to resonate beyond the particular that has so preoccupied science to the universal that echoes throughout art.

Les Deux Femmes Nues 6th state
26 November 1945

Les Deux Femmes Nues 3rd state
21 November 1945

CHAPTER THREE

ON CONTEXT

Illumination

Framing the Terrain

Sara Lawrence-Lightfoot

Like all researchers working within the phenomenological framework, portraitists find *context* crucial to their documentation of human experience and organizational culture. By context, I mean the setting—physical, geographic, temporal, historical, cultural, aesthetic—within which the action takes place. Context becomes the framework, the reference point, the map, the ecological sphere; it is used to place people and action in time and space and as a resource for understanding what they say and do. The context is rich in clues for interpreting the experience of the actors in the setting. We have no idea how to decipher or decode an action, a gesture, a conversation, or an exclamation unless we see it embedded in context. Portraitists, then, view human experience as being framed and shaped by the setting.

This perspective on context—as a rich resource for examining and interpreting behavior, thought, and feeling—contrasts sharply with the view of traditional positivist research, where context is a source of distortion. The positivist tries to create conditions and design controls that will permit study of a phenomenon without distractions and messy intrusions from the natural environment. In its most rarified form, the positivist approach leads the researcher to work purely in the laboratory, establishing experimental conditions for a controlled, systematic examination of the phenomena under study. The experimental method—used initially in agricultural studies and later embraced and refined by researchers studying humans—aims to isolate the effects of specific variables in hopes of making inferences to more general settings.

In a provocative and influential essay titled *Meaning in Context: Is There Any Other Kind?* (1979), Elliot Mishler posed what he thought was a rhetorical question. How can we, he asked, understand human experience and behavior unless we see it evolve out of its natural setting? To create ephemeral, isolated laboratory settings for the study of human science, he argued, is to risk misinterpretation of people's meanings, perspectives, competencies, and actions, and to risk inflicting the researcher's lens and standards on the subject's reality. Mishler criticized this practice of "context stripping" as problematic to rigorous scientific method and limiting to the subject's expressiveness and productivity.

> In pursuit of general laws, [methodologists] have been directed to the stripping away of contexts. Context stripping is a key feature of our standard methods of experimental design, measurement, and statistical analysis. To test the generality of our hypotheses, we remove the subject of our studies from their natural social settings; their normal roles and social networks are left behind as they enter our experimental laboratories. . . .
>
> Our procedures are aimed at isolated variables from the personal and social contexts in which they operate. Through factor analysis and scaling procedures, we search for pure variables, for measures of unitary dimensions that will not be contaminated by other variables. Ideal measures are independent, freestanding, orthogonal—that is, unrelated to measures of other variables [pp. 4–5].

But it is important to recognize that even the researcher's laboratory—long considered the optimal controlled environment—is not without context. A laboratory is not context free. It is a particular type of context, often experienced as unfamiliar and uncomfortable to the subjects who enter it. This strange environment can alter and distort responses. A young child in a laboratory, examined by a benign but unfamiliar researcher, may fail to perform on a reasoning task that she is given, her performance compromised by her discomfort in the strange setting, her lack of relationship with the examiner, or her inability to see the task as having any real significance or purpose in her life. In her own neighborhood—with friends and family members—this same child may show sophisticated reasoning skills as she navigates the streets, interacts with peers, or buys bread at the corner store. Likewise, an adult who seems inarticulate and reticent in a formal interview at the university may be self-assured and discerning when talking about what he knows, to people he knows, in a setting that he knows. Surrounded by a familiar place, rich in memories, cues, and experiences, he becomes the authority. He becomes more perceptive and expressive; he is free to be himself.

The portraitist, then, believes that human experience has meaning in a particular social, cultural, and historical context—a context where relationships are real, where the actors are familiar with the setting, where activity has purpose, where nothing is contrived (except for the somewhat intrusive presence of the researcher). The context not only offers clues for the researcher's interpretation of the actors' behavior (the outsider's view), it also helps understand the *actors'* perspective—how they perceive and experience social reality (the insider's view). In addition, it allows the actors to express themselves more fully, more naturally. Surrounded by the familiar, they can reveal their knowledge, their insights, and their wisdom through action, reflection, and interpretation. It is also true, of course, that the actors' natural environments will inevitably present constraints, restrictions, and barriers—but they will be familiar ones and the researcher will be able to observe the ways actors negotiate these points of resistance.

Just as people move from being subjects of inquiry in the laboratory to being actors in their own natural environments, so too does the researcher shift position from being the one defining and controlling the experimental conditions to being the one learning to navigate new territory. The researcher is the stranger, the one who must experience the newness, the awkwardness, the tentativeness that comes with approaching something unfamiliar, and must use the actors in the setting as guides, as authorities, as knowledge bearers. In qualitative inquiry this is a crucial shift of perspective and role between researcher and actor that has important implications for how the inquiry is approached and what is learned.

As newcomer and stranger to the setting, the researcher inevitably experiences surprises: events, experiences, behaviors, and values that she had not anticipated, and to which she must adapt and respond. Whether she is coming to the setting with a well-developed, discrete hypothesis, or with a theoretical framework that she is testing and refining, or with a number of relatively informal hunches, the realities of the context force the reconsideration of earlier assumptions. There is a constant process of calibration between the researcher's conceptual framework, her developing hypotheses, and the collection of grounded data. Working in context, the researcher, then, has to be alert to surprises and inconsistencies and improvise conceptual and methodological responses that match the reality she is observing. The researcher's stance becomes a dance of vigilance and improvisation.

Ethnographers—who describe this adaptive, improvisational behavior of the researcher working in context—often claim its relationship to validity in qualitative inquiry. Judith Goetz and Margaret LeCompte (1984), for example, argue that "validity may be the major strength" of ethnography. Participant observers working in context are forced to confront the distance (and dissonance) between their theories and categories on the one hand, and the actors' realities and perspectives on the other.

> First, the ethnographer's common practice of living among participants and collecting data for long periods provides opportunities for continual data analysis and comparison to refine constructs and to ensure the match between scientific categories and participant reality. Second, informant interviews, a major ethnographic data source, necessarily must be phrased close to the empirical categories of participants and are less abstract than many instruments used in other research designs. Third, participant observation—the ethnographer's second key source of data—is conducted in natural settings that reflect the reality of the life experiences of participants more accurately than do more contrived or laboratory settings. Finally, ethnographic analysis incorporates a process of researcher self-monitoring, termed disciplined subjectivity, that exposes all phases of the research activity to continual questioning and reevaluation [p. 221].

In observing and recording human experience in context, the portraitist's work joins with the practices and craft of other phenomenologists, ethnographers, and a variety of other qualitative researchers. But the portraitist makes deliberate and specific use of context in several ways that reflect her focus on descriptive detail, narrative development, and aesthetic expression, as well as her interest in recording the self and perspective of the researcher in the setting. Specifically, I will address five ways in which portraiture employs context, offering a delineation and illumination of each mode and excerpted illustrations from our texts. The first use of context depicts a detailed description of the physical setting; the second refers to the researcher's perch and perspective; the third underscores the history, culture, and ideology of the place; the fourth identifies central metaphors and symbols that shape the narrative; and the fifth speaks to the actor's role in shaping and defining context.

INTERNAL CONTEXT: THE PHYSICAL SETTING

Portraits are always framed by the ecological context: a vivid description of the geography, the demography, the neighborhood, and a detailed documentation of the physical characteristics of the place that evokes all the senses—visual, auditory, tactile. The reader should feel as if he or she is *there:* seeing the colors of the autumn leaves, feeling the temperature of the gentle breeze, and hearing the rustling branches. That is, he or she should not only see the contours and dimensions of the terrain but also feel placed in it, transported into the setting. Usually—though not always—the description of context opens the portrait, beginning with the larger macrosphere and moving to a more detailed examination of the immediate setting. The description works from the outermost circle inward, macro to micro, large to small, backdrop to foreground, general to specific, public to private. We see a sketch of the city, then move to the neighborhood, then to the school filled with individuals. With each layer of the ecology the description becomes more discerning, more specific and detailed.

When the portraitist is working in the field collecting data, she tries to capture all the specifics of the physical setting; no detail is too small to warrant attention and record in the observational notes. The documentation—on site—is purposefully all-inclusive. In creating the narrative, however, the portraitist makes judicious decisions about which contextual details to employ—selections shaped by the central themes of the portrait that she wants to foreshadow in the opening passages. In other words, the dimensions of context that appear in the portrait are carefully chosen, using only those elements that provide a physical framework, a feeling of embeddedness in the setting, and a forecasting of values and themes that will shape the narrative.

In *Safe Havens* (1993), Davis offers a classic contextual description in the opening of her portrait of the Artists Collective, a community art center in New Haven, Connecticut. She describes the city, the community, the neighborhood setting and demographics—all in terms carefully chosen to frame and inform the story and selected to foreshadow the themes of the portrait.

The Artists Collective

Downtown Hartford in midday steps off the glossy pages of a business magazine. Well-dressed professionals carrying briefcases dart across the moderately busy streets in and out of the moderately high skyscrapers that outline the business district in a particularly orderly fashion. A handful of conference hotels take advantage of the city's easy access to and from the highway that leads to New York or Boston.

The gold dome that is visible from the highway belongs to the rococo state house. Hartford is the capital of Connecticut. Two storybook castle–like towers flank the entrance to Bushnell Park: a spread of green not far from the venerable performance hall that Hartford residents simply call "The Bushnell." The castle towers, like the old park carousel, appear incongruous in a city center that seems otherwise devoid of outlets for play. No movie theaters or rows of stores peek out among the smooth tall office buildings. This is apparently a city for work, and the most visible work at hand is the managing of insurance companies. Hartford is the insurance capital of the nation.

Judging from the bustle of working people, a visitor might be surprised to learn how hard-hit financially Hartford has been in recent years or the high percentage of Hartford's residents who are actually unemployed. Judging from the predominance of white pedestrians downtown, a visitor might also be surprised to know that almost three-quarters of Hartford's population is either African American or Latino—many living at or below the poverty line. The white executives who crowd the street by day leave the city for the suburbs at night, and the African American and Latino residents maintain their respective places in the North and South Ends of Hartford.

The rooftops of the small two-and three-decker homes of the largely African American community of the North End are visible from the upper floors of the downtown buildings. It is difficult to convince a cab driver to take a fare there, but the North End is an easy walk from downtown. The dividing line between downtown and the North End is at the fork of Main Street and Albany Avenue. Almost at the juncture but just over the line is a small stone building labeled "The Craftery."

Unlike the sleek cool buildings of downtown, the Craftery is worn and warm. On its side, a mural—once lively, but now faded—depicts bigger-than-life musicians playing horns and swaying to music. The mural was painted by local high school students years ago. The artists' signatures are now hard to decipher, but their presence resounds. Craftery director Jonathan Bruce explains that the mural has never been vandalized because it is *owned* by the teenagers of the North End.

Across the line into the North End the vista of clean sidewalks peopled by well-dressed pedestrians disappears. In contrast, the streets seem littered and unpopulated. As if strewn across the sidewalks, bits of paper and other debris are lifted in momentary swirls of a February wind and gathered in heaps in occasional fenced-in corners. A lone pedestrian walks through an empty playing field. A drab cemetery; small houses in poor repair. This is a neighborhood in which people live, but that reality is belied by the emptiness of the streets.

The houses on Clark Street evoke this "empty" residential feeling. A shelter for battered women, another for the homeless, a burned-out former crack house—all appear to be vacant. The content of these houses is only by report. To the surveying winter eye, there is little if any activity visible on the street. By report, the vista changes in warm weather and gangs, drug dealers, and users make for an active if dangerous "street life." A 16-year-old local comments, "When it's light in the summer in the hot nights, people start bugging out and shooting themselves."

Housed in what used to be a Catholic school, situated between a church and a public school, the Artists Collective maintains anonymity in an old brick two-story building. A simple cross adorns the threshold and a barely visible sign mounted across the front of the building bears its name. A story below, another sign—rusted with time—declares the building's former use: "The Clark Street School." The frame of a disassembled swing-set remains standing to the left of the driveway alongside the entrance to the center. Speaking of the Collective, one North End resident makes the point: "I am thirty-five years old and I grew up in this neighborhood and I never knew about it and it was right down the street" [pp. 14–15].

This is a great example of placing an institution in the context of a larger environment that shapes it—in this case, the city of Hartford. The vision of Hartford as an elegant, efficient business center, flanked by Bushnell Park but devoid of community artifacts such as movie theaters or stores, points to the hollow desolation of downtown at night and foreshadows the stark divisions of race and class in this city. This is a city where well-groomed, rapidly rising white folks work but don't live. The demographic statistics are telling and stand in sharp contrast to the reality experienced by a visitor to downtown Hartford during working hours. The segregation of the city and the unemployment levels suggest areas of concentrated poverty, divided by race and ethnicity. These are the parts of town where cab drivers fear to go.

Travel to the North End displays new contradictions. This residential neighborhood seems barren, except for the litter swirling in the February wind. The weather accounts for some of the drab, vacant appearance, but Davis's description warns us that the warm weather will not give rise to greenery, flowers, or neighborhood congeniality. Instead, hot days may lead to violence and bloodshed in the streets.

Davis's descriptions of Hartford and the North End are crucial to understanding the mission and work of the Artists Collective. This nearly invisible, anonymous building, marked by a religious and educational heritage, is a safe haven, a welcoming asylum for the poor African American children who navigate these dangerous streets. We know these children are fighting long odds living in Hartford's North End. Maybe the Artists Collective is a place that will offer them challenge, solace, launching, and hope.

In a second illustration, from *The Good High School* (1983), I use the same contextual template as the *Safe Havens* example. This context development takes the reader on a journey to the school: it names streets, describes neighborhoods, identifies storefronts, and notes architectural patterns as it draws the relationship between the idyllic Milton campus and the city of Boston. The school is far enough away from urban life to feel safe and separate but close enough to feel its cosmopolitan pulse.

Milton Academy: City Backdrop

From Boston you travel along the Southeast Expressway, a three-lane highway crowded with fast cars and roaring trucks. You pass the great hulking oil drums with splashes of Corita-painted designs and the modern architecture of the University of Massachusetts Harbor Campus. I. M. Pei's Kennedy Library stands sleek and poised over the water, drawing a clean line in the sky. From the swiftly moving traffic you can spot the gaudy billboards, fast-food joints, and crowded shopping centers just off the expressway. After fifteen or twenty minutes of driving, the East Milton exit approaches quickly and the landscape abruptly shifts. During the late afternoon rush hour, it takes an hour to travel that same stretch of highway. The traffic is bumper-to-bumper. In the heat of summer, car radiators and human tempers rise to match the soaring temperature. In the winter, the slick, icy roads cause traffic to move at a slow, cautious pace and accidents are frequent.

The lush green landscape of Milton comes as a welcome surprise after negotiating the tortuous traffic. If you turn toward town, you find a small suburban village—a collection of drug stores, a twenty-four-hour grocery store, dry-cleaning and laundry establishments, dress shops, and luncheonettes. The tone is quiet, motley, and unpretentious, reflecting mixtures of this town's affluent and middle-income styles and tastes. Traveling further in that direction, toward a section that some of the wealthier residents call "the other side of the tracks," there are modest suburban dwellings on small plots.

But if you turn in the opposite direction when leaving the expressway, you soon approach the more affluent sections of Milton. Stately homes built of solid brick with sturdy white columns or New England wood-frame, century-old structures sit on large parcels of land surrounded by well-tended lawns and elegant gardens. A few turns later, Center Street becomes the central artery of Milton Academy, and you are advised to go twenty miles per hour. It is difficult to recognize the boundaries of the campus because it blends so easily into the residential landscape. For several days I thought the imposing brick mansions, close to the school and along Center Street, were extravagant private homes and discovered later that they were the girls' dormitories for Milton Academy. Some faculty view the town street running through the center of Milton's campus as important symbolically. "It reflects our close connections to the wider community, to intercourse with life beyond our borders," says one.

Eclectic architecture combines to form a handsome campus. The modern angular buildings face restrained old brick struc-tures. It is not an opulent, overly precious scene. The buildings are sturdy, the grass is green, and the campus has lovely scenic spots. Yet there is a well-used, slightly frayed feeling to many of the older buildings, and the new ones are not extravagantly built. The Yankee restraint of upper-class New Englanders is evident in many of the structures.

On the day I arrive in early April, the sun is golden, the air is clear but still brisk, and the budding crocuses promise spring. Students have shed their coats and are pushing the season in their warm-weather regalia. Many girls look light and feminine in spring frocks and flowered skirts. A girl with straight blond waist-length hair smiles broadly as she twirls barefoot on the grass. "I'm celebrating spring!" she explains to me. The boys wear corduroys and khaki pants with open-necked, long-sleeve shirts. (The dress code that does not permit boys and girls to wear blue jeans causes some complaints from students.) It is midmorning break and several students are gathered in small groups on the square lawn in front of the library. Some are completely sprawled out, trying to soak up the sun's rays. Others are engaged in casual conversation while they sip coffee, and a few are leaning against a nearby wall reading school-books. Three boys and a girl are tossing a frisbee to one another. It is the day following spring vacation and many stu-dents find it hard to make the transition back to school. "It is always awful returning after the holidays and facing the grind . . . simply distasteful!" complains a plump sophomore who is carrying a pile of books into the library.

I follow him into the Cox Library, a modern building with comfortable spaces for sitting, reading, and studying. It is a well-equipped and functional facility with 40,000 volumes,

121 periodicals, microfilm, and nonprint materials. It is also an aesthetic place with original artwork, comfortable furniture, and lovely patterns of light and shadow coming through tall windows. As you enter the library, two prominent pieces of art mark the extremes of human emotion. A metal sculpture called "The Tense Man"—tall, thin, and brittle—exudes tension and anxiety. On the wall close by hangs a modern quilted tapestry called "Planted by Living Waters." Done in soft, warm colors, it is a hanging that symbolizes calm and peace [pp. 246–248].

PERSONAL CONTEXT: THE RESEARCHER'S PERCH AND PERSPECTIVE

It is not only important for the portraitist to paint the contours and dimensions of the setting, it is also crucial that she sketch herself into the context. The researcher is the stranger, the newcomer, the interloper—entering the place, engaging the people, and disturbing the natural rhythms of the environment—so her presence must be made explicit, not masked or silenced. Noting the perch and perspective of the portraitist, the reader can better interpret the process and product of her vision. In portraiture, then, the place and stance of the researcher are made visible and audible, written in as part of the story. The portraitist is clear: from where I sit, this is what I see; these are the perspectives and biases I bring; this is the scene I select; this is how people seem to be responding to my presence.

This explicit perspective-taking is particularly important at the beginning of the piece, when the researcher arrives on the scene and describes what she sees and feels through the eyes of the newcomer, capturing details and nuances that may fade (or escape her notice altogether) as she becomes more accustomed to the setting. In revealing her first impressions, her initial moves into the context, and her place on the landscape, the portraitist invites the reader to join her on the journey and experience—step by step—the unfolding reality. The researcher's description of perch and perspective does *not* necessarily lock the reader into looking through the same lens or from the same angle. Paradoxically, it does the opposite. Vivid, discerning (and restrained) articulation of the researcher's stance allows the reader to entertain a contrasting view—to move to a different point on the landscape that might shape a different vision.

The following excerpt, from *I've Known Rivers* (1994), describes my first entry into Professor Charles Ogletree's class at the Harvard Law School. It is in many ways a classic classroom description. In the first two paragraphs—through concise but rich language—I describe the details of the physical setting, sketching the time, the place, the ambience, and the mood and tempo of the inhabitants.

But, in addition, I make my presence explicit, reporting my perspective, my biases, even my place in the room. I want the reader to know my ruminations and reflections, my place of witness as I perch in the second arc of seats.

> On a breezy, warm afternoon in April, I visit Professor Ogle-
> tree's 4 P.M. class, "The Defense Perspective." The corridors
> of Pound Hall, the main classroom building at the Harvard
> Law School are filled with casually dressed students—in jeans,
> shorts, T-shirts, warm-up suits—with only an occasional conser-
> vative suit. The classroom in which Charles teaches this third-
> year course is like all the others in its tiered horseshoe shape,
> although it is smaller in size than most, with only thirty gray
> swivel seats and two rows of tables. In front of the seats there
> is a large square table below a long blackboard. One wall of the
> classroom is all glass, looking out on a partly cloudy day and
> Massachusetts Avenue traffic. In the low ceilings, recessed lights
> shine down through the gray grid of acoustic tiles. The class-
> room feels functional, spare. The students seem slow and
> lethargic as they wander in to take their seats. Some sit alone
> daydreaming or reading; others are gathered in small clumps
> talking about their other courses or their court work in Roxbury,
> the "clinical" site for this course. These third-year students are
> apprentice attorneys learning the real-life activities of criminal
> defense lawyers. They are being tutored by practicing lawyers,
> their supervisors in the field, and they are receiving the counsel
> and guidance of their professor, but they are doing the work of
> real attorneys. This is not a class on abstract legal theory or a
> rehearsal of hypothetical cases. These students are defending
> real clients—a fact that contrasts sharply with their casual
> conversations before class. A very Cambridge-looking young
> woman dressed in light gray stretch pants, a magenta T-shirt,
> and running shoes calls across the classroom to a classmate,
> "Are you driving over to Roxbury tomorrow morning? . . . oh,
> you're taking the bus . . . what time are you leaving?"
>   The students seem so young to me, so cavalier—not mature
> enough to be doing the serious work of public defenders. Maybe
> I am projecting my own cynicism, but my first response in hear-
> ing their before-class chatter is to doubt their sincerity. I am,
> however, suspicious of my own doubts. After all, these students
> are much younger than most of my graduate students and do
> not seem to possess the seriousness and humility that often
> grow out of experience. For three years they have survived the

> elite, competitive, combative environment of the Law School
> and their easy arrogance (if it was not there before they arrived)
> is now firmly in place. I try to hold back on these immediate,
> harsh judgments. After all these are the twenty-five third-year
> students who *chose* to take Charles's course. Their choice must
> signal some inclination on their part to learn about (and maybe
> practice) the relatively low status, low paying, high demand
> work of defending poor folks. I perch myself in the second arc
> of seats, take out my pen and note pad, and work over these
> competing ruminations as the students saunter into the class-
> room [pp. 131–132].

In this illustration we see the portraitist at work, notebook in hand, pen poised. But we also look inside her head and heart and see the ambivalence, the contradictions, and the turmoil. We hear the self-reflection, the thought cycles that move her from "harsh judgment" to respectful regard. In other words, the portraitist has not just drawn herself into this classroom scene—she has also revealed her inner stirrings, opening herself up for scrutiny and, in turn, allowing the reader the space to make his or her own interpretations.

HISTORICAL CONTEXT: JOURNEY, CULTURE, IDEOLOGY

In the drawing of context, the portraitist is not only interested in recording the contemporary physical setting, she also wants to sketch the institutional culture and history—the origins and evolution of the organization and the values that shape its structure and purpose. It is often true that there are signs and symbols in the physical environment that reflect the organizational priorities and goals. In this case, the contextual description can weave together the external ecology within the ideological and developmental odyssey of the place. The portraitist should always be alert to the convergence (and contrast) between the external signs of the physical environment and the interior culture, noting the synchrony and the dissonance.

In the following excerpt from the portrait of St. Paul's School found in *The Good High School*, I purposefully blend the physical and the philosophical, the contemporary and the historical, the demographic and the cultural, the architectural and the evolutionary, into the opening description of context.

St. Paul's: The Aesthetics and Comforts of Abundance

> It is a magnificent spring day. The sky is clear blue, the air
> crisp, and the sun golden in the sky. The landscape is lush
> green and the azaleas are exploding with blossoms of magenta,

lavender, and deep orange. In short, it is the perfect day to visit St. Paul's School, which seems to stretch on for miles before me—aristocratic, manicured, perfect. I arrive midafternoon, the time for athletics, and see playing fields full of hockey and base-ball players—lithe, graceful, and practiced bodies moving across the grass.

Everyone is helpful and welcoming. A man in a blue truck—probably one of the custodial crew—finds me lost on the road and tells me to follow him to my destination, the School House. Everyone waves greetings. A young man on a small tractor mower offers a wide, enthusiastic grin, and a tall, distinguished, slightly graying man gives a stiff and formal wave. I park behind the School House, next to a car with windows open and a young child inside. Having just arrived from the city, I wonder immediately how anyone could feel safe about leaving a precious child in the car. Fearing that I will frighten her, I smile and speak softly to the little girl. She babbles back, unafraid. The child's mother returns after a couple of minutes. A plainly attractive woman of about thirty-five, she is one of the five females on the teaching faculty. She greets me warmly, intro-duces me to her daughter, and drives off quickly to play tennis. I am struck by how safe, secure, and beautiful it feels at St. Paul's. It is a place where windows and doors are left open, people exchange friendly greetings, and babies wait in cars unattended.

The land belonging to St. Paul's seems to stretch on forever. There are 1,700 acres of woods and open land surrounding over 300 acres of lakes and ponds, and over eighty buildings. A shimmering lake carves out a graceful shape in the central campus landscape. On an early evening walk from the School House to dinner in the dining room, you can cross the lake by way of a quaint stone bridge. The evening light makes the lake a mirror; the lily pads that dot the water gently sway back and forth, and all feels serene and still. The traditional and graceful architecture of New England characterizes the campus build-ings—sturdy brick structures with ivy growing up the walls and white, flat-faced houses with black and green shutters.

Among these quietly majestic old buildings are three sleek modern buildings that house the programs in dance, theater, and the plastic arts. A parent of a student at St. Paul's, who was interested in supporting the development of the arts programs, gave $3 million for these new buildings. Elegantly designed and highly functional, the buildings were conceived to be adaptive to the artistic mediums that they house. The theater in the drama building is layered, movable, and sparse, allowing for myriad rearrangements of space. The stage can be dramatically transformed from one performance to the next.

Mr. Sloan, the director of dance, worked closely with the architects and builders in the design of the dance building, and it shows the wisdom and inspiration of the artist's experience. The major dance space in the building is used for both classes and performances. Bleachers and balconies surround two sides of the dance floor, with mirrors and dance bars lining the other walls. Sunlight sweeps in the high windows and casts tree shadows on the dance floor. The internal lighting is soft and effective. The most extraordinary detail can only be fully appreciated by dancers. Mr. Sloan takes me into his office and proudly shows me the miniature model of the dance floor. It is a five-layered construction that took several months to build, and it moves and ripples when it is jumped on. "It is the best in the business," says Mr. Sloan. "The American Ballet Theater has the same floor."

The arts buildings symbolize one of the major missions of St. Paul's School. In his ten-year leadership of the school, the rector says that the building of the arts program is one of the developments of which he feels most proud. Along with the superb physical facilities, new faculty positions have been added in the arts; students can receive academic credit for coursework; and there are numerous opportunities for students to give concerts, performances, and exhibitions. In his 1979 Annual Report, William Oates, the rector, stressed the connections between art and culture, art and intellect, and art and personal growth:

"Work in the arts provides an opportunity for participants to learn about themselves. And this opportunity is particularly valuable for students at St. Paul's School because it allows, and in some ways demands, consideration of fundamental issues through observation, and testing, and experimentation. From fourteen years through eighteen this chance is eagerly sought and required. This is the period of questioning and exploring, of self-doubt and braggadocio, the period of developing self-confidence and of maturing personality. In the arts are found cultural contradictions and conflicts, insight, informed speculation, tradition and discipline, and a general pattern for testing achievement and apparent success. The arts afford the use of uncommitted space for thoughtful and considered growth through consolidation of experimentation. And increasing knowledge of the self promotes and supports its realization."

In stark contrast to the angular lines of the art buildings, the chapel of St. Paul and St. Peter stands as a symbol of classic beauty. The hundred-year-old brick structure was the first building on the St. Paul's campus and its stained glass windows, ornate wood carving, and regal dimensions mark the history and roots of this school. It is in these modern and traditional edifices that St. Paul's reveals its connections to past and present, its commitment to sacred traditions and contemporary change [pp. 221–223].

The first few passages of this portrait locate the school in a genteel, beautifully manicured asylum safe from the harsh realities of big city (or even small town) life. This idyllic setting is not only safe and lovely, it is also enriched by abundant resources: parents bestow gifts of $3 million arts buildings; the campus is carved out of more than a thousand acres of land; the dance floor "is the best in the business." This is a place of great privilege and abundance.

Moving beyond the refined splendor of the place, the contextual description also reveals St. Paul's educational philosophy. The arts buildings, chapel rituals, athletic contests, and references to faculty standards—as well as the rector's statement from the Annual Report—suggest the school's holistic, developmental approach to learning, one that seeks to blend mind, body, heart, and spirit. The architectural contrasts drawn between the stately ivy-covered buildings and the sleek modern arts complex also seem to reflect a philosophical stance that balances rich tradition with measured change. A visual scan of the physical setting, then, also helps the reader anticipate themes—both historical and philosophical—that characterize this place. The portraitist chooses these environmental symbols carefully; they echo with the school's values and vision.

AESTHETIC FEATURES: SYMBOLS AND METAPHORS

Related to the joining of the physical context with the philosophical currents of an institution is the portraitist's use of metaphor. Embedded in the contextual frame, metaphors capture the reader's attention, call up powerful associations, and resonate through the rest of the piece. These metaphors, well chosen (actually they are often heard first—and repeatedly—in the *actors'* observations and reflections), serve as overarching themes and rich undercurrents that resound throughout the portrait. The metaphors act as symbols pointing to larger phenomena that will emerge as significant and be developed more fully later on in the narrative.

In the following contextual description, opening the portrait of Tony Earls in *I've Known Rivers* (1994), boundaries become the central metaphor for speaking about contrasts between the real world and the academy, between chaos and serenity, between the rich and the poor, between elitism and diversity, and between research and clinical work—all themes that will thread through the narrative, gaining meaning and depth as the data are gathered. We also see, again, the portraitist in action: waiting, watching, witnessing, massaging the metaphor.

> The Harvard School of Public Health, a gray hulking building, sits on Huntington Avenue, a wide street usually clogged with traffic between downtown Boston and the suburbs—Brookline, Newton, Wellesley. Before Huntington Avenue turns into Route 9 and travels through the suburbs, it passes through what one of the students at the School of Public Health describes to me as "a very tough, black neighborhood." He is trying to explain to me why "security is so tight" at the school, why only one major door is open for visitors to come through, and why I have been firmly and abruptly stopped at the door for my University I.D. card. The School of Public Health, appropriately enough, is situated on the boundary between the academy and the "real world." It is part of the more sedate medical school complex and there are courtyards and stairs that connect it to the hospitals and laboratories of the Medical School. But it also looks out on housing projects, noisy trolleys, grocery stores, banks, beauty parlors—the bustling sights and sounds of city life.
>
> Inside the building at midday, students of all ages, dress, language, size, and color are jammed into a huge cafeteria, some in tight knots of serious conversation, others scanning notebooks or reading alone, others in raucous dialogue, laughing, gesticulating. The high ceilings do not absorb the sound; it ricochets off walls, floors, and tables. Trying to escape the noise and chaos, I find a chair slightly out of the action and close to the front door, and settle in to wait for Dr. Felton Earls.
>
> He arrives a few minutes later looking very calm against this bustling backdrop. He greets me warmly and leads me through the crowded cafeteria to a small quiet room with a simple sign, "A New Season." We enter into this soundproofed oasis where the tables are covered with white cloths and decorated with vases of flowers. It is a tiny restaurant run by caterers who used to provide food for special occasions and now have opened this noontime restaurant in a corner space carved out of the larger

cafeteria. There are five or six entrees on the menu and one
quiet, smiling waitress who serves all the tables in the room.
We settle into a reserved table and hear about the items on
the menu that are no longer available (it is now 1:30 P.M.
on Friday and we are the "last of the last diners" for the week).
We make our choices and almost immediately the food and the
setting become totally secondary to our intense conversation
[pp. 291–292].

The boundary crossing first takes us from a classic ivory tower image of Harvard University to the "gray hulking building" of the School of Public Health bordering the noisy, crowded city streets on one side and the more refined and stately Medical School cloister on the other. The School of Public Health is poised on the edge of the real world. Images of the students also echo the boundary crossing. Compared to the Harvard Law students depicted in an earlier excerpt—whose advocacy and activism in Roxbury barely masked their privilege and well-developed sense of entitlement—the students here seem colorful, diverse, alive, and vibrant; worldly and ready to take on the world. And as Tony and I navigate the boundary between the cacophony of the cafeteria and the quiet oasis of the exclusive dining room, we are also marking the metaphor—hinting at a central contrast that shapes Tony's professional life: the dialectic between activism and research, between passion and science.

SHAPING CONTEXT

As the researcher documents the context—rich with detailed description, anticipatory themes and metaphors, and allusions to history and evolution—she must remember that the context is not static and that the actors are not only shaped by the context, but that they also give it shape. The portraitist, then, must be vigilant in recording changes in the context, some as visible and anticipatable as the shifting seasons—the stark, dreary gray cast of the winter landscape fading into early spring with crocuses forcing their colorful heads through the brittle ground. Other changes in context are far more subtle—a painting that has been placed on a different wall, the mysterious darkness in a normally well-lighted corridor, a new smell in the environment that surprises and intrigues. The portraitist must be alert to documenting these changes and to observing whether the actors perceive and experience them. Each time the researcher visits the setting, she must scrutinize the environment for small and large transformations. It is also, of course, interesting to note when there is no change in the setting—when it remains constant and undisturbed by human occupancy.

Just as the portraitist needs to think of context as dynamic, she must also recognize the ways it is shaped by the people who inhabit it. Sometimes we—who underscore the power and significance of context in our work—begin to overstate its shaping influence in the lives of actors, assuming that institutional structures and ecological domains are far more powerful than they are. But in developing portraits we must also observe and record the ways in which people compose their own settings—the ways they shape, disturb, and transform the environments in which they live and work. The portraitist, then, hopes to capture this dialectic of contextual structures and forces defining individual action and perception *and* of actors inventing and shaping the contexts they inhabit.

The following illustration from *I've Known Rivers* shows Cheryle Wills in her environment. We see how she creates it, shapes it, embellishes it, and moves through it. And we also see how she is shaped by it—how it expresses who she is.

> Today, when I arrive at Cheryle's house, she is ready and eager to resume. She greets me at the door and immediately tells me that she will be turning the telephone off so that we will not be interrupted. I find it impossible not to notice Cheryle's wonderful costumes; they are such bold declarations. This morning she is wearing an emerald green and black striped silk skirt and blouse, trimmed—around the bodice and in a wide band at her waist—in black leather. Sheer black stockings and black patent leather shoes, again with three-inch heels, complete the picture.
>
> Cheryle has been away for several days in Chicago fulfilling her duties as a board member of National United Way. The Search Committee, on which she sits, is reviewing applications for an Executive Director. ("We've gotten four thousand applications; three thousand nine hundred ninety of them you could toss out immediately.") After the controversial departure of the former Executive Director, this search process has become highly politicized and Cheryle is in "the thick of it." After returning from her Chicago meeting in the late afternoon, she raced out to a fundraiser for a political candidate whom she is backing. Before I arrived she has gone out "to do her domestic thing" and when I arrive she is in the midst of unpacking groceries. "You'd be so proud of me," Cheryle chirps. "I've gone shopping!" She holds up a jumbo package of blue toilet paper— "the bare essentials." A few minutes later she zooms down thirty-five floors to park her car, which has been waiting at the curb, and returns with a huge bunch of gladiolus. "Now they

(the doormen) are convinced that I *live* here. . . . They think 'she's bought flowers. She must call this home.'"

From one of the grocery bags Cheryle pulls out a couple of bottles of raspberry-flavored soda, finds some fancy wine glasses, and pours us each a drink. We settle into our places in her pastel-colored living room. This time she kicks off her high heels, stretches her long legs under the coffee table, and sits with me on the soft rug. "I'm a floor sitter," she explains. With the tape recorder set up between us on the glass table, and both of us on the same level, facing each other, Cheryle is ready to work [pp. 429–430].

In summary, the portraitist views the context as a dynamic framework—changing and evolving, shaping and being shaped by the actors. The context is not only a frame for the action, it is also a rich resource for the researcher's interpretations of the actors' thoughts, feelings, and behaviors. Working in the natural environment, the portraitist scrutinizes the connections (and disconnections) between the theoretical predispositions and the actors' realities, seeking to accommodate the former to the latter, monitoring the growing convergence between scientific abstractions and the actors' empirical categories. In sketching the context, the portraitist captures the details of the physical setting, hoping to create a picture into which the reader will feel drawn—a palpable picture that allows the reader to see, feel, smell, and touch the scene. In addition, the portraitist places herself in the picture—not in the center dominating the action and overwhelming the scene, but on the edge witnessing what is happening and revealing her angle of vision. Finally, contextual description includes references to the history and culture of the setting and the use of well-chosen metaphors, foreshadowing central themes that will be further developed and enriched throughout the portrait.

Implementation

Setting the Site

Jessica Hoffman Davis

In implementing portraiture, the researcher is engaged in a discourse between two mutually informative aspects of the methodology: the process of data gathering and the process of shaping the final portrait. The product—the portrait—is at the forefront of both aspects of process from the inception of the research, even before the first interaction with site or subject. The process—the act of collecting and making sense of the data—continues beyond the time spent at a site or interacting with a subject, throughout the actual writing of the finished product. The requirements of the product stimulate insights into the process; the direction of the process actively shapes the finished product.

When outlining strategies for implementation, it is necessary to consider both parts of portraiture's dynamic and ongoing interchange between process and product. Indeed, the repeated methodological question that portraitists must ask of process is, How does this line of investigation inform (give shape to) the product—the developing portrait? And the repeated question that portraitists must ask of product is, How does this mode of representation inform (clarify) the process—the developing understanding? With slight variations, these two overall questions recur throughout our discussions of implementation.

SETTING THE SITE

In our discussion of the implementation of context, we follow the same thematic structure as in our illumination section, with a different emphasis and direction. Here, we consider practical strategies for discovering, including, and representing context as it is located in literal space and time (*internal context*), determined by the researcher's particular background, agenda, and presence (*personal context*), and situated in terms of the ideological and cultural journey of the subject or site (*historical context*).

Our suggested strategies for implementing context necessarily include discussion of particular process issues such as how the portraitist prepares for a first visit or encounter with a site or subject, and how she recognizes and attends to possible sources of contextual information. Product considerations address issues such as how to decide what to include as context in the final portrait and how to actually incorporate the various resources for context that the portraiture process uncovers. We also consider the differences in implementation from a group as opposed to an individual perspective and situate context in relation to the other operative features of portraiture.

INTERNAL CONTEXT: THE PHYSICAL SETTING

Although the finished product may not be very long, the footprints of process that lead up to the portrait form an extensive trail. In negotiating portraiture as a group process, Co-Arts researchers worked first as a group, establishing a set of shared procedures, priorities, and hypotheses that would give our productions consistency across portraits. In the creation of each portrait, one portraitist took the lead in writing, but researchers otherwise worked in pairs, preparing for the visit, collecting data on site, and reviewing the final production with input from the entire group.

An industrious pair necessarily generates more information and observations than individual researchers working on their own. For each of the six portraits of approximately thirty-five pages included in *Safe Havens,* there was almost a whole file drawer filled with data, including folders of background materials, audiotapes of on-site interviews, transcriptions of on-site and phone interviews, sorted transcriptions and field notes, outlines, and developing drafts. Portions of all these sources of data informed the construction of the portrait's internal context as physical setting.

In Co-Arts's work, we called the portrait's opening description of context, moving from what Lawrence-Lightfoot calls the macro to the micro environment, the *outside in.* From the beginning of the physical journey to the first encounter of the site, from wider setting to close surrounding neighborhood, from nearby architecture to specific building or campus, from exterior to interior space, portraitists are always attending to context. They are looking carefully, absorbing details of sight, sound, and ambiance—always collecting more information than will find its way into the final portrayal.

Just as the portrait's contextual introduction helps to locate the site or subject in time and space, it also helps to introduce and situate the essential features of the narrative—the various parts of the aesthetic whole. As the developing parts of the whole congeal, the portraitist gains a better sense of which aspects of physical context will warrant inclusion and which will not. But in first encountering a site or subject, the portraitist needs to be open to input from all sources of potential contextual material.

Traveling as we did to so many far-off cities, Co-Arts researchers often began their early attempts at writing *outside ins* with descriptions of their first direct experience of unfamiliar cities: the airport. Although most of these airport descriptions included information that would ultimately be excluded, it turned out that the striking similarities one researcher found between the circles of light flooding Pittsburgh's new International Airport and the skylight-lit lobby of the Manchester Craftsmen's Guild was no coincidence. The two facilities were designed by the same architect.

The Guild's executive director, Bill Strickland, sees the provision of a state-of-the-art facility as integral to his mission in educating at-risk youth. His hiring of the same well-known architect chosen for the airport typifies his efforts to convince students, as he says, "Hey man, you're worth something. Hey man, I care about you. You're going to college. Your life's going to change. We're going to turn the sunshine on and let it bathe you; you're going to be bathed in sunshine. Sunshine is free, it doesn't cost nothing. You don't need to be rich to walk in the sun, you can be anybody to walk in the sun" (Davis et al., 1993, p. 83).

As introduced in this statement and verified through progressively more intimate knowledge of the center, *A Place in the Sun* was identified as an emergent theme of the portrait of the Manchester Craftsmen's Guild. With that structural component in place, the portraitist was able to return to early field notes and glean relevant information to include in the *outside in*. Because it informed one of the Guild's emergent themes, the airport warranted inclusion in the presentation of physical context as internal backdrop to the portrait.

The few pages of researcher notes of careful description of the architecture and background of the airport were reviewed with this end in view. As example of the amount of thought and documentation that infuses every line of a research portrait, note the final space given to the resolution of these considerations in the contextual introduction (*outside in*) to the portrait of the Manchester Craftsmen's Guild. Here, we enter the Guild:

> Double glass doors open on to a lobby that is spacious, clean,
> and bright. Archways and windows repeat the motif of circles
> and light found throughout the building. The facility is designed
> by architect Tasso Katselas, who lent a similar touch to Pitts-
> burgh's new International Airport. Skylights line the two-story-

> high ceiling on opposite sides of the lobby and sunlight falls
> in patches on the beige and brown tiled floor. Two tall grayish-
> green ceramic sculptures, the work of a part-time artist-in-
> residence at the Guild, guard the entrance hallway. Other
> pieces of ceramic art, all by professional artists, decorate
> various corners of the building [Davis et al., 1993, p. 82].

The inclusion of this contextual detail begins to inform an understanding of the actual physical configuration of the Guild's facility, the underlying philosophy of the site in terms of aesthetic and personal mandates, and the structure of the unfolding portrayal.

In deciding what or what not to include, the portraitist needs to consider the question, Will this description inform the reader's understanding of the site or subject as it is portrayed herein? As the portrayal begins to take shape, a number of observed physical details that may at first seem potentially important end up not warranting inclusion as contextual information.

This mode of rapprochement between the clarification of the portrayal and the sorting and selecting of relevant data begins with preparation for the portraitist's first encounter with site or subject and continues as long as the portrait is being written (and rewritten). The final integrated prose that the reader experiences as a unified whole results from the portraitist's compilation of relevant documents, various on-site observations, diverse stories of actors on the scene and in the wings, and, as always, ongoing consideration of the developing whole of the portrait.

In collecting relevant documents, it is helpful to engage the assistance of the subjects or actors at the portrait site. Portraitists should ask to see copies of potentially informative resources when someone mentions them in conversation. An evaluation of a facility's current state and specific needs, like a founding mission statement or five-year plan, can be most helpful informants of context.

It is appropriate to ask to see materials such as year-end reports, questionnaires to students after graduation, scrapbooks of newspaper clippings, and publicity materials. Other rich resources may be found in lesson plans, meeting minutes, correspondence, or student evaluations or portfolios. By sharing an open interest in reviewing such materials, portraitists invite the actors into the portraiture process. From the existence of historic proposals to the identification of outsiders who possess intimate knowledge of the site, insiders will be able to suggest and provide more relevant resources than portraitists would think to request.

Evidence of the use of various sources is apparent in the passages cited in our illumination section as examples of internal context as physical setting. In the *outside in* to the Artists Collective, background research uncovered simple information such as the city's identity as state capital and as "the insurance capital of the nation." A review of the relevant neighborhood profile from the *Hartford Sociodemographic Profile* (compiled in 1991 by the Institute for Community Research in conjunction with the Urban League of Greater Hartford) supplied the demographics concerning the African American and Latino populations of Hartford and the percentage of residents living below the poverty line.

The discovery of an arts gallery, the Craftery, at the edge of the North End and embellished with a mural of performing artists, prompted an interview with Craftery Director Jonathan Bruce. The exchange with Mr. Bruce helped illuminate, as did interviews with numerous neighborhood residents, the community's understanding of the Artists Collective.

Other interviews uncovered the identities of surrounding houses as shelters and former crack houses. Similarly, Lawrence-Lightfoot's prior knowledge identified buildings along the Southeast Expressway on the way to Milton Academy and the names of the artist and architect defining the view from the road. In each of these instances, as with the airport reference for the Manchester Craftsmen's Guild, extensive inquiry informs small parts of a developing layered and nuanced whole.

Reaching beyond the immediate experience of subject or site for contextual elucidation is an important step in informing context. Although a lens is being focused on a particular setting and stage, the context determines the curvature of the lens and the illumination of the view it provides. The result of far-reaching attention to multiple sources of data is a collage of carefully chosen facts, views, voices, and impressions. This contextual collage situates the portrait's central players and images and points the way for reader and researcher.

In the openings of both the Artists Collective and Milton Academy portraits, the reader is situated in season (February in Hartford; spring in Milton), and in a journey to a physical location. In outlining the literal journey to the site, the portraitist needs to synthesize a plethora of information that, unchecked, can read like a road map or driving directions.

A description of the dividing line between the North End and Hartford's downtown provides important contextual information. The number of left and right turns between the fork of Main Street and Albany Avenue and the final right onto Clark Street does not. In the opening to the Milton portrait, it is sufficient to know, "A few turns later, Center Street becomes the central artery of Milton Academy, and you are advised to go twenty miles per hour."

Additionally, in both excerpted examples, you receive *alternative* information as part of the contextualization. We see Hartford's North End in winter, we hear about it in warm weather. We approach Milton swiftly and with little traffic, and hear about the journey in rush hour or during other seasons. These elements of alternative contextual information set the site as a vibrant changing locale that we encounter as moving through time and space, appearing one way at this moment, and another at the next.

The move from *macro to micro* continues from outer to inner layer in the researcher's and reader's growing understanding of the subject or site. Each subsequent layer of internal context moves closer to the micro as the site comes more clearly into focus. The following excerpt from the Artists Collective portrait clearly represents context as a collage of multiple sources of data, balanced with the emerging theme of *Safe Havens* and the center's overarching mission of providing positive African American role models while offering the arts as an alternative to life on the street:

> Early in the day, the Collective building is as apparently vacant as its neighbor structures on Clark Street. But in the late afternoon when classes begin or on a hectic Saturday of classes, the stream of people flowing in and out acclaims the vital presence contained behind the lifeless facade. Approximately six hundred students a year participate in classes at the Artists Collective.
>
> The door to the center is protected by a brick archway, and each individual must ring a buzzer and declare his or her name into the intercom before gaining entrance. The buzz of the doorbell syncopates intrusively the background hum between classes, punctuated now and then with greetings: "Hello." "How are you?" "How ya doin' man?"
>
> From outside to in, the change in atmosphere is as dramatic as the change experienced crossing "the line" into the North End. Opening the double doors into the main floor's hallway, eyes are drawn upward to the colorful banners hung from the ceiling in rows of three. Neatly hung posters line the hallways. Some announce performances by noted black artists, others advocate a drug-free America: "Drugs don't care about you; connect with people who do!"
>
> On the tops of skirted tables lie well-ordered stacks of free brochures: "Cocaine/crack, The Big Lie"; "Thinking about Drugs? Think about this." There are brochures that announce local arts events, tours of West Africa, and programs to help "if someone close has a problem with alcohol or other drugs." An order form for a new publication announces, "Finally, a guide for the unique issues facing black parents: Different and Wonderful, Raising Black Children in a Race-Conscious Society."
>
> Photo displays of Collective performances and visits from well-known black artists in music, dance, and drama are carefully compiled in large framed collages mounted against the shiny brick walls. Everywhere the touch of aesthetic order transforms the cold old school halls into what members of Hartford's

African American community have called an oasis. One mother who has just begun to bring her daughter to piano lessons explains that she had been urged to try the Artists Collective and had resisted: "The outside of the building looks so drab and uninviting." Her face lights up: "But inside, an oasis" [Davis et al., 1993, pp. 15–16].

PERSONAL CONTEXT:
THE RESEARCHER'S PERCH AND PERSPECTIVE

The researcher does not come as an empty slate to the job of interpreting the subject of the portrait. Individual characteristics and experiences shape the portraitist's voice. Preliminary research into or prior experience with the broader field of which the portrait is representative generates theoretical expectations that contribute to the researcher's personal context entering the work.

Lawrence-Lightfoot brought years of experience doing research in schools and classrooms to her portrayal of the selected sites in *The Good High School.* Project Co-Arts spent two years studying hundreds of community art centers through reviews of written materials, questionnaires, in-depth phone interviews, and brief site visits before even selecting the subjects of the *Safe Havens* portraits.

Individuals or groups of portraitists begin by researching the questions that drive their selection of a portrait subject or site. If the research question, for example, concerns the necessary ingredients for success in a particular educational setting, portraitists will want to review what has been written about similar sites. They will want to become familiar with the most frequent markers of success that have been identified in other inquiries. While these markers need not delimit on-site observations, they will serve as a contextual backdrop to the interpretation of the range of evidence that emerges from the site.

In collections of portraits, as in both *The Good High School* and *Safe Havens,* prefaces can introduce the methodology of portraiture, the sites selected, and underlying principles of goodness or effectiveness that inform the voices of the portraitists. In this way, prefaces can begin to offer overall *historical* (relating to the methodology), *personal* (relating to the researcher's perspective) and *internal* (providing a backdrop for the sites) context.

Unlike many other empirical investigations, portraits are not usually prefaced with a traditional review of the relevant literature. Nonetheless, such a preface may serve a portraitist well. For example, a student interested in the question of how identifying oneself as an artist contributes to self-esteem among adolescents may provide a small review of the literature on identity and self-esteem as a preface to her portrait of a teen arts program. This introduction, though external to the portrait, serves as a contextual backdrop illuminating the expectations that prior research instills in the portraitist approaching the site.

Regardless of the final articulation of prior research, portraitists prepare for the job at hand by developing a level of expertise that will inform the personal context through which they negotiate the challenge of interpretive description. That preparation—which may include a behind-the-scenes review of the literature—will help shape the conceptual framework and hypotheses that Lawrence-Lightfoot indicates need to be considered and challenged in light of the unfolding data gathered on site.

Most important, portraitists need to reflect on their personal contextual frameworks and become clear about the assumptions and expectations that they bring to the work at hand. Without such clear understanding, portraitists working in the context of the site will not be open to surprises and inconsistencies—let alone to the affirmation of expectations. Informed portraitists encounter the contextual features affecting the setting with an eye that is ever on the lookout for the expected and persistently open to the unexpected.

As an aspect of personal context, portraitists alert the reader to the fact that contiguous with the literal journey to the physical location is the researcher's personal journey in gaining familiarity with the site. Lawrence-Lightfoot asserts the importance of the portraitist *sketching herself into the context* and doing so at an early point in the portrait. This assertion of researcher perspective invites the reader to join actively in the journey of discovery of understanding.

The sketching in of self can be accomplished with an open declaration of "I" or with an implied presence suggested throughout. Referring again to the passages quoted in the previous chapter, when I say of the North End, "This is a neighborhood in which people live, but that reality is belied by the emptiness of the streets," I am sharing gained knowledge and first impression—but with implied and not directly stated presence. Lawrence-Lightfoot, on the other hand, directly reveals her growing knowledge of the buildings surrounding the Milton campus: "For several days I thought the imposing brick mansions, close to the school and along Center Street, were extravagant private homes and discovered later that they were the girls' dormitories for Milton Academy."

The difference between Lawrence-Lightfoot's explicit and my implicit self-reference marks a clear distinction in individual versus group portraiture. It is in the form of the imprint of self on every aspect of portraiture that the group process necessarily differs most from the methods of the individual researcher. Where the individual researcher can effectively use an articulated self in implementing personal context, a diverse group of researchers is less able to introduce and maintain a consistent "we" throughout the text.

In the example of Lawrence-Lightfoot's observation of Professor Ogletree's law school class, her articulated self-reflection on the age and intention of the students gives context to the reader's view of the individual researcher's particular perspective. A contemporary of the students might respond strongly to Lawrence-Lightfoot's comments, measuring their significance in terms of the age and experience of the portraitist, perhaps even thinking, "If I were there, I would not have had these doubts." And this is precisely what Lawrence-Lightfoot means by "allowing the reader the space to make his or her own interpretations." A pair or group of researchers cannot assert their separate personal contexts in the same way as the individual portraitist. A discussion, for example, of the differing impressions of a middle-aged and a younger researcher encountering Ogletree's students might distract from or cloud rather than enlighten the vision that the portrait seeks to provide.

Although the "I" is not stated in the North End excerpt, the reader is invited into the discussion because of the nuanced perspective that the reflection contains. For example, for someone living within the neighborhood, "the emptiness of the streets on a cold February day," like the unrealized expectation contained in the statement, "This is a neighborhood in which people live" may evoke a variety of responses. A resident might question the researcher's implicit expectation or think, "I wouldn't be surprised to see few people on the street." Active responses are invited by the speculative nature of the statement even without explicit reference to the researcher's inner thinking.

The removal of the overtly referenced "I" allows for the integration of various researcher observations into an implicit collective perspective. This researcher perspective can be introduced early on in context and maintained within and across a number of portraits of various sites. The implicit "I" or "we" not only reconciles a dilemma for a group of researchers, it also remains an option for the individual researcher. While the negotiation of personal context on a group level may seem particularly challenging, even for the individual researcher working on her own, the determination of "vivid, discerning (and restrained) articulation of the researcher's stance" is no easy accomplishment.

In our early gesture drawings, Co-Arts researchers worked independently and strove in our individual portrayals of subjects or sites to achieve a reasonable measure of direct articulation of self. In determining how much personal context to include, we repeatedly asked ourselves, "How much of the researcher's story is important for the reader to know in order to make sense of the data?"

For example, I am vexed by asthmatic symptoms that are particularly aggravated by contact with cigarette smoke. In an early gesture drawing of the Children's Art Carnival (1991), a community art center in Harlem, I described my initial encounter with Director Betty Blayton Taylor in terms of my distress over her heavy smoking: "Would I be able after all to stage this interview myself? I'd been so excited, but it was impossible for me to sit in a room with so much smoke!" Such inner dialogue initially seemed worth sharing with the reader. However, in light of the question of what was actually clarified by my personal dilemma, I saw that in my original draft, the reader learned more about my physical condition and personal distress than about the subject of my research.

Personal context is not meant to turn the reader's view away from the subject and onto the portraitist. Like all elements of context, personal context warrants inclusion only insofar as it illuminates the subject of the portrait. Lawrence-Lightfoot does not share her inner dialogue regarding Ogletree's students to educate the reader as to her own status as a professor teaching graduate students; rather, she includes the self-reflection to add skeptical nuance to the view of the scene. Measuring the ingredient of self throughout all phases of portraiture is a challenging procedure. It needs always to be guided by the contextual objective of informing vision.

PRESENCE ON THE SCENE

While our discussion of personal context has focused on considerations of shaping the portrait—what to include and the extent to which presence is explicitly or implicitly articulated—it is also important to consider how the portraitist negotiates actual entrance into the scene. The image of *fly on the wall* observation is not an objective in portraiture; nor, at the other extreme, is the status of *active participant,* engaged as an insider in the day-to-day workings of the site.

As examples of the inappropriateness of these two objectives for portraitists, consider the impossibility of two unfamiliar researchers with pads and tape recorders moving unnoticed through the halls of a small community center, or the futility of helping out as a teacher's aide while maintaining the wide purview afforded by a seat on the sidelines. The portraitist is an outsider to the scene and needs to accept and exploit that perspective, not only in the writing, but in the initial introduction to the site.

In setting the site in context, the portraitist must realize a researcher view that is sufficiently distanced to encompass the various sources of data, the broader physical and ideological landscape, and the developing vision of the whole. The elements of *self, voice, emergent themes,* and developing *aesthetic whole* (more fully discussed in their respective chapters) have already been mentioned in this discussion of *context*. The challenge of entering context touches on the remaining feature of *relationship*.

When negotiating entrance to context, self-awareness and an awareness of the impact of the portraitist's presence on the scene are essential. Such awareness not only helps guide the direction and shape of the interpretive description, but also helps mediate the developing relationship between researcher and site. In considering the contextual encounter with the site, the portraitist needs to be ever mindful of her own distanced relationship with the site itself (a Milton resident, for example, would not mistake the campus dorms for local mansions).

Beyond that, it is important for the portraitist to be clear about her own relationship with the actors—in the interviews that illuminate an understanding of the site (for example, with community members in Hartford like Jonathan Bruce or neighbors to the Collective)—as well as about the actors' relationship with the site (for example, "I am thirty-five years old and I grew up in this neighborhood and I never knew about it and it was right down the street.")

The portraitist is vigilant in the recognition of the differences in understanding of context that these various relationships afford and effect, as well as the difference that results from the researcher's necessarily intrusive presence on the scene (even as silent observer). As a result of such vigilance, the portraitist can collect and select relevant data that reliably represent the variations in understanding that enrich and lend nuance to context.

HISTORICAL CONTEXT: JOURNEY, CULTURE, IDEOLOGY

The implementation of context, *setting the site* in a framework that carefully illuminates the individual or institution, can be thought of as an introductory measure, but it is an activity that continues throughout the construction of the portrait. The initial move from macro to micro is not complete when the reader has entered the site or approached the subject. The portrayal does not move first from outside in only to continue with a strictly inward perspective. The portraitist continues throughout the work to weave into the narrative external contextual elements that help provide a clarifying backdrop to the action at center stage.

Throughout the creation of the portrait, the portraitist reaches beyond the site for input from multiple sources, draws on the insights derived from prior research, and keeps a watchful eye on the relevance of contextual details to the developing whole. This attention to parts and whole assures that context not only sets a physical site, but also situates the subject or site in reference to philosophical roots and directions, ideological and historical past, and practical plans for the future.

The portraitist needs therefore to offer context to the subject or site not only in terms of literal space and time, but also in terms of that place in the subject's personal or institutional journey in which the action is situated among past objectives, current realizations, and visions of the future. Various contextual elements allude to the philosophic or ideological journey of a site or subject as well as to the physical journey internally and externally.

We have already alluded to a number of these elements. The airport example from the Manchester Craftsmen's Guild portrait incorporates Strickland's original pedagogical purposes with regard to his students, the current realization of his particular objectives in terms of creating a setting for their learning, and his vision of the future for Guild students: one that is filled with the promise that sunlight will ensure.

The discussion of the Artists Collective's interior, while focusing on details of decor and ambiance, introduces the center's mission in terms of providing alternatives to Hartford's African American children, describes the Collective's realization of a safe haven in a drug-plagued community, and opens the readers eyes to the center's vision for African American children who will be raised positively as "different and wonderful" in spite of negative societal pressure.

A final example illustrates the multiple applications of context and the importance of journey as a contextual feature. In the following excerpt (the Artists Collective portrait's next layer of context), almost paragraph by paragraph, the reader is introduced to the center's mission in terms of offering a spiritual and educational alternative to Hartford's African American population, its historical origins in its founding by the McLeans twenty-five years ago, its educational philosophy in terms of providing students with a stronger sense of self, and its journey both ideologically in the notion of rites of passage and physically from current schoolhouse site to new facility.

Additionally, the passage introduces the emergent themes that shape our understanding of the center and the subsequent structure of the portrait. These themes inform and are informed by the portraitist's vision of the whole, and provide context for both the institution and the narrative that portrays it.

> "Oasis on Clark Street" is a popular descriptor for the Artists Collective, appearing as often in articles and promotional materials as it does in the conversation of advocates and constituents. In the summer of '91, one hundred young people in the Collective's summer program put on a musical at Hartford's Aetna Auditorium; its title, "An Oasis on 35 Clark Street." And that image of oasis as safe haven from the threatening realities outside is a resonant theme throughout this inner city community art center. Safe haven from drugs on the street and from the devaluation of African American culture and history in the media and in the schools. An oasis of culture, discipline, and high expectation.
>
> The hand exerting the aesthetic touch to school hall and ceiling belongs to the executive director of the Artists Collective, Dollie McLean. Ms. McLean is the wife of well-known alto saxophonist Jackie McLean, who—at the request of then executive director of the Connecticut Commission on the Arts, Tony Keller—founded the center almost twenty-five years ago. To think of the McLeans as the mother and father of the Oasis on Clark Street may obscure the parenting roles that so many

of the rest of the staff play. But all the surrogate familial connections at the Collective, taken together, evoke another resonant theme: the theme of family.

A third theme emerging from the fabric of life at the Artists Collective derives from the emphasis that is placed on performance, the positive performance that motivation, discipline, and high expectation can evoke. This emphasis is aimed toward what one parent at the center calls the realization that "I am somebody." At the Collective, students are trained as performers preparing each move and step and projection of voice for the audience of others they will meet throughout their lives. Founder Jackie McLean calls it a process, the "process of being somebody":

"We are trying to make kids love where they live and respect their elders and respect people, and if the kids in the Collective don't speak, we take them in and stand them up and if they look down at the floor, 'Hey, look at me.' There is love. . . . There is the process of being somebody . . . respecting someone else, saying, 'Good morning, How are you?' You don't have to be mad at the world."

Finally, across all three themes (safe haven, family, and the process of being somebody), and resonating throughout is the spirit and substance of Yaboo. Pronounced Ya-BO, it is the Nigerian word for "coming out" or "freedom": an African American version of what Master Choreographer and Collective teacher Aca Lee Thompson calls the universal phenomenon of rite of passage. All of us, Mr. Thompson explains, experience rites of passage "from minute to minute and day to day. Every birthday is a rite of passage; every transition." Our ability to recognize, negotiate, and learn from these rites of passage relies on the knowledge of self and culture that the Collective strives to instill: within the safe haven of the cultural oasis, supported by the foundational family structure, and realized through the process of being somebody. It is what Mr. Thompson calls one's realization of oneself as a person on the earth: "It is where you have come from and where you are going to go—not end up—because there is no end to it."

Individuals at the Collective experience rites of passage from class to class, day to day, and year to year. But nowhere is the coalescing theme of rite of passage played out more thoroughly than in the encompassing rite of passage the Collective itself is currently experiencing in its ambitious plans for a move from modest close quarters on Clark Street to an impressive $5 million performance center (part of a $7.8 million capital campaign) on upper Albany Avenue [Davis et al., 1993, pp. 16–17].

Artistic Refrain

Priming the Canvas

Jessica Hoffmann Davis

onsider the following two drawings of Happy, the first by a five-year-old child, the second by a professional artist (pp. 76–77). These different portrayals of the same emotion offer vivid examples of the effect of context from a *personal, historical,* and *internal* perspective. For both artist and research portraitist, these three interrelating contextual forces frame, elucidate, and animate the portrayal.

Personal context is evident as the experiential repertoire of the artist or researcher, *historical context* places the portrayal in a setting that transcends the limits of the aesthetic space, and *internal context* comprises the contextual details included within the aesthetic space. Personal context, then, is most specifically associated with the artist or researcher, historical context with the subject of the portrayal, and internal context with the portrayal itself.

In the child's drawing, personal context resounds in the wide open arms of the joyful figure. Michael spoke as he drew of how big and strong the figure is, "You can see the muscles . . . and fat and full, you can see the belly." Representing his own presence in context, Michael's Happy has a physiognomy (his own) expressively conveyed in his portrayal.

Situating his interpretation of Happy among contextual images of strength and amplitude (*historical context*), Michael is almost undifferentiated from his drawing. He displays the emotion in self-referenced form (*personal context*) that depicts both Michael and the larger human condition to which he is visibly connected. More aptly describing "humanness" than an individual child, Michael's drawing fulfills art psychologist Rudolf Arnheim's criterion for symbolic meaning, that is, "the sensing of the universal in the particular" (1974, p. 454).

The achievement of universality derives from what has been chosen by the child for inclusion as *internal context:* the powerful simplicity of a voluminous image defined by rounded and strong black lines against a simple white background. The line added at the top of the page balances the figure within the boundaries of the aesthetic space or edges of the page. The line also emulates the shapes that describe the head and shoulders of the figure and, in that echoing, reinforces and illuminates the articulation of the artistic statement.

Turning to artist Maxine's depiction of Happy, we are struck by the similarity of configuration between the five-year-old's open-armed figure and the artist's expansive sunflower, similarly dominating the aesthetic space with rounded open forms admitting the white background of the page. The leaves of the flower reach out like the five-year-old's figure's arms. The center of the flower almost embraces a smile. The petals framing the head of the flower resemble the muscles decorating the arms of Michael's figure.

These internal contextual elements selected by both artist and child situate their images in the wider historical human context from which they draw their similarities. But there is a difference. The artist has transported the emotion of Happy from the context of the human form and relocated it within the contextual realm of the flower. The relevant data that inform the internal context of the artist's drawing are provided exclusively through line and form and their interrelationship within the frame of the drawing. Unlike Michael's smiling figure—a happy person—Maxine's nonhuman sunflower, as a subject in itself, represents no emotion in particular.

Compare artist Maxine's drawing of Happy with her drawings of Sad and Angry (pp. 78–79). In the differences among these drawings, we see the importance of contextual information. The drooping lines of Sad and the refusal to admit background space through the close dark lines of Angry alter the internal context of the drawing and allow the same nonhuman subject to express different human emotions.

The personal context of the artist, rich with the resources that expertise will provide, allows Maxine to distance herself from the emotion and give it new internal context in an unexpected vehicle. The result is a visual metaphor, the juxtaposition of two different entities (the thought of the emotion and the thought of the sunflower) united in one image. Where the child's drawing extends meaning from the emotion to the physiognomic embodiment of it, the artist's drawing invents new meaning through visual metaphor.

Where the information provided in graphic symbolization is conveyed through line and form, the information provided in portraiture is conveyed through

Five-year-old Michael's drawing of Happy

Adult artist Maxine's drawing of Happy

Adult artist Maxine's drawing of Sad

Adult artist Maxine's drawing of Angry

language and story. For both, however, the context in which the information is provided introduces and sustains meaning and therefore provides crucial illumination to the interpretation that the portrait or drawing will provide.

As these examples demonstrate, contextual information directly informs the heart of meaning, enabling a portrayal to reflect the *personal context* of the artist (manifest here as expertise and differentiation), the *historical context* of the image (here as it is grounded in the broader cultural view of humanity), and the *internal context* of the image (here as the extension or invention of meaning: the achievement of visual metaphor).

Portraitists attempt to emulate the mature visual artist and provide personal context to their portrayals with expert repertoires, and internal context with details that lay the groundwork for such nuanced aesthetic achievements as metaphor. Also, like mature artists, portraitists strive to include sufficient historical context to allow the research portrait to achieve through narrative what is so readily accomplished in drawing by the child: *the sensing of the universal in the particular.*

La Taureau 1st state
5 December 1945

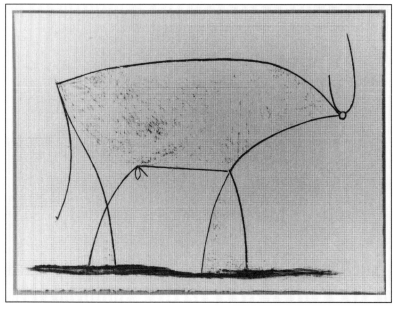

La Taureau 11th state
17 January 1946

CHAPTER FOUR

ON VOICE

Illumination

Expressing a Point of View

Sara Lawrence-Lightfoot

Every portrait that is painted with feeling is a portrait of the artist,
not the sitter. The sitter is merely an accident, the occasion.
It is not he who is revealed by the painter; it is rather the painter, who,
on the coloured canvas, reveals himself. The reason I will not exhibit
this picture is that I am afraid that I have shown in it the secret of my soul.
—Oscar Wilde, *The Picture of Dorian Gray*

In portraiture, the voice of the researcher is everywhere: in the assumptions, preoccupations, and framework she brings to the inquiry; in the questions she asks; in the data she gathers; in the choice of stories she tells; in the language, cadence, and rhythm of her narrative. Voice is the research instrument, echoing the *self* (or the "soul" as Oscar Wilde would put it) of the portraitist— her eyes, her ears, her insights, her style, her aesthetic. Voice is omnipresent and seems to confirm Wilde's claim that portraits reflect more about the artist than about the subject.

But it is also true that the portraitist's work is deeply empirical, grounded in systematically collected data, skeptical questioning (of self and actors), and rigorous examination of biases—always open to disconfirming evidence. From this vantage point, we see the portraitist's stance as vigilantly counterintuitive, working against the grain of formerly held presuppositions, always alert and responsive to surprise.

The portraitist's voice, then, is everywhere—overarching and undergirding the text, framing the piece, naming the metaphors, and echoing through the central themes. But her voice is also a premeditated one, restrained, disciplined, and carefully controlled. Her voice never overshadows the actors' voices (though it sometimes is heard in duet, in harmony and counterpoint). The actors sing the solo lines, the portraitist supporting their efforts at articulation, insight, and expressiveness.

From our point of view, then, Oscar Wilde is absolutely right *and* dead wrong. The portraitist inevitably renders a self-portrait that reveals her soul but she also produces a selfless, systematic examination of the actors' images, experiences, and perspectives. This balance—between documenting the authentic portrait of others and drawing one's self into the lines of the piece, between self-possession and disciplined other regard, between the intuitive and the counterintuitive— is the difficult, complex, nuanced work of the portraitist. In many respects, it is *because* the self of the portraitist is so present in the work, *because* she is the instrument of inquiry and the lens of description, interpretation, analysis, and narrative, that it is crucial that her voice be monitored, subdued, and restrained (though never silenced). The voice of the portraitist is poignant with paradox: it is everywhere *and* it is judiciously placed; it is central and it is peripheral.

This paradoxical paradigm contrasts greatly with the traditions and rituals of quantitative and experimental approaches to research—where the voice of the investigator is nowhere evident, where the first person is rarely (if ever) used, and where the structure of research design and text are predetermined and codified. In quantitative studies, researchers typically use the neutral "one" or "we" to refer to themselves, the subjects are called "Ss." Every attempt is made to disguise or mask the person of the investigator, designing an inquiry that will diminish (if not eliminate) personal perspective and bias. One of the ways the study is judged to be successful is if it can be replicated, if the experimental conditions, designs, methods, and findings can be reproduced, and if the investigators are interchangeable. The study must not be contaminated by the researcher's personality or idiosyncratic perspective. In this research tradition, then, personal view and judgment are considered distortions of an objective process. Voice is irrelevant. By design, it is neutralized out of existence.

Even though the voice of the researcher is purposely silenced in quantitative research where the structure and processes are relatively codified and routinized, it is important to recognize that the researcher's hand is, nevertheless, evident. We see the researcher's imprint in the selection of the research question, in the design of the study, in the data collection strategies, and in the interpretation of data. There is no voice, no soul, in traditional quantitative forms of inquiry, but the researcher's hand—revealed in the conceptual orientation, the disciplinary lens, the methods and design (and probably in personal disposition)—is certainly present and shaping the work.

In the various forms of qualitative research, investigators have struggled with giving definition to the notion of voice, seeking a way to represent *both* its omnipresence and its restraint, wanting to take full advantage of the insights of personal vision (that is, the self as research instrument) without caving in to personal prejudice (that is, research as self-expression). In qualitative inquiry and literature, *voice* has been used in myriad (often confusing) ways to refer to a variety of perspectives. In a welcome effort at discerning clarification, Donald

Freeman offers a nuanced examination of the various uses of voice in qualitative inquiry.

> The term "voice" is a messy and much used one that means different things; principally, it seems to refer to three inter-related sets of ideas. There is "voice" as an epistemological stance about the source of knowledge and understanding (Britzman, 1991; Belenky, Clinchy, Goldberger, & Tarule, 1986; Gilligan, 1982), there is *"voice"* as sociopolitical stance about who is doing the speaking and for what purposes (Freedman, Jackson, & Boles, 1983), and there is "voice" as a methodological stance towards what lies in the data to be heard, recognized through analysis, and advanced through the research process (Carter, 1993) [Freeman, 1996].

Voice in portraiture encompasses these three orientations—of epistemology, ideology, and method (with some variations in both framing and naming them)—but includes others, as well, reflecting the portraitist's explicit interest in authorship, interpretation, relationship, aesthetics, and narrative. In this section I will examine six ways in which the portraitist might use voice in developing the text, recognizing that the boundaries between these orientations are highly permeable and overlapping. Through explanation and illustrations from our texts I will explore first the use of voice as witness; second, voice as interpretation; third, voice as preoccupation; fourth, voice as autobiography; fifth, listening for voice; and finally, voice in conversation. The reader will notice that my examination of voice is purposefully sequenced to reveal the increasing presence and visibility of voice in the text, moving from the most restrained form of voice as witness, vigilantly listening and observing, to voice in dialogue, creating the story with the actors.

VOICE AS WITNESS

This use of voice underscores the researcher's stance as discerning observer, as sufficiently distanced from the action to be able to see the whole, as far enough away to depict patterns that actors in the setting might not notice because of their involvement in the scene. We see the portraitist standing on the edge of the scene—a boundary sitter—scanning the action, systematically gathering the details of behavior, expression, and talk, remaining open and receptive to all stimuli.

The portraitist not only uses her voice to express the outsider's stance, which looks across patterns of action and sees the whole, she also takes advantage of her position as stranger, which allows her to see through new eyes. As new-comer, she is able to perceive and speak about things that often go unnoticed by the actors in the setting because they have become so familiar, so ordinary, so habitual. The portraitist hopes to reveal those habits of behavior and per-spective that typically recede into the backdrop of human experience, fading into the background. As Malinowski—one of the first cultural anthropologists—put it, the ethnographer is always alert to the "imponderables" (1938, p. 306) of a cultural or social group, those things that the indigenous people would not even *think* to report. Geertz (1973) echoes Malinowski's search when he says that ethnographers are endlessly interested in the "cultural constitution of com-mon sense" (p. 11). The portraitist as witness, then, captures the terrain and its inhabitants with new eyes, from a position on the boundary. Through framing the scene and selecting the story, through her language and narrative style, we hear the portraitist's voice of witness.

In the following illustration from *The Good High School,* I describe the scene on the street bordering John F. Kennedy High, a magnet school located in the Riverdale section of the Bronx, one of the five boroughs of New York City. A huge school with nearly six thousand students, Kennedy High receives a diverse population of students from all over New York City, some traveling over an hour on the subway from their homes in East or West Harlem and the Lower East Side of Manhattan. Unlike other sections of the Bronx, which have a high pro-portion of black and brown families living in poverty, Riverdale is a relatively affluent enclave perched on the Palisades of the Hudson River. Riverdale dwellers respond to the Kennedy students with caution and some suspicion.

> The morning that I arrive in time to see the hundreds of students walk from the subway to the school's fourth-floor entrance, the community looks closed down. Windows are barred, shades are drawn, and almost no one is out on the street except the students, who by their massive presence seem to own the territory. I spot one elderly lady, dressed in a faded blue cloth coat and dark hat. She is leaving the corner grocery store, clutching her pocketbook close to her body. Four black girls crowd behind her because their gaits have suddenly brought them close and they are trying to figure a way to pass. As they chatter casually, the old lady's body seems to crouch in fear, and she ducks into a nearby doorway. In the vestibule of a square, four-story brick building across from the school I see a small group of black boys lighting up reefers. My com-panion says, in the residents' defense, "Now you know those boys don't live here. They've camped out there and they're get-

ting high. Who knows what they'll do next. You can't blame the neighborhood for being up in arms" [p. 91].

In this brief paragraph, rich in evocative description, we hear the portraitist's voice in her angle of vision, her selection of details, and in her choice of key words and phrases. The vision of the interloping students, owning the streets before school, feels almost apocalyptic. It is as if the windows are barred, the shades drawn, and the community closed down *because* of the students. The image of the elderly woman, bent and vulnerable, tellingly referred to as an "old lady," reifies the perceived power and menace of the students moving through this neighborhood by describing the way one resident seemed to fear for her life as the girls approached her from behind.

In a second illustration of voice as witness—also taken from *The Good High School*—I describe an advanced placement class called Literary Persuasion at Highland Park High, a school located in an upper-middle-class, largely Jewish suburb north of Chicago. Highland Park is a severely tracked school where academic competition is fierce and parental expectations are high. In this excerpt, I document the relatively sophisticated conversation between a teacher and her students, the teacher's meditative ruminations, and her efforts to inspire inquiry and discourse with them. Toward the end of this observation, I explicitly reveal my voice through a single question in which I express *my* discomfort and wonder out loud about the response of the only other African American person in the room.

> Ms. Wood is a short, curly-haired woman with a wry wit and an intense love of literature. She shows me "the original copy" of the book they are working with, tattered and worn from its many readings. With book in hand, she stands and leans casually against the front of her desk as she thoughtfully and carefully forms her first comments. The class seems to anticipate and enjoy her reflective, ruminative style. Before beginning the discussion, she remembers "the word for the day" written on the board, which is "phlegmatic . . . it is similar to sanguine . . . let's have a good sentence . . . What does it mean when you refer to a human being as phlegmatic, Lydia?" "Slow to act," responds Lydia without hesitation. This is a ritual that begins each day and most seem prepared to offer the answer.
>
> The discussion centers on Harriet Beecher Stowe's *Uncle Tom's Cabin*, a book the class has been reading and analyzing for the past two weeks. As they find the passages in the book, Ms. Wood begins, "This is a very didactic part of the book.

She [Stowe] uses Sinclair really as a mouthpiece. . . . His major character flaw is his indolence. . . . Don't you think he also represents a general human flaw? . . . Where he brings in his own opinion is in the analysis. . . . A slave owner might have a great deal to lose, at least from his own perspective . . . remember we have said that we can't judge the characters by our own standards; we must see them in historical and cultural context." To bolster her analysis, Ms. Wood reads excerpts from the text. She almost seems to be having a conversation with herself when she exclaims in the midst of her reading, "interesting idea, an unorthodox notion."

The discussion fastens on the author's attitudes toward slavery as Wood asks students to contrast Stowe with *Frederick Douglass,* an autobiography they have recently read. The class is silent and tentative, so the teacher leaps in and says, "Stowe mitigates—aha! one of your vocabulary words from last week— the horror of slavery, but Douglass's book is too extreme . . . it makes people feel uncomfortable, and if you are writing a book of persuasion, you don't want to turn people off." These notions of the limits of truth and the uses of distortion are clearly themes of this course that Ms. Wood often returns to. "Next week you'll be reading Saul Alinsky's book, *Rules for Radicals* . . . a Machiavellian essay that takes the extreme position . . . distortion is all right if it is for honorable ends." Some students— all the girls—are listening and taking notes, others are yawning and clearly bored by the esoteric distinctions.

Perhaps in response to the faraway looks in her students' eyes, Ms. Wood brings the discussion closer to home. She is trying to reveal the contemporary examples of enslavement all around them. "Having a slave in Highland Park is not the thing to do . . . it's also slightly illegal. But can't you picture how some of the folks here would deal with slaves . . . see them talk with the people who work for them. . . . They are just as despicable as Beecher Stowe's characters!" Maybe they hear the urgency in her voice, but the students' faces show no changes. I cannot see the face of the one black boy in the class who sits in the front by the window, but I project pain onto him. How must he feel as this conversation swirls about him? And how does he experience the disinterest and distance of his peers?

The interest of all students becomes suddenly charged when Wood says, "I'll give you a clue . . . in fact, I'll *tell* you one of the questions on the next exam. . . . On the basis of your reading of *The Jungle, Grapes of Wrath, Frederick Douglass,* and *Uncle Tom's Cabin,* which would you rather be, a slave or an English laborer? . . . You have to carefully examine the question of freedom." Hands are immediately raised and responses come from all corners. As students struggle for "the right answer," they do not seem to totally believe Ms. Wood when she claims there is no correct response. She is looking for a reasoned argument, a thoughtful interpretation, and creative insight. They are trying to come up with what she wants to hear [pp. 144–145].

VOICE AS INTERPRETATION

The second use of voice underscores the interpretive role of the portraitist. Here we not only experience the stance of the observer and her place of witness, we also hear her interpretations, the researcher's attempts to make sense of the data. She is asking, "What is the meaning of this action, gesture, or communication to the actors in this setting?" and "What is the meaning of this to me?" As Geertz reminds us in *The Interpretation of Cultures* (1973), the ethnographer's work is inevitably interpretive; it is a search for meaning. It involves the researcher tracing a path through a dense thicket of interpretations, "through piled-up structures of inference and implication" (p. 7).

As we mentioned in Chapter One, Geertz also makes a distinction between what he calls "thin description" (uninterpreted data, the systematic documentation of the who, what, where, and when of the action) and what he calls "thick description" (the information that the researcher needs to gather—in context and from a variety of sources—to begin to decode the environment in the ways the indigenous people do). The portraitist honors Geertz's distinction between thin and thick description, seeking to include both vividly detailed, low-inference description (thin) and thoughtful, discerning interpretation (thick) in the text. Both forms—thin and thick description—are important to the texture and authenticity of the portrait. But in making an interpretation, the portraitist must be vigilant about providing enough descriptive evidence in the text so the reader might be able to offer an alternative hypothesis, a different interpretation of the data.

In the following illustrations, we hear the voice of interpretation in the portrayal of two leaders, the first almost minimalist in its restraint, the second bolder in its interpretation of the person's demeanor, personality, and style. The first excerpt—from *Safe Havens*—is taken from a portrait of Bill Strickland, the executive director of the Manchester Craftsman's Guild, a community art center in Pittsburgh, Pennsylvania.

> Strickland himself seems to make a statement with his profes-
> sional appearance and aesthetically designed office. He is a tall
> African American man who dresses carefully in dark business
> suits, crisp shirts, and elegant ties. Seated behind a neatly orga-
> nized, polished wooden desk in his office, Strickland radiates
> ease and confidence. The walls of his office are covered with
> photographs: family portraits, photographs of art and of nature,
> and a picture of himself from years past when he worked as a
> pilot for Braniff Airlines. The image of the director of the Guild
> in pilot's uniform in the cockpit seems especially apt [p. 86].

This brief paragraph—marked by restrained and subtle interpretation—barely moves beyond the surface, simply reading the visual statement being made by Strickland's professional appearance and confident demeanor. The metaphor of Strickland as pilot of the Guild is telling, but still restrained.

By contrast, the description of Jerome Pieh, headmaster of Milton Academy—excerpted from *The Good High School*—is full of thick description. The para-doxical title of the section of the portrait from which this paragraph comes—"A Healing Authority"—seems to suggest a complex character and temperament that resists the conventional personification of authority.

> The tone of self-criticism at Milton is modeled and encouraged
> by Jerome Pieh, the headmaster. With a listening and gentle
> approach, he invites vigorous exchange, does not deflect harsh
> disagreements, and seems inspired by healthy debate. It is not
> that he seems to like confrontation, but that he deeply believes
> that institutional invigoration and change will only come with
> the difficult work of challenge and debate. He is aware of the
> differences in people's tolerance for uncertainty, and he recog-
> nizes the threats of institutional chaos and disintegration that
> often accompany a questioning climate. But he seems willing
> to risk the impending chaos in an attempt to encourage the self-
> criticism that he believes is the bedrock of a healthy educational
> climate. Pieh refuses to rely on the habits of tradition and yet
> he recognizes the need for roots and continuity to a rich past.
> He looks forward to the imperatives of the future, yet he resists
> the facile, trendy remedies. His is an uncomfortable posture,
> poised on boundaries and never comfortably settled. The last
> paragraph of his opening letter in the Milton catalogue reads:
>
> "Milton Academy introduced to you in these words is a constantly
> evolving school, neither shackled by its own past nor impatient to
> overturn its special traditions. Its focus on the individual student,

its commitment to rigorous standards, its rich store of experiences make it a challenging but friendly school. Welcome!"

This paragraph sits below a casual, quietly handsome photograph of Pieh. He is grinning, his hair is slightly tousled, and his eyes seem to express an edge of melancholy. The image is of one who appears wholly approachable, thoughtful, and empathetic. The picture is not of a distant, aloof, authoritarian headmaster [pp. 270–271].

In the physical description of Pieh that concludes this excerpt, the reader hears the portraitist's interpretive voice loud and clear, and perhaps learns as much about the researcher's eyes as about Pieh's face. Pieh's "grinning" and his "slightly tousled hair" are objective descriptors, close to the physical details of the photo. But when the reader comes to the passage about "eyes [that] seem to express an edge of melancholy," it is clear that the description must be read as symbolic interpretation; the descriptor points to a larger aspect of Pieh's personality. The eyes illuminate the warm, receptive side of Pieh—at least that is how the portraitist perceives him—and such terms as "handsome" and "empathetic" alert the reader to the evaluative nature of this description.

VOICE AS PREOCCUPATION

With increasing presence in the text, the portraitist's voice as preoccupation refers to the ways in which her observations and her text are shaped by the assumptions she brings to the inquiry, reflecting her disciplinary background, her theoretical perspectives, her intellectual interests, and her understanding of the relevant literature. Voice, here, refers to the lens through which she sees and records reality. This voice is more than interpretive description. It is the framework that defines—at least initially—what she sees and how she interprets it.

In another excerpt from the portrait of Highland Park High School, I reveal my intellectual interests and the conceptual preoccupations that guided my views of the school culture. As an educator, I was drawn to a drama class because I heard from many sources that it was an oasis for students, a place of refuge from the tough competition and strident ambition that characterized the rest of the school. In this class, creativity and disciplined inquiry were the currencies of discourse. I was also attracted to the teacher, Ms. Newbury, whose reputation as "a character" seemed to fit her, who relished her autonomy and flaunted her idiosyncrasies. And I was captured by this classroom, where relationships (between the teacher and her students and among the students) seemed to enhance trust, risk taking, and learning, and where emotional expression and high standards (both academic and artistic) were dual goals. *My* interests and *my* presuppositions thread their way through this passage, drawing me into the student theater, framing what I see, hear, and focus on, and leading to my unabashed admiration.

At fifty-one, Ms. Newbury is just as theatrical and enthusiastic as she was when she won the best actress award at the University of Wisconsin thirty years ago. With gray-blond hair swept back from her face, a voice that projects across footlights and into the balcony, and a carriage that is both confident and elegant, Ms. Newbury is a seductive force among her students. They crowd around her like disciples, worship the ground she walks on. In turn, she offers bountiful affection and personal caring. Her graduates return year after year for her hugs and reinforcement, and the student theater is a home away from home for Ms. Newbury's special group.

The student theater is a large room with a stage, scattered chairs, pieces of discarded scenery, and rugs to lie on. Students spread out on the floor and sit on tables and chairs as they listen intently to Ms. Newbury's words. She weaves the web of intimacy.

"My dears, this place offers an infusion—good word?—of comradeship. It is a built-in family . . . a built-in connection. . . . We will always have this tie. I look around for you because this is your place, your space . . . a magic place. . . . All our ghosts are here."

The delivery is perfect, her voice soothing and soft. No doubt it is a performance, but it is also experienced as genuine by students, who hear every word. Gone is the grubbing for grades and the cramming for tests. For this moment, the students seem far away from the rugged competition.

However, intimacy and good feeling is not all Ms. Newbury is after. She is also determined that her students will be introduced to the rigors and demands of acting and her standards are very high. She is fond of saying, "This is information that may be beyond you yet . . . you are so young . . . but you see I trust you enough to tell you this now and I know one day it will penetrate . . . and you will understand."

The class has just finished a screening of *Rebel Without a Cause,* a film classic starring James Dean and Natalie Wood. Students sprawled in front of the screen are still dazed by the powerful drama when Ms. Newbury begins her elegant critique of the film. Her comments are a mixture of lessons in technique, morality, and dramatic expression.

On morality: "I noticed you laughing at the black maid. Why? Why? She is a paid housekeeper in that very wealthy home. . . . She was the *only* one there to love and care for James Dean. Do you find that funny? I find that touching and unbelievable."

On technique: "There are all kinds of remarkable things about this film. Watch James Dean and you'll have a mini-course in acting. He does things so naturally that others of us would have to practice over and over. He's never, never melodramatic."

On emotional expression: "When Dean crumbles into tears and embraces the man, our first response to that is denial. We joke, experience disbelief. You say, 'I don't believe it. I'm numb. I refuse to feel this' . . . and then it hits you. . . . This, my dears, was a hard show to see. I wanted you to listen to Natalie Wood. Remember she said, 'I've been looking for someone to love me. Now I've found someone to love and it's easy.' Listen to her words carefully. Learn it and learn it soon" [pp. 146–147].

VOICE AS AUTOBIOGRAPHY

The fourth use of voice in portraiture reflects the life story of the portraitist. The researcher brings her own history—familial, cultural, ideological, and educational—to the inquiry. Her perspective, her questions, and her insights are inevitably shaped by these profound developmental and autobiographical experiences. She must use the knowledge and wisdom drawn from these life experiences as resources for understanding, and as sources of connection and identification with the actors in the setting, but she must not let her autobiography obscure or overwhelm the inquiry.

This balance—between self-possession and selfless, disciplined reporting of other lives (referred to at the opening of this chapter in response to Oscar Wilde's provocative assertion)—requires constant vigilance and calibration as the portraitist tries to avoid narcissism and yet use her self as research instrument. In the field, the balance is approached through self-reflection and self-criticism as the portraitist is engaged in observing, listening, and talking to people, always keeping the *actors* in the focus and in the light, always watching for the ways her shadow might distort her clear vision of them. The portraitist continues to work at this balance in her field notes and impressionistic accounts, identifying prejudice and bias growing out of her own life history along with the insights and resonance that enrich her inquiry. Finally, this balance must be explicitly reflected in the text as the portraitist sketches enough of *her* story into the narrative to inform the reader about the filter she brings to her interpretation of the data. Again, this autobiographical story must be expressed with restraint, sketching only those dimensions that bear some relationship to the themes of the portrait.

Paradoxically, the portraitist's reference to her own life story does not reduce the reader's trust—it enhances it. It does not distort the responsibility of the researcher and the authenticity of the work; it gives them clarity. A reader who knows where the portraitist is coming from can more comfortably enter the piece, scrutinize the data, and form independent interpretations.

In the beginning of *I've Known Rivers,* I tell a piece of my life story as a way of informing the reader how it will likely influence the way I will see, hear, and engage the actors portrayed in the book. The portraits in *Rivers* are deep and intimate, based on a year's worth of intensive dialogue with each person. The life stories of the actors call up powerful responses in me, shaping my interpretations and my construction of the narrative. It is crucial, therefore, that the reader hear my story as the framework, as the lens through which I will regard and investigate the journey of the book's protagonists.

The following excerpt from the beginning of *Rivers* reflects my explicit autobiographical stance and begins to reveal the personal history that I brought to this inquiry. The family themes (of intimacy, dialogue, and nourishment) and the sociocultural themes (of discrimination, oppression, and resilience) presage many of the central dimensions that will appear in the book's narratives.

> In my family's house, the dining room table was the center of gravity. Everyone was drawn to the table and once you settled there, it was almost impossible to move away. Friends and neighbors who dropped by claimed that any time of day or night you could find the Lawrences sitting around the table. Long after we finished eating, we would still be there—my parents, my maternal grandparents, my brother, my sister, and I, three generations under one roof. Generational contrasts and regional differences were reflected at the table, my grandparents' traditional Southern diet, fried catfish, cooked cabbage, corn bread, and yams alternated with our Northern dishes, broiled chicken, barely cooked asparagus, and corn on the cob from the local farm stand.
>
> Around the table we would tell stories, relive the day's events, explore new ideas, and compete for air time. It was here we always brought our tales from school, sometimes tales of victory and sometimes miserable laments. Sometimes my brother Chuck, a star athlete, would keep us on the edge of our seats with a detailed play-by-play of an "unbelievable"

touchdown scored at a football scrimmage, or a "gorgeous" jumpshot made in the final seconds of basketball practice. (We were present and cheering at every single one of his games.) Or else my sister Paula might do devastating imitations of our hapless teachers and I would follow with accounts of terminally boring lectures, our French teacher's excruciating pronunciation, or ridiculous rules regarding hall passes. One grievance would inspire another. If the accumulation of complaints became too heavy, my mother would step in. A child psychiatrist and psychoanalyst, she believed in the value of catharsis and always encouraged us in expressing our feelings. But after a lengthening parade of woes, she would deliver the familiar ultimatum. "If you can't say something good don't say anything at all." There would be a precious moment of silence as someone—usually a parent—tried to turn to more positive and productive conversation.

Even though my father was vice president of the local school board, there was much that was taught in school that opposed my family's teachings, and there was much that was not taught that my parents considered central to our education. Through twelve years of school, I remember being asked to memorize the verse of only one black poet, Langston Hughes. Around our table at home we recited the poetry of James Weldon Johnson, Gwendolyn Brooks, Countee Cullen, W.E.B. DuBois, Pauli Murray, Paul Laurence Dunbar, Margaret Walker, Arna Bontemps, and Jean Toomey, feasting on the rich language, rhythms, and imagery. We sang the Negro spirituals the way my parents had learned them growing up in black churches and schools in Mississippi. My father insisted that we not confuse spirituals with gospel music, that we honor the dignity and power of the simple verse. My parents knew that in our predominantly white school (often we were the only black students in our college preparatory classes) we would never learn about our African American heritage. Their family curriculum was ritualized, consistent, and intentional [pp. 2–3].

With this autobiographical backdrop, the following illustration from the portrait of Tony Earls becomes understandable. Tony Earls, a psychiatrist and epidemiologist, teaches at Harvard's School of Public Health. He tells me a powerful story from his experience as a psychiatric resident: a story that captures the challenge, guidance, and support he received from his mentor, Dr. Pierce, and symbolizes one of the greatest gifts ever bestowed upon Tony. My voice as autobiography threads through this piece, revealed in the nuances of our interactions, in the intensity of my questions, and in our raucous laughter that barely masks *our* pain.

It was the end of his psychiatric training and the third-year residents—"two black men, and about ten or twelve white residents"—were participating in a concluding seminar on "cultural sensitivity." The seminar, cotaught by Leon Eisenberg and Chester Pierce, was run "like a T-group" with the residents learning about their own cultural obsessions and defenses through interaction and introspection. With the reverberations of the civil rights movement surrounding them, the T-group became a microcosm of the larger societal struggles. "Week after week Chester would come with his sunglasses on," recalls Tony. "He was mysterious behind those shades. Leon would go on and on pontificating and occasionally he would manage to draw Chester out." But mostly, the tall, dark senior psychiatrist remained quiet, hearing everything and revealing nothing, threatening in his smoldering silence. During the last session of the group, the final opportunity to extract Pierce's perspective, Mel Williams, the other black resident, questioned Chester directly. He had been listening hard to Pierce's description of "racism as all-pervasive . . . a mental health disease." No white person growing up in our society could escape the malignancy of racism and no black person could be totally free of the experience of oppression and victimization.

Throughout the seminar, Pierce's assertions had been blunt and all-encompassing. Williams's final question asked him to be specific. "How many white folks do you know who you would not consider to be racist?" The question cut through the air and just hung there "for a very long time," while Chester slowly composed his answer and fueled the high drama. Everyone was visibly relieved when Pierce said that in his lifetime of knowing white folks, he could think of one nonracist. "Thank goodness Leon had made it under the wire," says Tony laughing. But the relief following Pierce's declaration lasted less than a minute when he whispered, "it's a woman in Texas." Eisenberg was not spared. He too was branded with the racist label. "Some white lady in Texas who had adopted a couple of black children" was remembered as a total anomaly, free of the most virulent societal disease. "Everyone was stunned," recalls Tony.

Then Pierce did something even more amazing, he removed his shades, squinted his eyes, and directed his gaze on the two black residents. For the first time he came from behind his dark glasses and let his black male students look directly into his eyes. His voice was dead serious. "I want to say something to Tony and Mel. . . . A lot of black men burn themselves out by the time they are forty. . . . You should have learned one thing here if you learned anything." He was both admonishing them and pleading with them: "You mustn't let yourself get burned out!" With those words, he put his dark glasses back on and fell silent. Tony's eyes are moist as he relives this extraordinary moment. "If someone ever gave me a pearl it was that . . . I will never, never forget it." He remains deeply thankful to Chester for the pearl of wisdom, for modeling the self-sustaining behavior that he was declaring as essential for black male survival, for directing his teaching to his young black colleagues. This was a special moment for Tony and Mel, a moment that would always be seared into their psyches [pp. 306–308].

VOICE DISCERNING OTHER VOICES (LISTENING FOR VOICE)

In this and the following section, we focus on the *actors'* voices; we listen for the timbre, resonance, cadence, and tone of their voices, their message, and their meaning. We make a subtle distinction between listening *to* voice and listening *for* voice (a distinction borrowed from Eudora Welty—referred to in Chapter One—in which she draws the contrast between listening *to* a story and listening *for* a story), the latter a more assertive stance than the former. When the portraitist listens for voice, she seeks it out, trying to capture its texture and cadence, exploring its meaning and transporting its sound and message into the text through carefully selected quotations.

In the field, the researcher records (in written notes or tape recordings) all that she hears—in interviews, dialogue, or informal conversations—trying to document the words, the gestures, and the tone, witnessing the voices in context, and seeking to understand the actors' interpretations of their talk. When the portraitist listens for voice, she also *observes* very closely, watching for the ways in which the actors' movements and gestures express and communicate what they mean. Sometimes the gestures speak much louder than the words, in which case the portraitist needs to vividly describe the visible cues and the body language. The young man jumps up suddenly, his pace quickens, and he begins to sweat profusely. His voice becomes staccato, halting. The child falls forward in her chair, she casts her eyes downward, and her face grows mournful. She whispers. At other times, there seems to be a dissonance between the actor's talk and his behavior, expressing confusion or ambiguity, uncertainty or ambivalence. His voice says "yes," but he shakes his head "no." Through listening *and* observation the portraitist documents these mixed feelings, the fusion of contrasting views and emotions that are so common in human experience.

Listening for voice not only requires listening, watching, and questioning, it also requires that the portraitist be attentive to silences. It is often true that the moments of silence are just as important to understanding the story as the message conveyed through words. Silences speak about points of confusion or resistance, or they indicate ambivalence or evasion, or they hide private feelings or make a dramatic point. So the portraitist listening for voice is also attentive to silence.

In addition, the listening portraitist is discerning of the idiosyncratic sound and use of language used by actors, describing individual variations in the way people express themselves—the flat, lifeless monotone of the school's principal delivering the announcements at school assemblies; the lilting, musical tones and lyrical language of the biology teacher describing the natural habitat of rare fauna. The portraitist is also listening for the range of sound and expressivity, the actor's repertoire of words and affect. The principal's dull monotone disappears when the subject matter is summer adventures or a favorite novel. The biology teacher's voice is harsh and menacing when a student breaks a piece of laboratory equipment. As the researcher listens for the nuance and range of individual voices, she is always alert to the metaphors actors use to symbolize larger themes, the images they keep returning to, the words and expressions they use most often. In describing the texture of voice, then, the portraitist is attentive to the sound and the silence, the talk and the gestures, the words and the emotions, the repertoire and the range.

In the following contrasting excerpts we notice the portraitist listening for voice, the first a rich cacophony of voices, the second a deep examination of a single voice. In the portrait of Plaza de la Raza, a community art center in Los Angeles that appears in *Safe Havens,* Davis and her colleagues include a range of voices—students, parents, and teachers—who speak about the warm, inclusive community they experience at Plaza. The voices—speaking Spanish and English interchangeably—contribute to the researcher's knowledge and understanding of the place and begin to capture the texture of sound and expression heard there. The voice of the dance teacher is an exhortation, challenging his students with a fast-paced, rhythmic chant that jumps off the page. The reader hears the shift of mood and tempo, experiences the drama and energy, and is drawn into the dance class.

> Plaza is a place where, one staff member points out, "people
> can feel a sense of togetherness." A student who has been

attending *folklórico* and acting classes at the center for seven years waits with his mother for his younger sibling to finish a music lesson. When asked what they like about Plaza, they respond together in Spanish:

Student: My mother sends me to this school. I need to practice
   folklórico. I like Plaza because I like to walk, I like the ducks,
   the lake.
Mother: And to be in a convivial atmosphere with his friends.
Student: And gather with my relatives.
Mother: Parents get together and we have conversations.

At Plaza, children and teenagers chat as they run from one class to the next, parents speak in English and Spanish interchangeably. "It is like a social event," says one mother who brings her daughter to *folklórico* three times a week. A twelve-year-old student appreciates that at Plaza, *"conoces más amigas"* (you meet more friends). A teenage student who has been attending the center for seven years values "talking to teachers on a friendly basis." Choral and piano instructor Antonio Ayón explains, "It is not only about singing, it's about friendship. . . . If you put eighteen people together, and they're friendly, they'll sound pretty good."

Dan Morris, an Anglo drum teacher at Plaza, suggests that "music and arts is one of the few things that human beings have that is universal and that is the place to start to bridge the gaps between us." Sandoval says that what Plaza is about is beyond the perpetuation of traditions: "It is the perpetuation of the human race." She explains:

"We live in a society that dehumanizes you. . . . You need to have the support system that makes you a human being again. Plaza is one of the few resources this community has for making this humanization process for our kids."

In the sparse dance studio with shiny wooden floors, off-white walls are intersected by a black horizontal bar. Two male and four female teenage modern dance students in leotards or sweatshirts are reflected in a long mirror that covers the entire back wall. Antony Balcena teaches the intermediate and advanced Modern Dance Limón Technique. He has very short brown hair, a silver hoop earring in one ear, and is dressed in a black unitard. He describes his students as "really human."

Balcena instructs the students with a level of animation that demands high energy: "Inhale and exhale! Beautiful! . . . And a

two, and a one! Let's just release! . . . And a one and a three . . . burst and pump!" [p. 122].

The second illustration is all about voice. It comes at the end of my portrait of Toni Schiesler, a research chemist, a former nun, and an Episcopal priest in training. We are both grieving over the recent death of her mother Gladyce (a jazz singer who never got the chance to express her art and lived a life of transience and poverty) and mourning the conclusion of our time together. In a tender dialogue—our farewell song—Toni and I explore voice as legacy, power, and insight. Her *singing* voice is her sole inheritance from her mother and it offers her solace and comfort. It gives her spiritual nourishment.

> It is hard to know how to give shape to this final session, how to give words to the sadness we both feel. I am haunted by Toni's bereft feeling that her mother has left her so little. I remember that one of the most precious legacies left by her mother has been her wonderful voice. Toni has said repeatedly, *"My mother's power was in her voice."* She meant this in two ways, I think. First, she has always known her mother as outspoken, forceful in her candor, frightening in her honesty. She possessed the voice of power, clarity, and confrontation. "My mother always said what she thought. She was *not* like me. She was not worried about other people's feelings." Perhaps Toni's struggle to "find voice" is part of her determination to feel more identified with her mother, to draw on some of her mother's fight and power. But she is also thinking of her mother's beautiful singing, soothing, comforting—an expression of her artistry. Toni lives with both legacies. As we search for closure, I long to hear Toni's own voice. "Will you sing for me, Toni?" I ask. "In all this time, I've never heard you sing."
>
> Toni needs no prodding. Moving swiftly and gracefully to a cross-legged position on the floor, she opens her guitar case, takes out an elegant and brand new instrument and searches for her "purple pick." She pulls out a list of songs that she has titled "Sacred Songs for My Ordination," including "The Lone Wild Bird," "Here I Am Lord," "The Spirit of the Lord Is Upon Me." "I'm so tired of Bach, Beethoven and Brahms." She chooses a song from her list, checks the tuning on her guitar, and tentatively strums a few chords. She apologizes for her fumbling. But there is no tentativeness or fumbling in her singing. Her voice is powerful and large and surprisingly sweet. Her singing seems free and totally unself-conscious. She is wrapped up in the music, in the poetry of the words, in the

resonance of her voice. Sitting on the rug, leaning over her
guitar, Toni's body looks relaxed. Her face is glowing and all
the weariness seems to be washed away. I know why she has
spoken of "music as healing." I sit quietly on the rug, leaning
my back up against the bookcase. I do not want to break the
spell as she moves through a group of her favorite songs, so
I don't comment or applaud. When she stops singing, she
lets the silence linger and then muses, "My dream is to have
a music group in a parish . . . to help people understand the
possibilities for worship. Singing is not just performing, it is
praying" [pp. 285–286].

This excerpt offers a kind of *metaview* of voice, an inquiry into the expression and meaning of voice in Toni's life, a view of voice as development and declaration, and a portrayal of the interplay of voices between us. We witness the healing power of singing, but we also hear the solace of silence. In contrast to the powerful presence of her singing voice, the silence seems to have a different but equally poignant resonance.

VOICE IN DIALOGUE

In this final exploration of voice in portraiture, we hear the voices of the researcher and the actor in dialogue. Here the conversation chronicles the developing relationship between them, the emerging trust and intimacy, capturing the dance of dialogue. The texture is very different from the portraitist's use of voice as witness, a position on the periphery of the action, a place from which she can observe patterns and see things that might not be visible to the actors. With voice in dialogue, the portraitist purposefully places herself in the middle of the action (in the field *and* in the text). She feels the symmetry of voice— hers and the actor's—as they both express their views and together define meaning-making. The reader also hears the researcher's methodology, her questions, her interpretations, her interventions.

In this illustration from the portrait of Katie Cannon in *I've Known Rivers*, I tell the story of our evolving relationship through the vivid display of our dialogue. *We* are talking, laughing, declaring, sharing. I am encouraging, prodding, supporting, and challenging her to participate. I am also trying to understand the origins of her reluctance. I'm empathizing with her, attending to what I perceive to be her vulnerability. And *she* is not only responding to my challenge, she is also expressing her concern for me. The empathetic regard is mutual as we struggle to find a place of comfort, balance, and symmetry. We are singing a duet.

Katie and I greet each other with a big, long bear hug. "How are you doing?" I ask. "I don't know, Sara," she says mischievously, then ominously. "I have nothing more to say." She is resplendent in a deep purple tunic from West Africa, which covers a bright gold long-sleeved shirt. Long amber and brass earrings are dangling from her ears, catching the sunlight that is filtering through the window and brightening up her dark face. She is a vision of intense colors. I beam across at her face admiringly, "You are looking so vibrant with color! What a contrast from your winter costumes." To which she responds, "Oh, I'm going through my midlife crisis . . . I've taken off all the heavy covering . . . I'm out there!" She spreads her arms like an eagle in flight. "The way you see me now is the way I'll always be . . . from now on." Liberation rings in her voice as she throws her head back in a long hearty laugh.

I have now heard Cannon refer many times to her "midlife crisis," to wanting to return home to visit her parents and talk about the pain, the distance, the closeness to them, to needing to visit her grandmother's grave and finally admit the enormous loss. In her references to midlife, she always links it to "crisis" and seems to welcome this tumultuous interlude with all its risk and drama. Her mention of it brings laughter and teary eyes. She is both joking and dead serious.

I assure her that she has *lots* more to say; we've only just begun . . . and that I will find the questions to ask that will inspire her talk. I am aware that she knows there is much more to her story, but might be reluctant to say much more.

I immediately suspect that our last interview has left her feeling vulnerable and exposed, as if she has given away too much [p. 44].

The listener will put up a shield to protect herself from the barrage of intense feelings. Katie worries that in her last interview she might have been "too raw" and too intense in telling of her experiences, that maybe some of the feelings are "too painful to even name." She ponders about the need to "filter" some of her emotions, dilute some of the pain, and hold back some of the tears in order that I will not feel assaulted or overwhelmed by her narrative. I see her look of concern, I hear her message of identification with the *listener,* and I am moved by her empathy. But, though I too have been "wiped out" by our last interview, I feel fully able to withstand the "raw feelings" and strong enough to hear her "name to the pain." I say as much as clearly as I can. Katie smiles, looking thankful and relieved, "Yes, I have no doubt you're sturdy enough to hear this" [pp. 46–47].

In summary, the portraitist uses voice in many modalities in the field and in the text. Voice speaks about stance and perspective, revealing the place from which the portraitist observes and records the action, reflecting her angle of vision, allowing her to perceive patterns and see the strange in the familiar. As the portraitist moves from thin to thick description, she uses the interpretive voice, which seeks meaning. The autobiography of the researcher (her history, experience, family background, and cultural origins) also informs and shapes the portraitist's voice, as do her intellectual interests, disciplinary background, theoretical frames, and ideological preoccupations. Finally, voice refers to the presence of the portraitist's voice discerning the sound and meaning of the actors' voices and sometimes entering into dialogue with them.

Each of these modalities of voice reflects a different level of presence and visibility for the portraitist in the text, from a minimalist stance of restraint and witness to a place of explicit, audible participation. In each modality, however, the chosen stance of the portraitist should be purposeful and conscious. Whether her voice—always dynamic and changing—is responding to or initiating shifts in dialogue, action, or context, she should be attentive to the ways in which she is employing voice. And although it is always present, the portraitist's voice should never overwhelm the voices or actions of the actors. The self of the portraitist is always there; her soul echoes through the piece. But she works very hard *not* to simply produce a self-portrait.

Implementation

Defining the Lens

Jessica Hoffmann Davis

Voice is the individualistic impression of the researcher on the portrait. It is therefore omnipresent, ubiquitous, and most difficult to isolate in our disassembly of the methodology of portraiture. Like every element of portraiture, voice is imprinted both on the product—the portrait as a finished narrative—and on the two mutually informative aspects of the portraiture process: the collection of data and the analytic shaping of the final portrait.

The voice that resounds in a portrait can be thought of as having its own disposition as well as its unique articulation. By *disposition* of voice, we mean those individual qualities that uniquely shape the portraitist's interpretation of the subject of the portrait—the finding of the story. By *articulation* of voice, we mean those individual tonalities that uniquely distinguish the portraitist's representation of the subject of the portrait—the telling of the story.

Regarding voice, the methodological question that portraitists must repeatedly ask of process is How (to what extent) does the disposition of my voice inform (give shape to but not distort) the product (the developing portrait)? And the question that portraitists must repeatedly ask of product is How (to what extent) does the articulation of my voice inform (clarify but not mislead) the process (the developing understanding)?

These operational questions enable the portraitist to control an element that, unrestrained in process, can turn vision inward and distort outward interpretation. Unchecked in product, voice can result, as Lawrence-Lightfoot has cautioned, in self-portrayal. Mixing metaphors to make the point, voice necessarily and meaningfully imbues the lens of the portraitist's vision with particular facets and hues; when it clouds, distorts, or redirects the portraitist's view, it challenges the integrity of the aesthetic whole.

Since it is so closely connected to the researcher, voice most tangibly represents the self of the portraitist. The implementation of voice therefore differs substantially when the portraitist is representing a group as well as an individual perspective. It matters also whether the narrative portrays one individual actor speaking in one other voice—other than the portraitist's—or an institution, the story of which is told through numerous actors speaking in various other voices.

Project Co-Arts addressed the particular challenges presented by the scenario in which portraitists are working together to portray a variety of sites—speaking necessarily with their own voices but most deliberately also representing what we came to call "group voice." In this section, we note the differences and consider implementation in terms of these various situations, addressing separately the aspects of voice proposed in our illumination section as: *witness, interpretation, preoccupation, autobiography, other voices,* and *dialogue.*

VOICE AS WITNESS

As mentioned in our discussion of implementation of context, when writing on behalf of a group, portraitists necessarily avoid the explicit "I" or "we" and declare their present voices implicitly—an option available to individual researchers as well. In either usage, implicit voice is often implemented through the selection of expressive vehicles or agents for voice.

For example, in the illustration included in our illumination section from Highland Park High in Chicago, Lawrence-Lightfoot employs as agent for her voice as outsider witness an individual—a character in the story—who delivers implicitly the portraitist's perspective. In Ms. Wood's class at Highland Park, throughout the detailed account of the teacher's discussion of *Uncle Tom's Cabin,* it is when the portraitist's lens is focused on the one African American student in the class that we experience the researcher's presence and discomfort: *I project pain onto him.*

In our first encounter of the Artists Collective, my research assistant and I experienced our presence as outsider witnesses, but not just as conspicuous observers perched on the edge of a vibrant oasis of artistic energy and learning. We were also initially aware of our otherness as nonblacks in a predominantly black arena. Our voices as outsider witnesses guide the underlying inquiry and shape the narrative evident in the following passages from the Co-Arts portrait of the Artists Collective:

Nonblacks do not always feel comfortable in this oasis of color. Dollie McLean tells the story: "I had a young white girl who came here for one of our summer programs from Farmington [a predominantly white suburb] . . . and she was so upset; she said: 'I just can't get the African dance.' You know she just couldn't get the feeling in the music . . . and she really wanted to quit. I mean it was that bad . . . and I said 'I know what you are feeling and I don't think you should.'" Ms. McLean reassured the student that she would shine in ballet: "I said, 'the other kids are not going to be able to master ballet movements as well as you because you have been studying ballet for a while . . . ' and she shone and did very well and I also talked about the strength of being the only one—something that we feel all the time—'so you're learning something that I think maybe . . . will put a little armor on you. . . . You will sense the way others feel when you enter a classroom and there is only one black or one Puerto Rican child there . . . it can hurt.'"

When hiring staff, Dollie McLean is up front with the issue: "The question I ask almost immediately is: 'How do you feel about being a part of this organization that is very focused on African American culture? It is primarily black people. I think we will all care for you and . . . you will have protection here from me down to every bit of the staff. But I can't control it— especially if you are a receptionist—if some woman comes and she doesn't have a job that she thinks that she ought to have.' All of that is always working and I deal with that stuff head on and I don't mince my words in discussing it and one young woman in an interview when I said it, I could see the fear in her eyes. I could see it and she said, 'Oh dear, I would be scared to death.' She was really very nice and honest but that was the end of that and she was happy that I brought it up" [Davis et al., 1993, p. 27].

In this excerpt, the subjects of Dollie McLean's two stories are vehicles for the voice of the portraitist as well as for the voice of the actor. The stories cited in the excerpt were chosen because they were resonant—representative of many that were collected on site as data for the portrait. In modulating the outsider portraitist voice, researchers must listen for such resonance in the voices of insiders. At the Artists Collective, respondents' ready examples and thoughtful accounts—like Dollie McLean's endorsement of the importance of gaining insight and strength from "being the only one"—demonstrate that the question of exclusion in a haven of *inclusion* is an issue that constituents deal with regularly and ponder deeply. The discovery of such resonance assures the portraitist that pursuing the inquiry on site (process) and selecting stories to represent the issue in the final work (product) is justified—and not an overindulgence of self in voice as witness.

As our visit to the Collective continued, our initial sense of otherness was replaced by our overwhelming experience of welcome. The following two passages, also reflecting the perspective of voice as witness, introduce alternative views to the account of the center.

> There are also a number of white students who are drawn to the Oasis on Clark Street to participate in the ongoing performing arts classes, the summer program, and such musical performance opportunities as the Artists Collective Lila Wallace–Reader's Digest Youth Jazz Orchestra. One young teenager, a fine trumpet player, came to the subsidized summer music program as a paying student ($200 for five weeks) and ultimately brought other white friends to this Afro-centric oasis of art, culture, and jazz. Dollie McLean remembers that in the beginning the white students stood apart, "But not Mr. Jason, he was right in the middle of all the other black kids . . . because he had already experienced being with us the previous year." Jason's mother reports that when Jason came home from the experience of going into the North End for the first time, he said, "Now I know what it feels like to be a minority." But inside the Collective, he too found safe haven: "Once you come inside," he said, "you are so welcome" [Davis et al., 1993, p. 26].

> The Collective's administrative assistant, Barbara Southard, is dressed simply in slacks and shoes that look like they provide comfort for her daily walks to and from the bus that takes her to and from the South End of Hartford. Ms. Southard is a white woman with light brown graying hair who wears bookish eyeglasses and taught religion for seventeen years at the private Massachusetts boarding school, Northfield Mount Herman. She responds easily to the question of what it feels like to be a non-black at the Artists Collective: "I work with a group of people who are all individuals and except for people who come here from the outside, say to register, and are angry anyway, I have never been made to feel that I am of another race" [Davis et al., 1993, p. 27].

The accounts of Jason and Ms. Southard, again selected from many stories heard at the Collective, help to represent the complexity of the issue that has been raised, experienced, and represented by the portraitist's voice as witness. Lawrence-Lightfoot's experience of the *Uncle Tom's Cabin* story was not that of the majority of the students in that class—just as ours was not the dominant encounter of Collective constituents. But the selection of one representative insider—like the student in Ms. Wood's class or Jason and Ms. Southard at the Collective—assures the reader of the resonance of the portraitist's voice even when striking a dissonant tone.

The portraitist's outsider perspective, then, even when deviating from the majority insider view—gains veracity from its resonance among insiders. Indeed, without corroboration, the representation of the perspective is liable to tell the reader more about the portraitist than about the actor or actors in the portrait. These excerpts demonstrate the possibility and responsibility of voice as witness to tell a story that is neither just the portraitist's nor just the subject's, but instead belongs to both storytellers, attaining and reflecting an outsider-insider view.

That outsider-insider view is literally assumed by the researcher who is the lead writer of the Co-Arts portrait of Plaza de la Raza, which means Place of the Race. The passage from that portrait excerpted in our illumination section demonstrates that the events at Plaza are witnessed by a researcher who speaks Spanish as well as English. This disposition of the portraitist's voice as witness is revealed implicitly throughout the portrayal. By incorporating Spanish words and their translations throughout the narrative, pointing out that constituents spoke only in Spanish and explaining what they said, the portraitist shares the insider knowledge that frames the articulation of her interpretive description.

Clearly differences in voice shape portraitists' individual interpretations. A researcher who could not speak Spanish would necessarily focus on different stories at Plaza de la Raza and might even regard as rarities traditions that would be familiar to a Latino researcher. Similarly, a nonartist would not witness the education at a community art center from the same perspective as that of a researcher who is also an active participant in the arts. However, as it is with painted portraits of the same subject, it is in the differences in interpretation that the works find their artistry.

VOICE AS INTERPRETATION

As all of portraiture can be understood as interpretive description, it is difficult if not impossible to isolate moments at which voice is not acting as interpretation. Even in the delivery of the who, what, when, and where of a site (what Lawrence-Lightfoot cites as Geertz's "thin description"), the researcher selects and includes those factual details that contribute to the coherence she seeks in constructing an interpretation.

In the descriptions of both Bill Strickland and Jerome Pieh (as included in our illumination section), the portraitists have chosen to describe physical objects that surround the actors—the two photographs—that seem, according to their respective interpretations, emblematic of attributes of the two leaders. The photo of Executive Director Bill Strickland in pilot uniform at the helm of the plane offers metaphoric resonance to a view of a soaring leader whose garb has changed from pilot's uniform to corporate suit. The photo of Jerome Pieh juxtaposed with the passage from the Milton catalogue strikes a more discordant tone and alerts the reader to the portraitist's variegated view of a provocative educator.

These implementations of voice as interpretation are again accomplished, by both group and individual researcher, without the overt use of "I" and with the use of selected images. Nonetheless, Lawrence-Lightfoot as an individual portraitist does reflect in her own voice on the image she sees by sharing her personal judgment of Pieh's posture as "uncomfortable," his physical appearance as "quietly handsome," and the look in his eyes as "melancholy."

In working as a group of portraitists reaching for consistency across portraits, we tried to avoid explicit evaluative judgment of a personal nature—that is, to stay away from the use of descriptors like *handsome*, the designation of which would necessarily vary across our six separate interpretive voices. Instead, we tried to layer our interpretive descriptions with less negotiable representations, employing selected physical details, descriptions of actions, and direct quotations from voices on site that might achieve similarly effective imagery.

For example, in describing the imposing countenance of one of the lead actors at the Artists Collective, factual details of dress and stance provide an interpretive introduction. The following portrayals demonstrate what can be accomplished almost entirely through selected physical detail woven into description of sufficient depth to include an insider view.

In the reader's first encounter with Aca Lee Thompson, the simple detailed account of his particular outfit reveals without overtly expressed judgment what might otherwise be accomplished with more negotiable descriptors such as "stylish," "high profile," or "eclectic":

> Master Choreographer Aca Lee Thompson is dressed in street clothes in a slim fitting blue double-breasted suit with bell bottom trousers, a black tie with white dots, and a knit skull cap [Davis et al., 1993, p. 34].

In a later encounter, the actor's aura is seen and experienced:

> Students in the evening Yaboo class (fourteen adolescent girls and three boys) are learning the 'Feast of the Strong Man'—

a South African song that will lead into a stick fight in the Yaboo ceremony to be performed in May. The initiates sit attentively on the floor in front of Master Choreographer and Disciplinarian, Aca Lee Thompson—"Aca" (pronounced AKO) as everyone calls him. A mature and majestic figure, Aca wears a mesh sleeveless shirt; red silken bands are tied around his muscular biceps. He wears baggy black pants tucked into patterned wool leg warmers that are pulled up to his knees. A red silk scarf is wrapped tightly around his head. In hushed tones, Aca leans forward in his chair towards his fully attentive students, "This is Zulu" he says as he explains how the segment fits into the Rite of Passage [Davis et al., 1993, p. 23].

And at another juncture:

In the Choreographer's Workshop Ensemble class, fifteen teenage girls in black leotards, tights, and high-heeled tap shoes gather in clusters of three or four—teasing each other, telling stories, laughing, studying themselves and the other young women in the large mirror along the front wall. Aca Lee Thompson walks into the room without a word, and the girls immediately fall silent and arrange themselves in three neat rows. Aca strolls back and forth in the front of the room, scrupulously observing each dancer as she begins breathing exercises. Most of the students in this class have "grown up" at the Collective; all except one or two students have been studying there since age three. At age nine or ten, they audition for this class. Once accepted, students are expected also to take classical ballet, modern dance, and African percussion, as well as to attend master workshops with visiting artists. They are at the Collective twelve hours a week.

Aca's countenance is serious and watchful—eyes darting from feet to shoulders to abdomens to faces. His own movements are almost feline in their elegance. A parent standing with some other adults and children at the edge of the room whispers: "I don't care what anyone says, that man make me nervous." Aca is intent on what he is doing and doesn't seem to notice the cluster of observers staring from the edge of the room or the spirited adult African dance class going on in the next room. His students do not show the wear of a full day at school; they are alert and engaged [Davis et al., 1993, pp. 42–43].

Without the portraitist directly stating that Mr. Thompson is intimidating, demanding, and engaging, the reader experiences that view of the master choreographer and disciplinarian (an effective interpretive title invented by the Collective) through the description of the actor in action and the responses of coactors on the scene.

These examples demonstrate the implementation of voice as interpretation as the governing force in the portrayal. In terms of the portraiture process on site, voice as interpretation pursues particular lines of inquiry, listens for resonance, observes carefully, and reflects continuously on the input of data, searching for and testing the strength of the coherence that will unify the interpretation. In terms of the construction of the final portrayal, voice as interpretation determines language, frames and selects images, modulates articulation, and balances the separate parts of the portrayal into a cohesive aesthetic whole.

VOICE AS PREOCCUPATION

It was Lawrence-Lightfoot's description of voice as the "preoccupation of the researcher" that fueled Co-Arts's development of what we called our *group* or *collective voice.* The individual differences outlined in the section on voice as witness persist even without conscious awareness on the part of the portraitist. But the preoccupations of the researcher as areas of "mattering" that derive from knowledge of the larger field or domain can be consciously acknowledged and prioritized.

In the excerpts included in the previous section, we see examples of Lawrence-Lightfoot's particular priorities. In selecting Ms. Newbury's drama class, Lawrence-Lightfoot demonstrates her interest in the alternative learning situations that the arts can offer, teachers who distinguish themselves as unique, strong relationships between students and teachers, and attention to the student as an emotional as well as intellectual being. More broadly, in Lawrence-Lightfoot's study of good high schools, the dimensions of interest to the portraitist include classroom ethos; teacher pedagogy, personality, and values; authority relationships between teachers and students; and student learning.

These areas of interest or preoccupations are not quixotic or idiosyncratic; they are the result of knowledge and experience. As such, these preoccupations skillfully direct the focus of the inquiry. A group of researchers (or an individual researcher) can purposefully develop and consciously articulate a set of preoccupations that will help guide inquiry and shape interpretation. The early work of Project Co-Arts accomplished this objective and informed our implementation of portraiture as a group process.

GROUP VOICE: THE CO-ARTS PERSPECTIVE

At the same time that Project Co-Arts researchers were preparing for their foray into portraiture, we were studying the scene of community arts education on a wide scale, analyzing our reviews of 350 sets of printed materials received from centers, collecting and analyzing results from more than a hundred questionnaires, and conducting in-depth phone interviews with almost a hundred community art center or education directors. Out of this work, we developed a descriptive model of educational effectiveness and a set of strategies for self-assessment (see Davis, 1993a; Davis, Solomon, Eppel, & Dameshek, 1996).

By the time our in-depth phone interviews were staged, Co-Arts had already identified four closely related and mutually informative areas across which educational effectiveness in community art centers appeared to occur. As they were central to the realization of effectiveness, we called these areas *relevant dimensions:*

- *Teaching and Learning:* the pedagogic structure of the center
- *Journey:* the center's historical course and vision for the future
- *Community:* the community the center serves
- *Administration:* the organizational structure of the center

Furthermore, certain questions emerged as central to our quest for understanding educational effectiveness within and across these dimensions. We initially explored these questions in phone interviews and went on to use them in brief site visits and in our longer portraiture expeditions. These were broad-based assessment-related queries such as, "What counts as success to you?" or "If you had to tell someone who wanted to start a community art center like this what makes this place so successful, what would you tell them was the most important ingredient?"

While on site, these questions were useful for quick encounters in the hall with a wide range of constituents. More important, they provided ready openings to in-depth interview conversations. Co-Arts researchers were trained as interviewers to go beyond interviewees' quick responses and to listen *for* stories by framing open-ended questions and providing scaffolding for respondents by sharing their own perspectives. Nonetheless, the interpretive discourse was deliberately and continuously informed by Co-Arts's developing understanding of educational effectiveness in these settings.

Throughout this process, then, researchers were reconciling a number of different voices: the collective Co-Arts voice (made up of our growing and shared understanding of the field—Co-Arts's preoccupations); individual researcher voices (made up of our respective perspectives and interests—individual researchers' preoccupations); and, of course, the most important voices—the voices of the actors on the scene, which filtered through our various lenses into our final portraits. Individual researcher voice touched by collective Co-Arts voice was balanced by center voice as researchers were best able to hear and represent it.

Attending to both group and individual voice, in the preface to the collection of portraits in *Safe Havens,* we introduced the relevant dimensions that informed the group voice of Project Co-Arts. In brief biographical sketches included in an appendix, we introduced the individual researchers who were taking the lead in writing the various portraits. These descriptive sketches suggested what the preoccupations of the various portraitists might be.

In her biographical paragraph, the lead writer of the Manchester Craftsmen's Guild portrait informs readers that she has a master's degree in higher education administration, that her prior research focused on issues confronting students of color in higher education, that she worked in college offices of race relations and interculturalism, and that she grew up in India and came to the United States for her undergraduate education. Another of her research interests was in issues of leadership.

In the following brief excerpt from the Manchester Craftsmen's Guild portrait, the reader can hear the individual portraitist's voice as preoccupation with strategies for advancement of students of color as well as Co-Arts's group voice as preoccupation with its relevant dimensions. These individual and group preoccupations of voice resonate throughout the discussion of the emergent theme, *Winning the Right to Be Heard:*

> For students at the Guild, winning the right to be heard involves learning how to articulate both their artistic interests and personal beliefs. This requires reflection on motivations and goals. The Director of Ceramics says that when students are applying to college programs or for scholarships, staff members help students to voice explicitly "why they're making work, why they see themselves coming here voluntarily." Josh Green says of a student who has been learning ceramics for the past year, "I would expect that by next year he should have a body of slides together that looks something like a portfolio so that he can apply to the Governor's School. Then I'll ask him to start making some critical judgments about his work and why it's his work, why he's doing it." Green mentions a student whose application statement began: "As an African American Muslim woman. . . ." He questioned the student: "What does that mean? Why do you make art because you're African? The

student knows but nobody is generally asking this student these questions."

Winning the right to be heard also requires that college-bound students know how to negotiate financial aid and employment procedures in the higher education system. Strickland speaks proudly of a former Guild student who finished college in spite of financial hardship because he "hustled here, hustled there, got a little job on campus." Strickland reports, "We have never had one kid go to college and drop out because they couldn't afford to stay there." He believes that scholarships are available for students who are savvy enough to understand how to obtain financial aid and work opportunities in higher education:

"You have to figure out the politics of how to share [the resources]. I did it. My parents didn't pay for my college education, . . . they didn't have any money. I was slick enough to get on the campus, see this angle and that angle. It's part of survival. You've got to do that for the rest of your life anyway."

In keeping with the Guild's philosophy of art as a practical path to employment, students are taught how to price their work and develop a small source of income. The use of materials and equipment for ceramic art and photography is provided at no cost to students. Nancy Brown states that the upper limit for the sale of photographs by Guild students has been fixed at $50. Ceramic art is priced individually on the recommendation of the Director of Ceramics. She explains:

"One of the problems that we continue to have with our students when they go off to college is that they've been treated like the 'little stars.' Especially the ones that get a four-year . . . scholarship, the 'art jocks.' So to the best that we can, [we try to] control that attitude. You can charge whatever you want for your work later on, when the public thinks that's what it's worth."

Brown also points out that students at the Guild get used to celebrated artists or important officials visiting the center. "Living masters" in ceramic art and photography come to the Guild to do workshops, lectures, and sometimes, residencies. This is not only an important educational component but is also part of Strickland's strategy of doing outreach and "winning the right to be heard" for the Guild [Davis et al., 1993, pp. 102–103].

As examples of the preoccupations of group voice, in this passage's discussion of portfolio compilation and student reflection, we hear the Co-Arts dimension of *Teaching and Learning;* and in the discussions of selling student work and providing free materials, the dimension of *Administration.* In the discussion of outreach, we hear issues of *Community,* and throughout the excerpt, in the development of individual students into college *art jocks* and even in Strickland's personal development, we hear the dimension of *Journey.*

Co-Arts researchers attended to the preoccupations of group voice throughout the process of data collection. In interviewing constituents, for example, researchers purposefully included representatives of each dimension: students and teachers (*Teaching and Learning*); parents and neighbors (*Community*); board members and office staff (*Administration*); and the center's founder as well as current grant writer (*Journey*).

As illustrated in the Guild portrait excerpt, in the construction of the final product, researchers were also deliberate in representing these dimensions. For example, as will be explained more thoroughly in Chapter Six, once we identified a theme like *Winning the Right to Be Heard,* we considered its relevance to each of the four dimensions. Of course the different dimensions resonated more or less sonorously throughout particular themes or aspects of the whole just as particular encounters more or less audibly amplified the voice of the individual researcher.

Individuals, like groups of researchers, may want to enrich their portraitist voices by selecting particular preoccupations or relevant dimensions derived from preliminary research. Dimensions will vary according to the research questions and pertinent literature that focus and inform the portraitist's efforts. For example, a student writing a portrait on a community school of music was particularly interested in self-image as an artist and its impact on adolescent development. In her preliminary review of pertinent research, she identified four relevant dimensions that she incorporated into her individual portraiture voice: *Mentorship:* the impact of master-apprentice relationships; *Family:* the influence of familial support; *Flow:* a commitment to optimal experience; and *Performance:* the formation of identity in relation to an audience (see Powell, 1995).

In preparation for portrait writing, a group of researchers studying a K–6 science curriculum geared toward language acquisition brainstormed dimensions based on their understanding of the objectives and methods of the bilingual program. The dimensions they identified were used to frame their group voice and add consistency to their individual researcher efforts to portray five different classrooms or program sites. Their dimensions were: *Inquiry:* posing open-ended questions; *Reflection:* assessing one's own thinking and learning; *Interaction:* relating socially with other students and with the teacher; and *Transformation:* changing roles from learner to teacher and from teacher to learner (see Kaiser, Davis, & Dameshek, 1995).

The purposeful identification and application of preoccupations or dimensions can help focus the individual work of a veteran researcher studying multiple sites or a novice researcher approaching a research question and the portraiture methodology for the first time. Across the portraits of various researchers, a shared set of relevant dimensions establishes a group voice that is manifest both in its disposition throughout the process of data collection and its articulation within and across a number of final portraits.

VOICE AS AUTOBIOGRAPHY

We have noted that because another voice is telling the actor's story, the actor's story is no longer exclusively his or her own. Interpretation acts as an active link in the reconstruction and co-construction of narrative. In the process of data collection, a story is reconstructed through interview—co-constructed by the interviewer's listening and the interviewee's telling. In creating the final portrait, the story is reconstructed yet again, in its presentation by the portraitist within a particular context. In presenting the story, the portraitist is ever mindful of the intentions of the original storyteller and the responsibility of retelling another's story.

The interpretations of protagonist and portraitist contribute to the co-construction of the story, but the final contributor is the reader—who brings yet another interpretation into the discourse. The reader is an active force in the co-construction of story, applying available data to the elaboration of his or her interpretation of the narrative. As such, the reader can benefit from autobiographical information about the individual portraitist as well as about the actors or site.

For example, in *I've Known Rivers,* the protagonists—like Lawrence-Lightfoot—are accomplished African Americans who at midlife reflect on their life journeys. In this context, the articulation of Lawrence-Lightfoot's individual voice as autobiography, as in her reflection on family dinners, is crucial for understanding the intimacy of rapport that resonates throughout the shared telling of stories and the co-construction of emergent themes. Group voice, however, is less likely to be explicitly expressed as autobiography, and individual portraitists working in groups rarely articulate their separate autobiographical voices.

Indeed, in every situation, it is difficult to determine the nature and amount of autobiographical information that will be useful to and not distracting from the development of interpretation in portraiture. It is not easy to decide what biographical details should be included in add-on paragraphs describing individual portraitists. Within the structure of the narrative, the determination of the extent to which it is helpful to admit voice as autobiography is even more daunting.

The questions offered at the start of this section for modulating the disposition and articulation of overall voice can also inform the decision as to what auto-biographical information warrants inclusion within the narrative. As an example of restraining voice as autobiography, consider my personal reasons for being particularly moved by the notion and ritual of rite of passage so gloriously enacted on the Artists Collective stage.

Grappling at the time of my visit with a birthday perilously close to the half-century mark, I found myself absolutely fascinated with the Collective's study of Yaboo. When Aca Lee Thompson indicated that we all experience rites of passage *"from minute to minute and day to day. Every birthday is a rite of passage; every transition,"* he was unknowingly speaking to me and to my own personal moment of transition. Indeed one scene, sketched into my field notes, seemed an especially vivid candidate for inclusion in the final portrait:

> Dance Director Cheryl Smith notes my presence as observer in her class and asks the children to introduce themselves to me.
>
> Twenty-two straight-backed children, many in leotards sized to last a few years—boys and girls in shiny tap shoes—each declare: "My name is Nathan and I'm five years old." "My name is Leena and I'm six years old." I am greatly impressed by the sense of ceremony contained in the marking of each child's space in this universe and the noting of how long that space has been occupied. The pride and formality with which these children declare themselves is inspiring. When they are through, I can feel my own back straighten and my heart leap with excitement and relief as I speak clearly, and in what still sounds like my own voice, "My name is Jessica and I'm forty-eight years old."
>
> The children gasp and laugh and I am exhilarated with the marking of my own rite of passage at the Artists Collective.

On further consideration, I recognized that to share this story fully, I would need space in the portrait for personal context that would, in this case, detract from rather than illuminate the image of the Artists Collective. No matter how meaningful I found the experience, the detailed sharing of this manifestation of my own rite of passage would be self-indulgently autobiographical.

Ever mindful of the objectives of the portrait, the portraitist must modulate voice as autobiography through such hard decisions of selection and exclusion of individual stories. Personal resonance can enhance or consume the portrayal, and the portraitist needs to cautiously monitor the balance. Regardless of the exclusion of the birthday story, my scrupulous attention to the theme of rite of passage—confirmed as central by insiders at the Artists Collective—gave suffi-cient if not overt evidence of my individual voice as autobiography.

OTHER VOICES: LISTENING FOR VOICE

The method of listening *for* a story rather than *to* a story is at the heart of the process of co-constructing narrative. When listening *to* a story, the researcher records the account that the actor is sharing and structuring entirely on his or her own. When listening *for* a story, the researcher plays a more active listener role in the actor's storytelling. Through the dialectic between interviewer and interviewee, voice as interpretation contributes to the determination of the direction and shape of actors' responses. As example, you can hear my voice listening *for* the story in the following excerpt from a three-hour interview with Jackie McLean, founder of the Artists Collective.

We are at McLean's office at the University of Hartford's Hart School of Music. McLean has been telling me of his struggle with drugs, his experiences growing up in Harlem, and his dream of creating this center for the youth of Hartford's North End—a center in which students will find the skills, discipline, and self-esteem to combat life on the street. I come to our meeting with a growing awareness of a dissonant thread—a view of the Collective, in spite of its clear intentions, as somewhat of an outsider to the immediate community. We are exploring the neighborhood and its challenge to the well-being of the Collective:

> *JM:* At the collective it is like magic . . . every once in a while someone
> will break in; it used to happen a lot in the early days . . . but there
> has been so much good that the collective has done and it is so highly
> respected in the community that we don't get problems . . . and we
> don't like to raise any bully kids but I have always been an advocate
> of the martial arts because there have been a few times that bullies in
> the street see kids coming in with instruments and push them around
> and all like that and I say, "Dollie, we have got to do something about
> that and make them self-assured—"
> *JHD:* Do the martial arts help make them self-assured?
> *JM:* My kids are good at it. They can jump in the air, but they are
> trained not to hurt anybody and everybody loves the collective. [It's]
> just as a last resort to protect themselves—
> *JHD:* Everybody loves the Collective?
> *JM:* Of course there are some factions always that don't want to see
> you succeed. I come from New York so you know New York is a
> spread-out place and you don't have time to be suspicious of a stranger
> because you don't know who a stranger is . . . but once you come to
> New York and live there you are a New Yorker because nobody is going
> to ask you if you were born there or raised there . . . none of that . . .
> who cares? . . . But up here it is different and that is the problem that
> we had early on and it is very hard . . . being an outsider.
> *JHD:* Were they suspicious of you as outsiders in the North End?

JM: Oh are you kidding? Sure. Especially when they found out about my background, they thought what is he doing? They always think . . . some of these people think that somebody is doing something for some other reason . . . but I think that people found out early on and people that don't give us their total support, now they just don't understand and we don't have time to wait for them.

JHD: What are the misunderstandings?

JM: Just provincial stuff—you know: "Who do they think they are coming in here to help us? . . . We coulda done it. . . ." When I get them all together, I say, "Why didn't you do it? . . . You didn't do it. So stop talking about it. . . . We did it."

JHD: How do they respond to that?

JM: People know what is really happening . . . the kids really know what is real . . . so we keep the kids on their toes and all of our staff . . . we try to live what we preach over there . . . and try to give them love and that is the main thing—some kind of real understanding that they have a chance to come out into this world and be something positive because a lot of kids don't think that they can do it . . . TV shows fast life and a lot of money and their only chance of getting it is taking a chance in the street because they don't have enough support from the community to point a direction and say go to school and do this, do that . . . it was different when I was coming up. It is not there anymore.

Listening *for* the story, I note specific words spoken by the interviewee that herald possible directions of interest. After the first response, I am most concerned with this notion of tension between students at the Collective and the "bullies in the street," creating a need to make students feel more self-assured. Where a researcher pursuing curricular practices at the center might ask, "Can you tell me more about how you train students in the martial arts?" I probe the tension: "Do the martial arts help make them self-assured?"

Listening for the curricular story, I might follow the lead of "trained not to hurt anybody." I continue with the thread of the story I have begun to hear: "Everybody loves the Collective?" By holding to the language of the interviewee, I tangibly demonstrate my attentive listening. I literally enter the story by sharing the language of the narrative that *we* are co-constructing. In my third question, I pick up on the notion of suspicion—a term I would not have expected or selected on my own—and the dissonant thread is uncovered as prevalent and one with which the McLeans deal directly.

As Jackie McLean concludes with the connections between kids growing up today in the community and his own upbringing, I mark the connections between the Collective's growth in gaining acceptance in the community, the McLeans' work in that direction, and the struggle of the young people whom they are serving. These connections ultimately congeal in the final portrait's theme of *Rites of Passage,* in which the discussion of the dissonant thread of community resistance is addressed.

Listening *for* a story in interview—attending to what is said, marking down key words, and in one swift moment incorporating those phrases into a next question—is demanding and absorbing work. In addition to the multiple and simultaneous actions involved in active listening, the portraitist is also trying to attend to close visual observation. With so much happening in the moment of interview, it is useful if not necessary to tape and later transcribe interviews so that they can be revisited.

When transcribing on-site tapes, portraitists may be surprised to discover all that transpires beyond the active and absorbing co-construction of story. The pauses and changes in tone of voice—the expression of what Lawrence-Lightfoot calls "mixed feelings"—are often overlooked in the moment of interview as the portraitist works hard to find direction through the posing of questions. When portraitists engage others to transcribe interviews, they should insist that the transcriber indicate pauses, hesitations, and changes in tone of voice so that portraitists can attend to these markers of the texture of stories in the construction of the final portrait.

As has been illustrated, each juncture in listening *for* a story offers a range of opportunities for the portraitist to mount an interpretation that will follow one or more different pathways of understanding. In interview, the portraitist may help navigate the exploration, but the protagonist of the portrait is still at the wheel of the ship. It is in attending to the actors' authority and expert knowledge that portraitists can most responsibly and authentically give voice to a story that becomes, in part, their own.

VOICE AS DIALOGUE

In Lawrence-Lightfoot's example of voice as dialogue in our illumination section, she cites an excerpt representative of the intimate one-to-one dialectic between an individual portraitist and an individual subject. Certainly one-to-one settings are most propitious for the explicit declaration of the portraitist's voice in dialogue. But the voice of the individual researcher in dialogue with one or numerous actors at a site can also be heard through implicit expression.

In the following excerpt from the closing scene of the portrait of the Artists Collective, the portraitist is attending an off-site performance of the young dancers and musicians:

> Jackie McLean has arrived. He is smiling and clapping and
> speaking back to the musicians. The sparsity of the crowd
> has been overwhelmed by the intensity and electricity of the
> audience's experience. We are yelling and clapping; we are

entirely engaged. Dollie McLean, dressed in white, looks worried. One of the children is ill; she needs to get him back to Hartford. As the performance comes to an end, the announcer says there will be a second performance in just a few minutes. The thought that the performance will begin again is almost unbelievable. The intensity and accuracy of this work seems impossible to duplicate without even a rest. But in the dressing room, the energy is uplifting. Even an onlooker can experience what the Collective mother describes as "the self-esteem and the good feeling you get after a good performance—that natural high that will encourage you to do a lot of things. . . . " The audience has experienced the "high" Cheryl Smith noted in the prison audiences: "they are high not for one day but they are high for a year until we return. . . . " It seems possible.

All the Collective family members are there to celebrate the children's success, to gather and share in Jackie's that evening. Suddenly the woman with the cane is spotted. First Dollie, then Jackie, and Aca, and Sheila, and Cheryl are embracing her and her daughter. It's a family reunion. It seems as if all the training has been rehearsal for a moment like this. And Dollie McLean agrees, "Yes, you get to see the finished product . . . ," and she adds with a smile, "but it is never finished" [Davis et al., 1993, p. 51].

Here, the portraitist declares her presence by openly identifying herself as a member of the audience: "We are yelling and clapping; we are entirely engaged." She refers again to her own presence in the phrase "Even an onlooker," and in metacomments on the narrative such as "It seems possible." The last two sentences of the passage give subtle evidence of the dialogue between the portraitist and Dollie McLean. It is apparent that the notion that "all the training has been rehearsal for a moment like this" has been shared with Ms. McLean—perhaps as a question—because Ms. McLean is described as readily "agreeing."

This example makes implicit reference to a conversation that is not directly represented in the narrative. In instances such as this, voice as dialogue functions as a muted tone in the portraiture fabric's weave—making the dominance of other threads both possible and prominent. In group portraits in which the "I" remains unstated, it is in the seamless threading of implicit portraitist and explicit subject voices that the reader can experience the closeness of rapport that has been established. Resonating throughout the harmony of these interwoven voices is the sense of dialogue that has constructed the narrative throughout the portrait.

Artistic Refrain

Negotiating Perspective

Jessica Hoffmann Davis

Compare again the drawings of a young child and a professional artist (pp. 126–127). Five-year-old Adam's drawing of Angry holds many discernible similarities to adult artist Sarah's drawing of the same emotion. Artist Sarah explained her drawing, "When I'm angry, I can't move—the feeling of being inactive—you can't change anything, so you get frustrated. Then you learn that's the first phase of anger."

Through sophisticated manipulation of line and form, Sarah imbues her image with her personal interpretation of the emotion. She represents Angry in her own voice. Caged and spinning in ineffective motion, bearing the scar of a recent surgery, she shares her voice as witness to the display of the emotion, as autobiography identifying herself as the woman ineffectively spinning, as interpretation shaping the image, as preoccupation sharing her interest in self-reflection, and in dialogue with the more universal properties of the emotion itself.

As a result of my observation of Sarah as she draws and from my knowledge of her other work, I speak with some authority in reinterpreting the interpretation she has rendered. As Joshua Taylor points out, "A greater knowledge of an artist's production can sharpen our awareness of the subtleties of his vocabulary and often reveal new content which to our direct view may not have been accessible" (1981, p. 139).

Taylor's comment speaks directly to the importance of voice as a tangible feature in portraiture as well as in the creation of visual art. Our knowledge of Lawrence-Lightfoot's voice across her various portrayals of individuals and sites entitles us to more nuanced understanding of each distinctive portrayal. As we read any portrait and become familiar with the portraitist's unique voice, through her language and her composition of the whole, we assess the content of the interpretation with greater depth and understanding than if we had falsely accepted the account as objective reportage.

Adam's drawing holds the same staccato aura as Sarah's. The vertical jagged lines that motor and represent Sarah's painful spinning in place define the furious mouth of Adam's figure, an angry mouth that extends beyond the limits of the figure's central form. A scowling brow emphasizes the angular stance of the figure threateningly perched on the upper half of the page. This is an angry Adam. The child is one with his drawing and demonstrates his connection both in his process of constructing the drawing, throughout which he assumes the scowling face, and in his final product—the articulation of his own facial expression and stance in the interpretive image.

Artist and teacher Nicolaides addresses the need for carefully modulated voice negotiating perspective when he tells his students, "If I force myself completely on the model, that is wrong. Or if the model forces itself completely on me, that is wrong. There is a place in the middle where we meet and continually interact" (1941, p. 210). Nicolaides can be understood here as instructing the artist to achieve in the image a co-construction—a representation that is overwhelmed by neither artist nor model. He advocates instead a representation that embodies equally the voice of the subject and the voice of the artist. Again, conceptualizing the model or subject as the emotion of anger, what could we consider as Angry's voice as an entity apart from the voice of the artist?

Artists have long been interested in *synaesthesia,* what Ernst Gombrich describes as "the splashing over of impressions from one sense modality to another" (1969, p. 366). The comprehension of perceived "gestalts" for emotions (for example, downward drooping lines as sorrowful, upward rounded shapes as Happy, and jagged tense lines as Angry) are all synaesthetic understandings upon which most individuals agree. From a synaesthetic perspective, then, we can consider the jagged lines in both Adam's and Sarah's drawings as the voice or imprint of Angry.

Indeed the portrayals by professional artists Henry and Karen (pp. 128–129) confirm the resonance of Angry's jagged lines even as they demonstrate the different imprints of individual interpretations of the same emotion. In the four artistic interpretations, we see the constant imprint or voice of Angry as jagged frantic lines, but intermingled seamlessly with the different imprints or voices of four artists. For Sarah, we see the caged confined frustration; for Adam, the menacing self-portrayal; for Karen, the dark thicket of lines; and for Henry, the explosion of sharp angles. And for all of these renderings, we hear my voice as perceiver framing my own interpretations of the various portrayals.

Five-year-old Adam's drawing of Angry

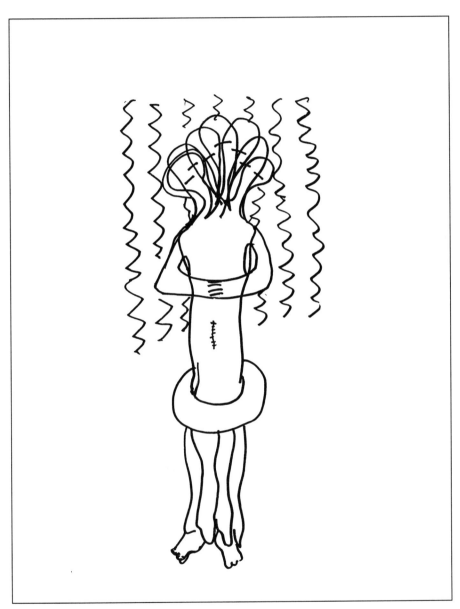

Adult artist Sarah's drawing of Angry

Adult artist Henry's drawing of Angry

Adult artist Karen's drawing of Angry

The portraitist strives to achieve a similar transgression of boundaries as persists between the understood imprint of content (inside) and the perceived visual image (outside). For portraitists, however, the boundary crossed is between the voices of insider (subject) and outsider (portraitist). The portraitist attends faithfully to the authentic voice of the subject and is simultaneously and ever aware of the disposition and articulation of her own voice. In this way, portraitist voice meets subject voice in the middle and continually interacts throughout the narrative of the portrayal. This Nicolaides-like meeting in the middle represents the achievement of a shared voice, an insider-outsider perspective constructing the narrative and opening the way to yet another voice: the voice of the reader who reinterprets the portrayal.

For both artist and portraitist, it is interpretation that facilitates the boundary breaking. Interpretation connects as if undifferentiated: artist, symbol, referent, and perceiver as well as portraitist, portrait, subject, and reader. In both situations, it is the artist's hand or the portraitist's voice that finds and expresses the interpretation.

Femme Assise et Dormeuse 3rd state
11 May 1947

CHAPTER FIVE

ON RELATIONSHIP

Illumination

Navigating Intimacy

Sara Lawrence-Lightfoot

ortraits are constructed, shaped, and drawn through the development of relationships. *All* the processes of portraiture require that we build productive and benign relationships. It is through relationships between the portraitist and the actors that access is sought and given, connections made, contracts of reciprocity and responsibility (both formal and informal) developed, trust built, intimacy negotiated, data collected, and knowledge constructed. Relationships are never static—they are dynamic, evolving, and fluid. They are negotiated and renegotiated, week by week, day by day, even minute by minute as the portraitist and the actors navigate lines of intimacy, trust, reciprocity, and boundary setting, and as they work to develop a level of comfort, balance, honesty, and authenticity in their communications with one another. It is in the building of relationships that the portraitist experiences most pointedly the complex fusion of conceptual, methodological, emotional, and ethical challenges.

Our examination of these complex challenges begins with the simple and profound insight voiced so eloquently by philosopher Martin Buber (1958) when he spoke about the "I-thou" relationship. The self, he said, is only experienced through connection and the I-thou relationship—of attention, empathy, trust, and intimacy—can only be achieved when people come to it as separate and whole individuals. Relationships are defined by individuality and contrast as much as by connection. Carol Gilligan (1982) echoes Buber when she underscores what she calls the "paradoxical truths of human experience." "We know ourselves as separate," she says, "only insofar as we live in connection with others, and we experience relationship only insofar as we differentiate other from self" (p. 63). This paradox is not only important for the researcher's documentation of others' lives, it is first—and most fundamentally—crucial for self-understanding. Bernstein (1992) speaks about this process of self-reflection and self-understanding that grows out of relationship. "It is in our genuine encounters with what is other and alien (even in ourselves) that we further our own self-understanding" (pp. 66–67, cited in Moss, 1996).

This self-understanding—which emerges out of the intersubjective experience of relationships—becomes the impetus for deep inquiry and the construction of knowledge. In his examination of a methodological approach that he refers to as "radical empiricism," ethnographer Michael Jackson (1989) traces the connection between the building of relationships and the development of knowledge, and between connection and mutuality in relationships and validity in research.

> Knowledge of the other is not just a product of our theoretical thought and research activity; it is a consequence of critical experiences, relationships, choices, and events both in the field and in the quotidian world of our professional and family lives. . . . Ethnography then becomes a form of *Verstehen*, a project of empathic and vicarious understanding in that the other is seen in the light of one's own experiences and the activity of trying to fathom the other in turn illuminates and alters one's sense of Self. . . .
>
> Self and other share the same world, even though their projects differ. To fathom another is not, therefore, all projection and surmise, or insular subjectivity blindly reaching out to an alien other. To compare notes on experience with someone else presumes and creates a common ground, and the understanding arrived at takes its validity not from our detachment and objectivity but from the very possibility of our mutuality, the existence of the relationship itself [pp. 34–35].

Like Buber, Gilligan, and Jackson—philosopher, psychologist, and anthropologist—the portraitist views relationship as fundamental to self-understanding, to mutuality and validity, and to the development of knowledge. We see relationships as fertilizing the "common ground" that Jackson refers to, as seeding discovery and insight.

But it is important to recognize that other researchers working in the qualitative realm often take a more limited and pragmatic approach to relationship. They have a more circumscribed view that focuses on relationship as a tool or strategy for gaining access to data—a boundary that must be negotiated to "get the goods" from the "insiders." From this point of view, relationship almost begins to be seen as barrier (to entry) rather than connection (to self, to other, and to knowledge), as something to be gotten through rather than something to be engaged and embraced. Maxwell (1996) criticizes this reductionist view of relationship—a perspective that sees it simply as the vehicle for "access" and "entry"—and suggests that we view relationship as dynamic, complex, nuanced, and ongoing.

> The terms *negotiating entry* (Marshall and Rossman, 1989) or *gaining access* (Bogdan and Biklen, 1992; Glesne and Peshkin, 1992) suggest that this is a single event that, once achieved, requires no further thought; those terms downplay the continual negotiation and renegotiation of your relationship with those you study. Clearly the process is much more complex than this, and rarely involves any approximation to total access. Nor is such access usually necessary for a successful study; what you want is a relationship that enables you to ethically learn the things you need to learn in order to validly answer your research questions [p. 66].

Just as there is some controversy among qualitative researchers about the goals and purposes of relationships in research design, so too is there debate about the optimal depth, quality, and intensity of research relationships. Should researchers seek distance or closeness, objectivity or subjectivity, scrutiny or alliance, asymmetry or symmetry in their connections with subjects? At one end of the continuum of opinion, traditionalists (such as Seidman, 1991) believe that relationships between the researcher and the subject should be clear, distant, and formal—that they must be seen as limited and pragmatic, with visible boundaries of decorum and responsibility. To blur the boundaries or reduce the distance would be to distort the researcher's objectivity and threaten the rigor and validity of the research. From this perspective, the very idea of developing a relationship with a research subject would challenge the subject-object separation that is the underpinning of traditional scientific methods and endanger the rituals of research design (Nielsen, 1990). To maintain the stance of a disinterested observer, the traditionalists claim that personal involvement must be monitored and circumscribed; intimacy must be avoided.

At the other end of the continuum, researchers (let us call them *revisionists)* believe that the formalized distance prescribed by traditionalists may not only be disrespectful and diminishing of research subjects (minimizing their authority and potentially masking their knowledge) but also may undermine productive inquiry. They claim that relationships that are complex, fluid, symmetric, and reciprocal—that are shaped by both researchers and actors—reflect a more responsible ethical stance *and* are likely to yield deeper data and better social science. Feminist researchers, for example, have been bold in their assertion of this position, arguing that traditional researcher-subject relationships are "descendants of hegemonic power structures" that need to be deconstructed. Authentic findings will only emerge from authentic relationships (Oakley, 1981).

Portraitists share this revisionist view of relationship, recognizing its dynamic and complex qualities, seeking to construct relationships of symmetry and reciprocity with actors in the setting, and working to negotiate (and renegotiate) fluid boundaries that mark distance and intimacy. We see relationships as more than vehicles for data gathering, more than points of access. We see them as central to the empirical, ethical, and humanistic dimensions of research design, as evolving and changing processes of human encounter.

It is important to recognize, however, that the quality and complexity of the relationship will be shaped by both temporal and temperamental dimensions—that is, by the duration of time spent and the frequency of encounters between the researcher and the actor, as well as by their personalities and the chemistry of their interactions. It is likely, for example, that a single encounter with an actor that is brief and largely informational will not have the same depth, complexity, or resonance as a research relationship that spans several months where the participants meet frequently and talk about matters of great personal meaning. In the former, the distance between actor and researcher is likely to be greater, the boundaries clearer, the interactions and information more focused, and the engagement more restrained. Both parties would be aware of the limits of their time together and would be less likely to invest their deepest feelings or their most intense emotions. In the latter case—of sustained relationships—the challenges of intimacy, rapport, and reciprocity would be enhanced. The relationship would evolve over time and require negotiation and renegotiation, shifts of roles and boundaries, greater emotional and intellectual investment, and an increasing sense of intimacy and connection.

In *I've Known Rivers,* my interviews with each of the book's six protagonists lasted about a year and we met frequently, usually weekly. These were sustained and sustaining encounters. Not only was the depth of these relationships defined by the duration and rhythm of the time we spent together, it was also shaped by the intensity of the discourse. The substance of the inquiry—an exploration into the development of wisdom and creativity in their life journeys—called up a range of deep and rich emotions, requiring great trust, intimacy, and commitment. Of course, the depth of the connection, the quality of the insights, the expression of emotion, and the timbre and range of the dialogue were different for each person—a reflection of differences in their life stories *and* differences in the relationships we created. As a matter of fact, *I've Known Rivers* tells two stories: the first chronicles the life journeys of each of the protagonists, and the second traces the evolution of our relationships. In the following passage from the opening chapter of *Rivers,* I speak about the many complex roles I played as these relationships developed over time—relationships of reciprocity and symmetry, of skepticism and appreciation, of trust and alliance, of challenge and support.

> As I listen to these extraordinary women and men tell their
> life stories, I play many roles. I am a mirror that reflects back
> their pain, their fears, and their victories. I am also the inquirer
> who asks the sometimes difficult questions, who searches for
> evidence and patterns. I am the companion on the journey,
> bringing my own story to the encounter, making possible
> an interpretive collaboration. I am the audience who listens,
> laughs, weeps, and applauds. I am the spider woman spinning
> their tales. Occasionally, I am a therapist who offers catharsis,
> support, and challenge, and who keeps track of emotional mine
> fields. Most absorbing to me is the role of human archeologist
> who uncovers the layers of mask and inhibition in search of a
> more authentic representation of life experience. Throughout, I
> must also play stage manager, coordinating the intersection of
> three plays—the storyteller's, the narrator's, and the reader's—
> inviting you to add your voice to the drama [p. 12].

In many respects, *Rivers* represents the extreme of depth, intensity, and range in research relationships in portraiture. "Human archeology"—the mode of portraiture used in *Rivers*—refers to a process of deep examination and penetration: an inquiry that is designed to uncover layers of mask and inhibition; a search for authenticity that is rich, ranging, and revelatory.

The more typical modes of portraiture tend to not go as deep or be as sustained or penetrating—less like excavation and more like rich ecological mapping. The resulting portraits are broader, more contextual, often institutionally defined, requiring the development of many relationships of shorter duration. The relationships may be very brief (an hour-long conversation with the football coach after the team practice) or somewhat more sustained (several encounters with a teacher, including classroom observations, three or four taped interviews, and some informal conversations at lunchtime). In both cases, the relationships are more contained than in human archeology—the topics of discourse more circumscribed and the boundaries clearer.

But there are surprises. Brief encounters do not necessarily mean superficial connections. Portraitists must always be ready for moments of revelation, insight, and vulnerability that suddenly transform the discourse and lead to unanticipated rapport and intimacy. They must anticipate the possibility that topics they consider relatively neutral may be experienced by the actors as emotionally charged and intrusive. And they must be aware that an immediate personal chemistry may develop with an actor that neither of them would have anticipated. Two examples:

> Maria, a fifteen-year-old Puerto Rican girl with a head full of
> unruly curls, clear penetrating eyes, and a raucous laugh, agrees
> to talk to me about her freshman year at John F. Kennedy High.
> We sit on the floor in the hall with our backs up against the
> metal lockers, our legs stretched out in front of us, and our
> faces turned sideways towards one another. The tape recorder is
> resting on Maria's lap. She seems to forget about it immediately
> as she talks to me about her friends, her family, her school, and
> her dreams. Once I get used to her lilting Spanish accent, I relax
> and give her my full attention—our eyes connecting, our heads
> nodding in unison, our voices in synchrony. At the conclusion
> of our hour-long conversation, Maria's eyes fill with tears and
> she asks me, out of the blue, "Do you know what this feels like
> to me . . . this talk you're having with me?" "No," I respond,
> surprised by the tears and the sudden urgency in her voice.
> "It feels like it feels when my grandmother brushes my hair,"
> she says. "Real soft, real gentle . . . you know, safe." In that
> moment, we both feel "real close"—an unexpected intimacy,
> a connection neither of us anticipated and one we will never
> forget [Impressionistic record, January 1981, field notes for
> *The Good High School*].

In a second example—from Davis's portrait of the Artists Collective—we witness another moment of intimacy between the portraitist and a young adolescent, a man-child who is both strong and vulnerable, enthusiastic and guarded. In a brief, penetrating encounter he lets Davis know about his admiration of his teacher's spirit and mentoring, his need for the protection and asylum offered by the Artists Collective, and his deepest fears about an untimely death.

> One sixteen-year-old student from the neighborhood says the
> Collective is his "second home . . . it's fun . . . I have fun with
> these people . . . they've taught me a lot but they're still fun
> to be around . . . especially Ra . . . he's like a father." Ra Atam,
> instructor of African percussion, is one of the Collective rela-
> tives who comes up from New York. Brought to the Collective
> by Aca Lee Thompson, he has been teaching there for seven
> years. A heavyset African American man wearing a Dashiki,
> Atam has a steadiness and aura of calm about him. He explains
> that it is "important that a child sees other role models."

Sounding more father than educator, he says he gives students his home phone so kids can call him.

Of the sixteen-year-old who thinks of "Ra" as a father, Mr. Atam says the boy "has had a hard life and needs to talk." For this boy who recently witnessed a killing, "right here [across from the Collective] on the street," following role models is only a possibility. The boy says, "I hang out with Ra and I play with him and accompany the classes sometimes." But when asked if he will himself grow up to be a drummer like Ra Atam, the boy responds without emotion, "It depends on whether or not I still have two hands or not and if I get older . . . depends on what the future brings" [Davis et al., 1993, p. 36].

Whether the encounters are brief or sustained, then, it is important that portraitists view relationships as potentially meaningful and significant to the lives of the actors, and that we try to make the time together comfortable, respectful, and benign. We want the actors to feel our full attention, our deep engagement, and our challenge—and we want people to leave the encounters feeling safe and whole. At the center of relationships, portraitists hope to build trust and rapport—first, through the search for goodness; second, through empathetic regard; and third, through the development of symmetry, reciprocity, and boundary negotiation with the actors. In the following pages, I will describe and illustrate each of these dimensions of relationship building.

THE SEARCH FOR GOODNESS

The portraitist's stance is one of acceptance and discernment, generosity and challenge, encouraging the actors in the expression of their strengths, competencies, and insights. She sees the actors as knowledge bearers, as rich resources, as the best authorities on their own experience. She is interested in examining the roots of their knowledge, the character and quality of their experiences, and the range of their perspectives. In supporting the expression of strengths, the portraitist also seeks to create a dialogue that allows for the expression of vulnerability, weakness, prejudice, and anxiety—characteristics possessed to some extent by all human beings, and qualities best expressed in counterpoint with the actors' strengths.

By *goodness,* then, we do not mean an idealized portrayal of human experience or organizational culture, nor do we suggest that the portraitist focus only on good things, look only on the bright side, or give a positive spin to every experience. Rather we mean an approach to inquiry that resists the more typical social science preoccupation with documenting pathology and suggesting remedies.

(For a fuller discussion of this research tradition, see Chapter One.) Rather than focusing on the identification of weakness, we begin by asking What is happening here, what is working, and why? But in focusing on what works, on underscoring what is healthy and strong, we inevitably see the dark shadows of compromise, inhibition, and imperfection that distort the success and weaken the achievements.

The shift of research stance—from focus on weakness to pursuit of strength, from preoccupation with disease to concern for health, from inquiry into dysfunction to examination of productivity—does *not* mean that the former attributes are neglected in favor of elevating the latter. Rather we assume that the latter qualities—of strength, health, and productivity—will *always* be imbued with flaws, weaknesses, and inconsistencies, and that the portraitist's inquiry must leave room for the full range of qualities to be revealed.

In the opening chapter of *The Good High School,* I describe my perspective on goodness—a complex, holistic, dynamic concept that embraces imperfection and vulnerability; a concept whose expression is best documented through detailed, nuanced narratives placed in context. The following excerpt refers to the search for goodness in *schools,* but it also conveys the particular and unique stance of a portraitist doing work in any setting—a stance that defines the portraitist's movement into the setting and shapes her relationship with the actors. This generous and discerning framework guides the work and the encounters of the portraitist, shaping the process and the product.

> Purposefully, I chose to study good schools—schools that were described as good by faculty, students, parents, and communities, that had distinct reputations as fine institutions with clearly articulated goals and identities. My descriptions of good high schools were, of course, shaped by my views on institutional goodness—a broader, more generous perspective than the one commonly used in the literature on "effective" schools. My first assumption about goodness was that it is not a static or absolute quality that can be quickly measured by a single indicator of success or effectiveness. I do not see goodness as a reducible quality that is simply reflected in achievement scores, numbers of graduates attending college, literacy rates, or attendance records. I view each of these outcomes as significant indicators of some level of success in schools. And I view these as potent shorthand signs of workable schools, but each taken separately, or even added together, does not equal goodness in schools. "Goodness" is a much more complicated notion that refers to what some social scientists describe as the school's "ethos," not discrete additive elements. It refers

to the mixture of parts that produce a whole. The whole
includes people, structures, relationships, ideology, goals,
intellectual substance, motivation, and will. It includes
measurable indices such as attendance records, truancy rates,
vandalism to property, percentages going to college. But it also
encompasses less tangible, more elusive qualities that can only
be discerned through close, vivid description, through subtle
nuances, through detailed narratives that reveal the sustaining
values of an institution. . . .

In offering this more generous, less absolutist vision of
goodness I am in no way trying to compromise standards
of excellence in education. Rather I am seeking to formulate
a view that recognizes the myriad ways in which goodness
gets expressed in various settings; that admits imperfection
as an inevitable ingredient of goodness and refers instead to
the inhabitants' handling of perceived weaknesses; that looks
backward and forward to institutional change and the staged
quality of goodness; that reveals goodness as a holistic concept,
a complex mixture of variables whose expression can only be
recognized through a detailed narrative of institutional and
interpersonal processes [pp. 23 and 25].

An illustration of this generous *and* critical stance—the mixture of strength
and vulnerability that is part of the portraitist's palate—is found in the following passage about Bob Mastruzzi, principal of John F. Kennedy High School.
The excerpt opens with the effusive declarations of Mastruzzi's many admirers.
He is idealized and idolized by all the school's people—teachers, students, parents, and other administrators—who speak about Mastruzzi's extraordinary
energy, passion, and commitment. As portraitist, I gather and display the long
litany of elaborate praise and introduce the powerful life-giving metaphors that
punctuate people's references to him. But I also search for the human side of
Mastruzzi. I look for the inevitable struggles of temperament and leadership
that compromise mastery and productivity in his work. Documenting the under-
side, I find that not all of his faculty hires have been exemplary; that his efforts
at inclusive leadership are often felt by the staff to be inefficient and unpro-
ductive; and that his reluctance to say no to the often-conflicting requests of his
various constituencies is seen by some as a tragic flaw in his character.

Overwhelmingly, the voices of Mastruzzi's staff sing his
praises and exclaim great loyalty for him. Over and over again,
superlatives are used. "He is the greatest human being I've
ever known," exclaims one. "I feel a tremendous sense of pride,

almost a rah-rah spirit, and I attribute that to Bob," exults another. A third speaks about Mastruzzi's "irreplaceable" qualities, "If that man were to leave this school and you were to come back three or four months later, you'd see a very different situation. The man is a great person, knowledgeable, wise, an extremely good administrator. . . . I would say he enjoys the total loyalty of his cabinet and ninety-eight percent loyalty from the faculty. . . . The man's got charisma!"

Almost everyone points to the personal qualities of Mastruzzi when they are asked to identify the origins of goodness at Kennedy. His "spirit emanates" throughout the school, says one teacher with almost religious fervor. He is "the life blood of this organism," she continues as she switches to a medical metaphor. What is fascinating about Mastruzzi's bigger-than-life role and imagery is that his self-conception is based on very different views of his power and style. Listening to his admirers, one might at first imagine that Mastruzzi's seductions are too powerful to resist—that he reigns through mysterious, otherworldly attractions, that he is a guru of sorts. But listening to Mastruzzi's perceptions of his leadership role, one is struck by his notions of participation and collaboration. He does not view himself as high on a pedestal, but as down in the trenches inspiring, cajoling, and encouraging people to "do their best and give their most." He rarely refers to the edicts and commands that he issues from his lofty station, but often to the listening, responding, and negotiating that are part of his everyday interactions. His charisma seems to derive less from his otherworldly qualities than from his very human qualities—his great ability to empathize and identify with others. When I ask Mastruzzi about his views on school leadership, he immediately refers to the collaborative dimensions of the principal's job. "First of all, I have a great concern for the quality of human relationships. I try to find ways of getting people involved in the process, using their strengths and assets. My big word is *participation*. I want to have as many people as possible join in deciding and acting. They must become responsible to something larger than themselves. If there is one fault some people say I have, it is that I try to involve too many people, and it is sometimes inefficient. But I'm willing to tolerate the inefficiency because in the end, people will feel more connected, more committed and pulled into the process."

Mastruzzi's strong and decisive views at first appear contrary to others' idealizations of him. But on closer examination, his words are echoed by the perspectives of faculty and students. Their loyalty does not seem to be an expression of idol worship, but a reflection of their connection to a communal process. When people refer to "feelings of connection," they often talk about the autonomy and independence that Mastruzzi permits and encourages. "He allows us scope, the space to develop our own thing," says one. Another points to the way that Mastruzzi protects his faculty from "the arbitrary regulations of the central authority. . . . He serves as a buffer between outside and inside. If it weren't for him, we'd feel more constrained. We have a great deal of freedom here." Some observers believe Mastruzzi is able to encourage autonomy among his faculty because of his own deeply rooted self-confidence. "He is the most secure principal I have ever known. He likes to see strength, not weakness, in the people who work for him," says a relatively new faculty member who believes there is a "fair exchange" between the freedom the faculty enjoy and the commitment that Mastruzzi expects.

One enthusiast claims that Mastruzzi not only encourages faculty creativity and autonomy, he also allows people the room to make mistakes. He is "forgiving" and believes that people often learn from repairing the damage they have created. The coordinator of student affairs, Pamela Gino, recounts the disastrous story of the first rock concert she organized for students at Kennedy. She had expected a couple of hundred students and eight hundred showed up, many high on alcohol and marijuana. "A lot of those kids think you can't listen to rock unless you're high. Booze and rock go together." Not expecting the great number of students, nor their inebriation, Gino had not planned for adequate security; it became a chaotic, treacherous evening. "After it all, I felt a tremendous letdown, a real sense of failure," remembers Gino. "But I also had learned a lot about how to plan for that kind of event. I knew I could do it better given a second chance." Mastruzzi greeted her request for a second chance with healthy skepticism and a battery of critical questions, but he allowed her to try again. The second rock concert was a "great success. . . . He's a generous man. He sees failure as an opportunity for change," beams Gino.

Just as Mastruzzi identifies his potential source of weakness as his unending attempts to be inclusive, to encourage all voices to be heard, so too do others point to the inefficiencies and ambiguities that this causes. But most do not identify the weaknesses as a problem of "participation" taken to its extreme; rather, they see it as Mastruzzi's difficulty in saying "no" to people. One sympathetic colleague, who sees many of the same traits in himself, justifies the weakness by saying, "There is something in Mastruzzi which won't let you say 'no' to him. Part of that is our expectation that he won't say no to us. I think that's fair." Others identify it as his single tragic flaw. Says a close associate, "If Bob has one fault, it is his inability to say no, to act quickly and decisively when he sees something wrong." One critic believes that Mastruzzi is "smart and calculating" and always wants to be seen as "the good guy. . . . Saying no would tarnish that image" [pp. 67–69].

The nuanced search for goodness is really a search for a generous, balanced, probing perspective. It is a search for the truth—or for the complex and competing truths that combine to shape an authentic narrative. In the previous illustration, we see the researcher on her search, checking her assumptions, pushing past the facile facade. She records first impressions and initial appearances, and then goes on to say "but on closer examination—" She layers the data; we hear from a wide arc of school people in a few short pages. As more voices enter the discourse, a more complex image of Mastruzzi emerges. We even hear Mastruzzi criticizing himself. While the portrayal is full of praise and admiration for this remarkable leader, it does not deify him. His frailties are unmasked, his uncertainties revealed, his critics heard.

EMPATHETIC REGARD

Not only are research relationships defined by the portraitist's search for goodness, they are also shaped by empathetic regard. In listening and responding to the actors, the portraitist tries to develop an understanding of their perspective. What would I feel like if I were in his shoes? If I was looking at the world through her eyes, what would I see? The portraitist tries to imaginatively put herself in the actor's place and witness his perspective, his ideas, his emotions, his fears, his pain.

For several decades, clinicians and researchers have considered the roots and purposes of empathy, and seen it as a crucial ingredient of productive and successful relationship building in therapy and in research—both being arenas of intimacy and intervention. Clinicians (including therapists and counselors of all varieties) have focused on empathy as a vehicle for identification, intimacy, and

the development of trust. Empathy is seen as the channel of emotional resonance, the vehicle for gaining a deep understanding.

Clinical psychologist Rollo May (1939), for example, devoted much of his pioneering work to examining the place of empathy in the therapist's shaping of
"constructive, affirmative, friendly, and upbuilding relationships" (p. 90). He
speaks about empathizing as developing deep connections that require "learning to relax mentally and spiritually as well as physically, learning to let one's
self go into the other person with a willingness to be changed in the process"
(p. 97). He claims that empathy is the opposite of egocentricity; the therapist
must be ready to both witness *and* experience change, to move beyond self-
reminiscence to a place of deep understanding.

> How does one personality meet and react upon another? The
> answer lies in the concept of *empathy,* the general term for
> the contact, influence, and interaction of personalities. . . . [In
> contrast to sympathy] empathy means a much deeper state of
> identification of personalities in which one person so feels him-
> self into the other as temporarily to lose his own identity. It is
> in this profound and somewhat mysterious process of empathy
> that understanding, influence, and the other significant relations
> between persons take place. . . . In this identification real under-
> standing between people can take place; without it, in fact, no
> understanding is possible [p. 75].

In *Counseling and Psychotherapy,* another classic work, psychologist Carl
Rogers (1942) stresses the supportive, healing qualities of empathy, but also
underscores the insights and generative knowledge that emerge during empathetic encounters. Therapists, like researchers conducting interviews, hope for
shifts in perspective, revelations, and new insights. Rogers defines insight as "a
process of becoming sufficiently free to look at old facts in new ways, an experience of discovering new relationships among familiar attitudes, a willingness
to accept the implications of well-known material" (p. 177). He goes on to
describe the counselor's role of encouragement and restraint, of talk and silence,
in the development of empathy: "The primary technique which leads to insight
on the part of the client is one which demands the utmost in self-restraint on
the counselor's part, rather than the utmost in action. The primary technique
is to encourage the expression of attitudes and feeling . . . until insightful understanding appears spontaneously" (p. 177).

Skipping nearly four decades and moving to the realm of research, Carol Gilligan (1982) uses the term *intimacy* to define the depth of connection to which
both May and Rogers refer and she speaks of *clinical interviewing* as the method
for nourishing this connection. Clinical interviewing embraces both diagnostic

and therapeutic themes—both the illumination and intervention that characterize intimate encounters. Intimacy, she says, is crucial to an understanding that honors multiple perspectives (much like Rogers's notion of looking at "old facts in new ways" and "discovering new relationships among familiar attitudes"). Gilligan links intimacy directly to the development of empathy. "Intimacy becomes the critical experience that brings the self back into connection with others, making it possible to see both sides—to discover the effects of actions on others as well as their cost to self" (p. 163).

Even traditionalists with a more circumscribed and pragmatic view of research relationships, those who resist the clinical language of intimacy and intervention, acknowledge that some level of connection is important. Seidman, for example, argues against close personal relationships with research participants but still speaks of the rapport that is necessary to lubricate dialogue and provoke perspective-taking in interviews. "There are times when an interviewer's experience may connect to that of the participant. Sharing that experience in a frank and personal way may encourage the participant to continue reconstructing his or her own in a more inner voice than before" (1991, p. 66).

In their approach to empathy, Marshall and Rossman do not support the notion that researchers should offer their own experiences in an effort to develop rapport. Rather they suggest a stance of receptivity and openness, welcoming the interviewee's perspective, "respecting how the participant frames and structures the responses." "The most important aspect of the interviewer's approach," the authors claim, "concerns conveying the idea that the participant's information is acceptable and valuable" (1989, p. 82).

Portraitists view empathy as central to relationship building in research. They share May's notion of identification, Rogers's view of empathy as impulse for insight, Gilligan's perspective on intimacy as critical for honoring multiple perspectives, and Marshall and Rossman's understanding of empathy as respect and open acceptance of the actor's views. None of these authors confuse empathy with sympathy; all of them recognize the quality of attention, the connection of life experiences, and the deep understanding that are key to its expression in research relationships.

Deep understanding and intimacy, of course, require that the researcher not only see the actor's reality and respect the actor's frameworks and perspectives, but also that she *herself* be self-reflective and self-analytic. That is, when the actor calls up haunting memories and vivid experiences, the portraitist must also be able to identify resonant experiences and similar feelings in herself. This does not mean that the experiences must be identical, or that the two must share parallel histories or like identities. But it does mean that there must be something in the researcher's personal experience or intellectual background that connects with what the actor is saying. The researcher does not need to be able to reflect back perfect mirror images, but the actor should be able to see refracted resonance in the researcher's eyes. This not only requires an open-minded, generous stance, it also requires a knowledge base, a level of understanding, and a body of information from which the researcher can draw connections and contrasts to the actor's reality. In other words, the more knowledgeable you are about the actor's reality and the more self-analytic you are about your own, the better you will be able to empathize. The next three illustrations express the rich roots and dynamics of empathetic regard in portraiture.

In the first illustration, from the portrait of Plaza de la Raza in *Safe Havens,* you see the immediate connections—in language, culture, and idiom—between the actors in the setting and the Mexican portraitist on the research staff. The Spanish-English dialogue about cultural identity echoes a deeper, more sophisticated level of identification and understanding between researcher and actors, and points to the place of knowledge in the expression of empathy.

> At the end of the office corridor, a shelf contains kitchen supplies one of which is a white mug that has imprinted in black the word "Hispanic" crossed out with a bold red line. "To me," dance instructor Juanita López says, "the title is not that important. . . . If people would quit putting everything into little categories it would be much easier to get along with everybody." Enrique Gálvez, the grounds manager, says he was born in Michoacán, Mexico, and explains that *"El Mexicano no tiene nada de distinguirse. Uno es Mexicano, donde quiera que va, uno es Mexicano!"* [Mexicans don't distinguish. One is Mexican, no matter where one goes, one is Mexican.]
>
> Computer operator Castañeda Trujillo, who was born in Mexico, finds "it hard when people try to coin me as a Chicano, and I do not identify with that because I still feel that I have been rooted in Mexico, so I consider myself Mexican." Rachel Pulido-Oakley says that for some time she hesitated to use the word Chicano because it carries "a lot of baggage":
>
> "Being a Chicano is by no means something that people embrace across the board. I'm the only person I know who calls herself that . . . no one [else] in my very large family . . . "
>
> Pulido-Oakley is a Chicana woman in her twenties who grew up in East L.A. She took piano lessons at Plaza when she was six and says, "I was always aware of [Plaza] as a resource." Pulido-Oakley attended a predominantly Anglo college on the East Coast and believes that "taking you out of your context is really great for making you realize what you are. . . . If I had stayed here, maybe I wouldn't have given it too much thought," and adds that when she has children, "I'm not going to tell

them 'you are a Chicano' or 'you are a Chicana' because that is something that you decide for yourself" [p. 136].

In the second illustration we see the knowledge, intimacy, and trust that can build over time to create a space safe for vulnerability and risk-taking. The passage records a moment in my evolving relationship with Katie Cannon (in *I've Known Rivers*) when we had been meeting for several months, when the rhythms and range of our encounters had become firmly rooted, and when the comfortable continuity of our sessions allowed for the expression (and recognition) of surprise. Each of my meetings with Katie would provoke reflections and inspire new stories that Katie would return with the next time. Her work was relentless, ongoing—it lasted well beyond our meetings, consuming her thoughts, her fantasies, and occasionally her dreams. Katie would sometimes record these between-session ruminations to remind her of ideas that needed expression and stories that needed telling the next time we would meet.

> Katie arrives at my office with a story to tell. The story has weighed heavily on her mind and needs immediate expression. She now seems to have become thoroughly immersed in and committed to our interviews, which echo through her hours and days after each session. Last time she burst into my office with the news that she had nothing more to say—an expression of her sense of vulnerability and exposure. She needed to tell me about the raw feelings, her wish to slow down, dilute the intense melodrama, contain some of the pain. She still needed to be assured that I could be trusted; that I would not recoil from the drama or the pain; that her stories were heard, received, remembered. This time, she needs no such assurances. She wants to begin by back-tracking to an important event that has left a deep imprint within her, but has remained unspoken since 1965, the year Katie was in the 10th grade.
>
> "I need to tell you about the time I drew a knife on my teacher," says Katie theatrically. Her opening draws a loud exclamation from me, *"Really*! Wow!" I have begun to sense that her life is full of extraordinary, dramatic, powerful moments—some having happened *to her* fortuitously, circumstantially; some having been created *by her.* Regardless of their origin, *all* of them are made more vivid by Katie's dramatic interpretations. Simple facts become complex and significant from her perspective. A beautiful thing may be seen as ugly (or vice versa) because of the context she places it in. Nothing in Katie's world is discrete or one-dimensional. It is not merely that her forty-one years have probably been more exciting and

complicated than most lives, but it is her lively interpretation of those life experiences that captivates and amazes the listener. She is the actor *and* the creator of her stories; the subject *and* the author; and these dual roles bring life to all her stories [p. 55; note that this excerpt is continued in Chapter Six].

At the end of this passage, I draw together themes that have emerged over time in my conversations with Katie: her unique take on the world, the way she sees the strange in the familiar, the complex in the simple, the light in the darkness. My ability to name these interpretive themes grows out of my increasing knowledge of Katie, our deepening relationship, and our growing trust. The authenticity of these interpretations echoes the empathy that we have achieved.

The third illustration of empathetic regard circles back to the pioneering work of Rollo May and Carl Rogers and underscores the merging of emotional and intellectual content, of inquiry and intervention, and of the insight and catharsis that can develop in relationships in portraiture, particularly when the research encounters are sustained. After a hiatus of several months—during which Toni Schiesler (in *I've Known Rivers*) has been feeling overwhelmed by the demands of her work, the rigors of her theological studies, and the burdens of nursing her invalid mother—we return to our work with relief and enthusiasm, picking up the threads from earlier encounters and weaving them into our reunion. Toni looks forward to the oasis of quiet and the nourishment of talk and self-reflection, the chance to refuel and recharge.

It is an unseasonably warm mid-February day and the air is heavy and damp. Several months have gone by since I last saw Toni and I am eager to see her and pick up the threads of her story. She bursts out of her front door, again dressed in bright purple from top to bottom. Her sweater is purple, her stretch slacks are purple, her leather walking shoes are purple. She smiles broadly and opens her long arms in a big, warm hug. We are like two squealing long-lost friends. The halo of curly white hair looks longer, bigger, wilder than I remember and it is a grand contrast to the vivid declaration of purple. But then I notice that her eyes do not mirror the vitality of her bold outfit. They are weary, swollen, and red. Her brown face has a gray cast. After the initial excitement of our greeting, her voice reveals the weariness as well. She speaks in low, measured tones as if there is no fuel left.

When we land in our chairs in her quiet study a few minutes later, she immediately picks up a book that she is in the midst of reading. "This is me. This is my condition," Toni says as she shows me Ellen Sue Stern's popular book, *Running on Empty:*

Meditations for Indispensable Women. "This has been a difficult time for me . . . too much to do, pulled in too many directions . . . I'm exhausted." I am unpacking my tape recorder, my notes, and my paper worrying whether our session will be another heavy burden on Toni or whether it might provide her with some measure of relief, and perhaps some insight into her weariness. Almost immediately I sense with relief that she has been looking forward to our time together as an oasis of quiet and self-reflection. So much of her life is responding to others' needs. She is hungry for the time and space to focus on herself. "I'm feeling change coming on, major changes." Toni explains to me. "And it scares me, exhausts me. You've come along at exactly the right time . . . to help me figure this out" [p. 242].

RECIPROCITY AND BOUNDARIES

The last two excerpts—from the portraits of Katie Cannon and Toni Schiesler— not only reflect the depth of intimacy and the rich emotional terrain of these long-term research relationships, they also point to the need for the portraitist to define and mark the boundaries of these encounters. In some sense, the deeper and more complex the relationship, the more important it is to be clear about the drawing of its contours. Although there is obviously a dynamic mutuality in these relationships—the researcher and the actor shaping the intellectual and emotional meanings—it is the *portraitist's* responsibility to define the boundaries and protect the vulnerability and exposure of the actor. This is both an ethical responsibility (a moral stance) and an empirical responsibility (a concern for the validity of the research). The parameters of the relationship must be drawn to protect both the people and the work. The navigation of boundaries, then, must be seen as counterpoint to the development of intimacy.

In the encounter with Toni Schiesler, for example, we witness her weariness, her anguish, her need for receptive and clarifying dialogue. She comes to our interview with great anticipation. She wants to hear her own self-reflections; she wants to listen to her own voice; she wants to revisit ancient traumas; she wants to discover the missing stories in her past. In the several months in which we were not able to meet, Toni has stored up stories she is eager to tell. This is deep emotional work—but it is not therapy. (Toni *has* a therapist whom she has been seeing for several months, and she brings some of the insights from her therapy to our dialogues. But she—and I—know the difference between her therapy and this inquiry.) The focus of our work is on telling her story, on chronicling her developmental journey, not on identifying and analyzing her traumas or on searching for a remedy for her angst and weariness. These are hard lines to draw, of course, because life stories are packed with emotional content and narratives fuse ideas and feelings, experiences and epiphanies, insight and affect. In excavating the story, then, the portraitist must keep focused on the research questions and must be vigilant in underscoring the central themes of the inquiry, guiding the actor away from the emotional minefields that will dilute or distort the inquiry, or that will evoke feelings of vulnerability. These research encounters reflect mutuality and empathy, but the boundary drawing is the responsibility of the portraitist.

In the process of navigating intimacy, the researcher learns to discern her own motivations, sensing the difference between legitimate inquiry and voyeurism, between the curiosity that is crucial to probing investigation and the prying that is invasive and presumptive. Using his typical homespun wit, chronicler Studs Terkel (1976) defines the appropriate limits and stance of the inquirer: "You should never ask anything that is not your business," he says adamantly. He means that the motivations of the researcher should never be self-serving—they should always be in the service of the work. And the questions the researcher asks should probe universal human themes, not be guided by individual, idiosyncratic intrigue. The researcher must ask, What in this life would have resonance in other lives? How might this individual experience inform others like it?

The challenge of boundary marking is not as complicated with research relationships that are less deep and less intense than the ones I had with Katie and Toni. But in all research relationships, the portraitist navigates the distance, the depth, and the intensity of the encounters by seeking a symmetry and reciprocity with the actors, by staying focused on the work, and by developing a contract (written or oral) with the participants that clearly articulates the commitments and responsibilities of the relationship.

The reciprocity in research relationships is sometimes named and explicit, and other times more fluid and implicit. It grows out of a sense of respect, acceptance, and appreciation for the actor's contributions to the work. After all, the actor is bringing his or her most precious resources—time, energy, experience, and wisdom—and the researcher must give something back in return if the inquiry is going to bear fruit and be productive. In exchange for the actor's contributions to the research, the portraitist might, for example, promise a service (tutoring, child care, counseling), or a document (a portrait, a journal), or an educational experience (training in research, access to courses). But it is also possible that the reciprocity will be embedded in the research process—that the experience of reflection on life and the insights derived from that will be viewed by the actor as a rare gift, and that the full attention and discerning questioning of the portraitist will be clarifying, energizing, and inspiring to the actor.

I will never forget the woman who, in the midst of an interview, suddenly asked me to stop the tape recorder, rewind the tape, and play it again. "Let me hear *me,"* she exclaimed. "I never knew I felt that way." The interview—in this case brief and focused—had allowed her to think aloud and discover her insights. It gave her a new appreciation for her perspective, a new view of herself. To her it felt like a "big opportunity," more than she ever expected to gain from the experience. "Have you gotten what you wanted?" she asked me tentatively at the end of the hour together. "*I* got more than I ever bargained for!" she concluded, with a smile both radiant and meek.

Marshall and Rossman (1989) speak about reciprocity as a reflection of the researcher's commitment and they underscore the myriad ways it can be expressed in relationship building: "Qualitative studies intrude into settings as people adjust to the researcher's presence. People may be giving their time to be interviewed or to help the researcher understand group norms; the researcher must plan to reciprocate. Where people adjust their priorities and routines to help the researcher, or even just tolerate the researcher's presence, they are giving of themselves. The researcher is indebted and should devise ways to give time, feedback, coffee, attention, flattery, tutoring, or some other appropriate gift" (p. 69).

Marshall and Rossman also point out that expressions of reciprocity can be used to gain the confidence and trust of informants. For example, they note that confidentiality may be experienced as one form of reciprocity that can be used in exchange for sensitive information. Reciprocity can also be embedded in the accuracy and subtlety with which the actors' lives are portrayed by the researcher. The actors see their experiences and perspectives vividly and authentically reflected in the researcher's work and they feel the satisfaction of a fair exchange. Goetz and LeCompte (1984) describe the participant's feeling of legitimacy as the core of ethnographic reciprocity: "Ethnographers' involvement with their participants is . . . governed by an informal tradition that expects a special kind of commitment from the researcher. This involves sympathizing and identifying with the people studied to the extent that the materials produced represent the participants' life in ways that are not just true to life and authentic to outsiders, but that feel legitimate to the participants themselves" (p. 98).

We recognize the reciprocity embedded in sensitive portrayals in the following excerpt from the Artists Collective portrait in *Safe Havens.* Dollie McLean, the cofounder and director of the Collective, describes some of the tough and painful choices she has had to make in order to maintain the clear values, ideology, and vision that are key to the Collective's coherence and success. The level of trust and reciprocity between Davis and McLean is evident in the intimate tales—both poignant and powerful—that she shares. And Davis demonstrates regard for that trust in the carefulness with which these intimacies are retold and couched in the aesthetic framework of "family" that is the Collective's signature.

Real parents may have different priorities than Collective parents. Ms. McLean tells the story of the child of a single mother who was enjoying her preparation for the Yaboo ceremony. The question arose as to who would serve as the male elder presenting the young woman at the ceremony and the mother protested. She felt she had raised the child alone and should alone present her for the Rites of Passage. In this instance of a real parent intervening in the Collective family, the Collective drew the line. To honor this mother's wishes would ruin "the choreography" of the performance. "But more important," Dollie McLean adds, "[it] would destroy the concept of traditional family values which the rite of passage is based upon, with mother and father image." The mother withdrew the child from classes.

The different priorities of real parents can also get in the way of the development of a Collective child's life as an artist. Ms. McLean explains that when her husband spots a "natural musician," he knows that the child's chances of becoming a "great artist" rely on whether "his family doesn't interfere and push him in some other direction . . . if they support him" [p. 36].

Reciprocity between the portraitist and the actor is more likely to occur when the structure, boundaries, and commitments of the relationship are made explicit from the beginning. The actor needs to know what the portraitist intends, needs, and wants. Will it be one hour-long session, a few meetings over a week's time, or several months of frequent encounters? What will be the focus of their conversation, the central agenda, the guiding themes? Will the sessions be taped? Will the actor's identity be revealed? Will there be an opportunity to review the final manuscript, correct errors of fact, or negotiate interpretive differences?

These questions need to be asked and discussed, and issues need to be resolved before embarking on the work. For research relationships—of great intensity and long duration—it is wise to record the final agreements in the form of a written contract. But it is important to know that however specific and explicit the contract, there will always be room for differences of perspective and interpretation along the way that will require new adaptations and renegotiations on the part of the researcher and the participant.

The portraitist comes to the actor as a supplicant, earnest and beseeching (but *not* begging). She is careful to be clear and honest about her expectations and she is open and responsive to the actor's needs and desires. The portraitist must not be too aggressive in urging the actor to participate in the inquiry, nor overly anxious or solicitous. In her efforts to gain the assent of the actor, she must be careful not to promise too much. The dignity of both parties is at stake, and the actor must be able to feel comfortable saying no.

Once the researcher negotiates the terms of the contract (written or oral) and gains the actor's consent, the external boundaries of structure and time begin to shape the contours of the relationship. But the internal boundaries—of intimacy and distance—continue to be challenging and shifting markers of discourse. With each encounter the researcher must make judgments about what to ask, what to pursue, and how far to probe. She must sense the mood of the moment, the tenor of the talk, the thrust of the conversation, and the resilience of the actor. She must be sensitive to the developmental phase of the research relationship and know enough about the actor's range and repertoire of responses to be able to read them accurately.

In the following illustrations from *I've Known Rivers,* I am navigating these internal boundaries and respecting the silence that is often defining of intimacy and distance. In the first example, from the portrait of Tony Earls, we are finding our way with one another during our initial meeting. Tony is searching for a point of entry, a place to begin his story, and I am listening very hard, offering reassurances, and trying to understand a way to help him get started. I do not follow some of his elliptical wanderings as he struggles to get rooted in the narrative, but I sense that he is expressing a pain that is inchoate. I choose not to ask, not to probe or push, not to challenge, because my priority—during this first encounter—is to be fully accepting and receptive. Later on in our relationship, I will become much more assertive and challenging, seeking clarity and depth. In this excerpt, Tony—a full professor at Harvard's School of Public Health—is offering a critique of what he perceives to be the University's reluctance or unwillingness to face issues of racism and discrimination from a moral (rather than a political) position. He faults Harvard's facile, pragmatic response to problems that have deep ethical—even spiritual—implications.

> Tony looks to Harvard for leadership, for a special sensitivity to the dilemmas of institutional racism. He sees Harvard as having a unique responsibility because of its elite status. "The minority issue is one that has deep moral implications for all of us. Harvard should be creating some leadership in this area. If it doesn't come from this place, where is it going to come from?" He seems to be casting around, talking to himself, as he searches for the clues to some way out of this "depressing scene." "Maybe the church," he says half-heartedly. "But I don't have a strong allegiance to the church . . . I'm an atheist, not a believer . . . I'm not identified with the metaphors . . . I have

used the church for political purposes. In St. Louis, I worked with a lot of the churches on antiapartheid stuff. . . . So the university and the church are two spheres I've worked in . . . but both of them disappoint me—the church because of its metaphors, the university because of the way it insists upon administrative rhetoric and reasoning."

Tony's language sounds abstract to me, sweeping in its assertions. I want to know what he means by the "church's metaphors," "avoiding the moral and ethical issues," the "administrative rhetoric and reasoning." But I choose not to probe. This is our first session and I am listening for the cadence and style of his talk. I also feel that he has entered his story at the most vulnerable place—the place within him that is questioning how he is using himself in this world; whether he is being true to his values, his identity, his roots; whether he can be productive and worthy in a place that often feels resistant and alien. This vulnerability, I think, is expressed in the abstractness of his language, in the pain in his voice, in his choice of where he will begin his story [p. 299].

In the second illustration, I am reflecting on the moments of reluctance and resistance in the encounters of each of the storytellers in *Rivers*—vulnerable and painful places that persisted even as our relationships deepened and matured; boundaries drawn by the actors that I respected, that went unchallenged by me. These are the moments—on the boundary lines—when the portraitist feels most sharply the convergence of empirical, ethical, and humanistic currents.

With each of these storytellers there are silences that must be respected, moments when the conversation stops, when the storytellers resist, when their faces close down or they look away. These are the places I dare not tread, the points beyond which—by silent mutual agreement—I must not go. Ogletree's brief, flat description of his sister Barbara's murder does not permit my entry. There is anguish underneath his lawyerlike public rendition and I know it would be cruel to pursue it. Toni Schiesler hints at the abuse (possibly sexual abuse) of her stepfather. "He was the meanest man I never knew . . . I often fantasized about picking up a knife and stabbing him." "What did he do to you?" I ask quietly. "I don't remember . . . but he always made me come home every day directly from school . . . my mother wasn't around." Her voice trails off. Her eyes fill with tears. We let the silence sit there.

Each time I must decide whether to risk opening a wound. There are also other dimensions of their life experiences that all the storytellers are deliberately reluctant to address. These are not the traumatic places that cause silence. They are places where storytellers fear public exposure. . . . Katie Cannon, who has no children, worries that her version of her life experiences might not be the story her family wants told. She does not want to cause her family humiliation. She knows the active grapevine that winds its way through the small southern town of Kannapolis, and she knows the damage it can cause. Katie is particularly concerned about her mother, who has been bruised and confused by earlier writings by and about her daughter, and who has had to absorb all the "rage" of her home folks who did not like the way they were portrayed. Her mother asks in disbelief, "Katie, did you forget that the tape recorder was on?" "You see," says Cannon, "my mom will take all the heat" from the relative whom everyone knows—but no one will admit—is an alcoholic, or from the light-skinned aunt who has always rejected and demeaned the Cannon children because of their dark skin. "I'll be safe way up here in Cambridge but my mom will hear about it from everyone."

I understand and honor the storyteller's judgment about who and what needs to be protected from scrutiny and exposure. Very occasionally, I even choose to edit out those parts of stories that would seem potentially damaging or hurtful even though they have been offered freely and spontaneously [pp. 610–612].

In summary, relationship building is at the center of portraiture. It is a complex, subtle, dynamic process of navigating the boundaries between self and other, distance and intimacy, acceptance and skepticism, receptivity and challenge, and silence and talk. And it is the challenging process of negotiating the often-conflicting demands and responsibilities of ethics, empiricism, and emotion.

In developing relationships, the portraitist searches for what is good, for what works, for what is of value—looking for strength, resilience, and creativity in the people, cultures, and institutions she is documenting. This generous stance opens up a space for the expression of the weakness, imperfection, and vulnerability that inevitably compromise the goodness. The portraitist is not interested in producing a facile, idealized portrayal; rather she is committed to pursuing the complex truths, vigilantly documenting what supports and distorts the expression of strength.

The search for goodness is embedded in relationships marked by empathy. In offering empathetic regard, the portraitist tries to imaginatively place herself in the actor's chair, see through his eyes, and share his angle of vision. Empathy grows out of knowledge of the actor's world, out of symmetry and mutuality of regard, and leads to increasing trust, intimacy, and understanding.

But as intimacy grows and the relationship deepens, there is the paradoxical realization that boundaries must be drawn marking the contours and limits of the relationship and offering structure, coherence, and focus to the work. The external boundaries of time, commitment, and responsibility to the demands of the work can be reflected in an explicit set of agreements forged beforehand by the researcher and actor. Internal boundaries, however, require constant vigilance and negotiation as the portraitist navigates the tender and treacherous emotional terrain, the complex arena of intellect and insight, and the spaces of resistance and silence.

Implementation

Declaring Boundaries

Jessica Hoffmann Davis

The construction of an authentic interpretation—one that is acknowledged by the actors as well as by the portraitist—results from the redefinition of those boundaries that traditionally separate insider from outsider knowledge. The actors graciously open their lives and work to the portraitist, knowing that the portraitist is only visiting for a while. Reciprocally, the portraitist enters the scene—a grateful and supplicant learner—mindful of the power of her intrusion and the limits of her participation. The boundaries declared by this purposeful and respectful rapport scaffold the endeavor of co-construction and determine the faithfulness of the resultant interpretation. Where our discussion of voice centers on the portraitist as the *finder* and *sharer* of story, our consideration of relationship considers the portraitist as the *forger* and *keeper* of rapport.

As it is with every feature of portraiture, relationship is not confined to the process of data collection, it is imprinted as well on the final product, the research portrait. The rapport forged in the process of co-constructing narrative is respected in the final product through which the narrative is shared with the reader. When Lawrence-Lightfoot describes the portraitist's objective of forging and maintaining relationships that are *benign*, she speaks to the researcher's covenant to do no harm. The keeping of this covenant requires that the boundaries declared between self and other admit intimacy even as they forbid trespass.

The territory delineated by these boundaries (as proposed in our illumination section) is distant and close, accepting and skeptical, receptive and challenging, and filled with silence as telling as talk. In establishing and maintaining such relationships, the question that portraitists must repeatedly ask of process is, How can I forge a relationship sufficient to inform (authenticate) the product (the developing portrait) while doing no harm to the subject? And the question that portraitists must repeatedly ask of product is, How will the representation of what I have learned through relationship give shape to the whole (the developing understanding) while protecting the actors on the scene?

As already mentioned, the terms and outcomes of relationships differ greatly depending on the duration and circumstance of the rapport—the length of time in which the portraitist and actor are in dialogue together and whether the focus is on an individual or an institution. The challenges and intricacies of long-term one-to-one relationships, as negotiated by Lawrence-Lightfoot in the creation of *I've Known Rivers,* have been explored in the illumination section.

Here, drawing on the experiences of Project Co-Arts, we consider the relationships that groups of portraitists forge with individuals and institutions before, during, and after limited (about a week in residence) intensive on-site visits. Beginning with a discussion of the implications and outcomes of the search for goodness, we consider implementation of relationship in preparation for the visit, during the on-site gathering of data, and beyond the visit, in the analysis of data and the creation of the final portrait.

THE SEARCH FOR GOODNESS

Project Co-Arts's relationship with community art centers that focus on education began two years before we visited our portrait sites in our preliminary discovery and close study of the field. Beyond our portrayals of five exemplary centers, our objective was to develop and disseminate a viable and accessible assessment structure. The structure promised to be of use both to centers seeking to establish and maintain educational effectiveness and to funding organizations eager to assess the educational practices of their grantees. In short, we came to the field bearing the promise of gifts.

The need for assessment structures was great and the recognition of these educational centers long overdue. Accordingly, the field welcomed us and our efforts. Prospective portrait sites were selected on the basis of their diversity in terms of location, operating budget, arts media, and specific educational objectives. Judging from comments in recent promotional materials, selected institutions felt honored that they had been chosen as exemplars. Furthermore, they were assured that our study of the education they provide could ultimately benefit the field at large. Our relationships began on this high note of admiration and interest on our part, and pride and contribution on the part of the subjects of our portraits.

These positive feelings reverberated throughout our visits and did not seem to inhibit actors' willingness to present themselves to us fully—replete with flaws that were often more vigorously shared than strengths. Indeed the field's clear acknowledgment of flaws as a reality of effective practice was reminiscent of the view of goodness that Lawrence-Lightfoot presents in *The Good High School.* A brief overview of the model of educational effectiveness that we found in these centers clarifies the point and suggests potential commonalties between the process of assessment and the methodology of portraiture. Portraitists eager to forge trusting relationships with actors on site should be aware of such potential similarities.

Beginning with the identification of the four closely interrelated relevant dimensions within and across which educational effectiveness was observed to occur (*Community, Teaching and Learning, Journey,* and *Administration*), Project Co-Arts discovered effectiveness in these settings, not as the static achievement of articulated goals, but as an active process powered by ongoing reflection on the interplay among goals, practices, and outcomes. Furthermore, that reflective process was seen as balanced over time across a course of action in which opposite poles were recognized and reconciled as *generative tensions.* The observed generative tensions included *acceptance* (commitment to the individual) and *expectation* (commitment to the center), *innovation* (creative vision) and *tradition* (historical perspective), *seamlessness* (a way in which the center was one with the community) and *individuation* (a way in which the center was unique), and *flexibility* (responsiveness to changing needs) and *integrity* (accountability to articulated goals and mission).

Underlying this reflective process-based model was a view of a field in which artists were administrators and educators. We recognized this field's approach to education as the artist's approach—one in which the center (as we were often told) was regarded as "a work of art in progress." In this context, two guiding principles held sway: persistent interest in and careful attention to process (as opposed to product), and fascination with mistakes as generative—as a place to begin: "what's right, you have to work around."

These discoveries were certainly in line with goodness as Lawrence-Lightfoot presents it in *The Good High School,* incorporating both mistakes and attention to process: "It is not the absence of weakness that makes a good school, but how a school attends to the weakness" (1983, p. 24). Indeed in her introduction to *The Good High School,* Lawrence-Lightfoot declares goodness in terms that also encompass Co-Arts's relevant dimensions. For example, she recognizes the manifestation of leadership that is fueled by partnership and alliances—

reflective of the dimension of *Administration,* and the presence of opportunities for teacher autonomy as well as visibility and accountability among students—relevant to the dimension of *Teaching and Learning.*

Lawrence-Lightfoot also embraces a view of generative tensions among constituents at good high schools. For example, she articulates the tension between *acceptance and expectation* in two instances in good high schools: in students' struggle to balance peer group demands and adult requirements, and in the academic curriculum's struggle to balance "equity among student groups and the quality of academic pursuits."

These observations grew out of Lawrence-Lightfoot's portraiture expeditions, interpreted through her experienced lens. Our observations largely preceded our portraiture forays and resulted from analysis of data from a variety of sources. Lawrence-Lightfoot had these understandings primarily in place as she framed the final portraits of good high schools, but we reached the understandings much earlier, as we approached our portraiture expeditions. Importantly, in framing both process and product, the understandings that inform the methodology do not define it. The portraitist is always open to the unexpected and to the reshaping of understanding that surprising discoveries will require.

Both Lawrence-Lightfoot's discovery of goodness and ours of educational effectiveness began with the presumption that positive educational encounters were there to be found—and, moreover, to be learned from. The declaration of this positive approach is of the utmost importance in forging relationships with future portrait subjects. Institutions are accustomed to reviews designed to ferret out problems—the location of malfunctioning parts with no regard for the coherence and productivity of the whole. Prospective sites may therefore be apprehensive, if not terrified, of any process that seems evaluative. Furthermore, for many culture-specific centers, the fear of letting others tell their stories is grounded in painful histories of misrepresentation by mainstream voices.

There is an important distinction between one-shot outsider evaluations that tell an institution that it is "good, better, or best" and ongoing insider assessment through which an organization reflects productively on its day-to-day efforts. The Co-Arts Assessment Plan was being developed to facilitate such integral self-assessment by providing a flexible structure that would admit a wide range of manifestations of effectiveness. A few of our collaborators suggested that the methodology of portraiture seems to achieve similar objectives and that our various portrayals, so different in detail, texture, and content, aptly represented the diversity of the field's display of successful educational practice.

Though not often linked directly, the making sense of experience that constitutes the interpretive process of portraiture has much in common with the assessment process of careful reflection on daily practice. While not of the "good, better, best" variety, judgment—as our discussions have demonstrated—prevails throughout the implementation of the methodology of portraiture. The portraitist's judgments of what to include and exclude, what comes together and what does not, determine the impact of the final portrait. In forging relationships, portraitists must be aware of these commonalties and of the probability of actors on the scene feeling that they are being judged and needing the assurance of a benign if not even a beneficial end in view.

PREPARING FOR RELATIONSHIP: PRE-SITE VISIT PLANNING

A group of researchers seeking integrity in their relationship with the subjects of their portraits must realize that the work done in preparation for the visit plays an important role in setting the stage for positive rapport. Researchers should consider role-playing introductions to themselves, to their specific research project, and to their work in portraiture. Toward that end, Project Co-Arts logged a list of common questions that we expected might be asked on site and on which we wanted to present a unified perspective.

The questions included, What is Project Co-Arts? Why are you here observing this center? Were we selected as a site because we are one of the best in the country? Are you going to write this interview down? May I have a copy of the transcript of the tape? In anticipation of these questions, we prepared a one-page overview of our work that we could share with actors on the scene. We also agreed on the wording of our explanation that centers were chosen on the basis of their diversity and we decided together that none of us would share in-house transcripts with interviewees.

While these issues may seem purely technical, the group's agreement and assurance on our responses to frequent small questions would help to present a consistent and reliable countenance to the many constituents whom we would meet during a week's visit to a site. We agreed that if a technical question arose about which we were uncertain, we would explain that we would call the project and check before we made promises to one constituent that we were not prepared to make to another.

Our numerous brief site visits during the creation of our gesture drawings provided us with experiences on which we could draw in presenting ourselves to portraiture centers. Based on these experiences and in preparation for all our visits, we met as a group to role-play interviews and critique our respective developing skills. We also generated a list of reminders that we shared among the team and to which we added new suggestions as our forays into the field continued. That list was divided into two sections: Nuts and Bolts, which included specific technical issues that might influence the development of relationship, and Heart of the Matter, which addressed more overarching principles for relationship building.

Among the technical issues in our Nuts and Bolts list were decisions regarding spending money on site, securing transportation into reluctantly trafficked areas, and dressing ourselves and addressing actors on site with visible respect. We noted detail-oriented suggestions like prioritizing on-site observation, requesting written materials whenever the opportunity arose, and marking down key players' names so that we would be sure to remember them.

In the Heart of the Matter part of our list, we emphasized our mandate to do no harm and reminded ourselves of the potential to do good: that careful observation and attentive interviewing done well are positive interventions. We reviewed details of interview protocol such as the importance of preparing for the interview, listening *for* a story without being invasive, and reaching for open-ended questions rather than those that seem to have right or wrong answers. We reminded ourselves not to make personal assumptions (avoiding phrases like "Does your husband—") and to keep a respectful distance with interviewees.

Overall, we emphasized the importance of maintaining careful boundaries in relationship—not trying to forge new friendships or act like the players on the scene: "People will be watching us and casualness is too easily misinterpreted as disrespect." Our final reminder on that list was to "overcome the love affair" we expected to have with the site and to listen for the hard discoveries below the surface: "What's not quite right won't dull the light" was one of our maxims.

While these examples of suggestions may seem most relevant to our project, the preparatory activity of compiling a list of agreed-upon guidelines is worth replicating by other portraitists preparing as a group for various site visits. The objective of such preparatory guidelines is to help a diverse group of portraitists lay consistent and fertile groundwork for the forging of productive relationships with actors at a site. Brainstorming approaches together as a team not only prepares a group of researchers for careful entry into the scene, it also provides an opportunity for important early reflection on the particular site and its relationship to the research initiative in which portraitists are involved.

Before portraitists arrive on site, they may want to send a letter ahead outlining the details of what a portrait is and what is involved in preparing to create one. Additionally, it is helpful to introduce the researchers who are traveling to the site, with brief biographies including the nature and length of their involvement in the work and their particular preparation for portrait writing. Such letters of introduction initiate a sense of reciprocity—a willingness to share the sort of information about the group that portraitists hope to glean from actors on the scene.

FORGING THE RELATIONSHIP DURING
THE SITE VISIT: NUTS AND BOLTS

It takes time for an institution to begin to become used to researchers' presence and for the establishment of smooth dialogue among portraitists and key players. Most often, the director or some other inside actor takes on the responsibility of helping portraitists make connections with the individuals they want to interview and the classes they want to observe. If portraitists have reviewed class schedules in advance, they can more easily ask to visit classes that are of particular interest.

Careful review of written materials prior to the site visit will also help portraitists identify key players with whom they want to speak. It is important for sites to know in advance, for example, that portraitists may have an interest in speaking with members of the community who have relationships with the institution, or individuals who were involved with its inception. Occasionally, a surprisingly apt candidate for interview, like the institution's accountant, will unexpectedly drop in and be willing to be interviewed. More often, portraitists will have asked to meet with selected players and will have these meetings scheduled by their hosts.

Actors on the site frequently have an agenda of classes and events that they would like portraitists to observe and particular people whom they would like to see interviewed. It is very important to prepare a schedule that can honor such insider requests for self-presentation while at the same time leave room for scheduled meetings that seem important to the portraitist. It is also most important to leave space for unscheduled time to roam the halls and speak spontaneously with actors on the scene. Each portrait site may have a cadre of individuals who perhaps unexpectedly demonstrate sustained and intimate knowledge of the institution.

Beyond the important allowance of time to wander, portraitists also need to be ready to observe the unexpected, to be open to serendipitous encounters, and to consider each individual as a resource. In discovering an unexpected issue of interest, portraitists can ask the interviewee to suggest other actors who might be able to tell them more about the topic. When an instructor speaks of a particular student, for example, the portraitist can ask to meet with that student to obtain another version of a given story.

Occasionally individuals with whom the site has prearranged visits appear to have prepared remarks that may seem canned or be off-putting in their polish. It is important to remember that no matter how much players sound as if they have been prepped by a development officer, they really do have personal stories to share about a site. If the interviewee is going on about the great things the site does for children in general, portraitists can ask questions like, Is this what happened for your own child? How did your child happen to come here?

Portraitists can help set interviewees at ease on this count by being up front with their interest. "Yes, I have read about the number of classes offered. We are speaking to individuals like you to learn more about what happens within this place for participants like you—what makes *your* experience here special." Interviewees are usually more comfortable telling their own stories, but are not certain that is what the portraitist wants. Actors at a site often have the sense that the portraitist comes to an interview to gain particular information. There is the frequent fear that the interviewee may not be able to deliver what the interviewer wants.

Interviewees may also be reluctant to share negative experiences of a place and may need assurance that the portraitist's intention is to gain a whole picture, not to do harm. Actors on site may need to hear, for example, that the tape recorder is a vehicle for documentation, not indictment. Portraitists can anticipate the question "What will happen to these tapes?" and from the start of an interview explain that they are taping the encounter so as to record every word without having to make note of it. It is useful to ceremoniously and carefully record the respondent's permission to tape the interview—no matter how brief.

This gesture not only takes care of an important technical issue, it also serves to reinforce the formality and importance of the moment of the exchange. In brief encounters with students in the halls at institutions we visited, this gesture was generally met with amusement, excitement, and ultimate engagement. The procedure said to the student, "We are about to have an important discussion. Please take these questions seriously and provide your best responses." Beyond that, the formality also tells the interviewee that he or she is part of an important place and that the content of the interview really matters, that daily experience that is often taken for granted is something others respect and learn from, and that the interviewee's responses may be incorporated into researchers' writing so that others can also learn from the experience.

The example of introducing the use of the tape recorder illustrates how careful and courteous explanations of simple activities can act as positive interventions in the forging of relationships. If portraitists maintain the attitude of respectful learners, insiders have the opportunity to perceive themselves as experts and teachers. Such self-perception is enlarging and a benefit of the portraiture process—one of the gifts that portraitists offer in exchange for the enormous gift that the site extends in opening its doors to research.

If portraitists feel too greatly the burden of their intrusion, suspect rather than respect the actors at a site, or pry too deeply in their inquiries, they violate rather than honor their covenant to do no harm. Portraitists must always be mindful of the seriousness of their work on site and the ease with which their actions can unintentionally be injurious. For example, the portraitist's knowledge of the general field that the site represents may inadvertently be threatening to constituents. If the portraitist is being shown a performance of which the site is most proud, it is detrimental (no matter how well-intentioned) to point out, "Oh this is the sort of performance I have seen at so many places in our study."

On the other hand, knowledge of the field can be serviceable in exchanges over painful issues. For example, when Co-Arts centers shared their frustration over lack of funding for sustained operation, they seemed comforted by the knowledge that researchers were aware of that problem, that we knew many other centers that struggled as they did, and that we were committed to bringing attention to the issue in our writing.

In short, the portraitist needs to remember that a site is at the same time representative of the larger field and unique in its own right. No individual or site wants to be reduced to the status of "typical phenomenon." In forging relationships, portraitists need to be open about the methodology's celebration of what is unique and its intention to reveal what is universal within the portrayal of uniqueness.

FORGING THE RELATIONSHIP DURING THE SITE VISIT: HEART OF THE MATTER

In individual interviews, the negotiation of boundaries plays a pivotal role in forging and protecting relationships. While most interviews are enlightening, in some, as Lawrence-Lightfoot has mentioned, the chemistry that can develop between portraitist and actor is profound. One of my interviews at the Artists Collective was particularly moving and illuminating for me. It was an example of an exchange in which chemistry and empathy between portraitist and actor were surprisingly achieved in a brief encounter.

The meeting with Derek's mother was prearranged. Knowing that I wanted to interview parents, the Artists Collective had invited a few veteran parents to come in and talk with me. While several parents took the opportunity to meet with me as they dropped their children off at classes or waited for them to be finished, Derek's mother came specifically for our meeting.

Unlike most of the parents I met, Mrs. Raymond (I use fictive names) was dressed for the occasion. She was a heavyset middle-aged African American woman with a warm but worried face, made up with visible blush and dark red lipstick. She wore an ornate hat and carried a formidable pocketbook, reminiscent for me of truly "grown up" women in the 1950s—women who wore double-breasted coat dresses, stockings, and sensible but high-heeled shoes. She carried—and immediately pointed out to me—her notebook from the class she was off to after our meeting in which she was training to become a teacher's aide. Mrs. Raymond seemed intoxicated, high on something, and I felt considerable guilt. Was she so nervous about meeting with me, so anxious about being chosen to represent the Collective—so eager to represent them well—that she had fortified herself for the experience? Was I misreading her demeanor?

I was both nervous about the encounter and overwhelmed by the thought of what might happen. Could she answer my questions? Was I competent to handle the potentially uncomfortable dialogue that might ensue? I began with simple factual questions, the nuts and bolts approach we had chosen to put respondents at ease and assure them that participating in the interview would not be difficult.

How had she heard about the Collective? How long had her son been coming here? She answered my questions graciously, thoughtfully. Her son was a great dancer. Thanks to the Collective he had dance scholarships at other programs as well; he worked at a radio station after school. She was filled with admiration and affection for the Artists Collective. As I listened to her responses and wrote down key words with which to frame my next questions, I noticed that I stopped hearing a slur in her speech or an occasional unprovoked laugh. I no longer felt the intensity of her wary eyes following my every gesture.

In an economically impoverished community, the Artists Collective charges students, albeit very small amounts, for attendance at its classes. I was told by constituents that this was because students and parents did not respect what they got for free. Furthermore, the opportunity to provide parental services in lieu of payment not only made it possible for children who could not otherwise afford it to come, it also opened the way for the essential ingredient of parental involvement. Still, I had heard from a community service provider that people in the neighborhood thought of the Collective as expensive and therefore exclusive.

When Mrs. Raymond began to tell me how she came to enroll her son, I realized that she was very much a part of the immediate neighborhood, in touch with the individuals who could not pay and did not appreciate being asked to do so. Mrs. Raymond told me of her friends who did not take the time or were otherwise unable to realize the advantage of the Collective for their kids. She tried to convince them to participate but some who wanted very much to have their kids there could not afford it.

She felt lucky that Derek had been able to come to the Collective for so long, that he was so talented, that all his friends were dancers and that they hung together and did not drink or steal, that their dancing took the place of life on the street. Derek had been in trouble with the law before he started dancing, but now he was "clean." She smiled as she told me that in the fall he had had to choose between football and dancing because his schedule would not allow both, and of course, he chose dancing. Having met Derek, a stalwart sixteen-year-old, the dream of any high school football coach, I understood the significance of this decision. I was fascinated with what she was telling me about the way these "jocks turned dancers" brought their competitive spirit into their dancing. When kids at school teased them, they'd put down their books in the hall and dance. "Can you do this?" "How about this?" and the jeering would turn to applause. I made note of our exchange:

> She speaks with pride about her son, but it is guarded. As one who is outspoken in my proud accounts of my three sons, I "Oooo" and "Wow" supportively at every word of praise she shares. But every one of my "Wows" is met with cautious optimism. Her tone is level and sure. This mother does not accept her son's current success as a given. She tells me that for now he is "off the street" and she hopes it will stay that way, but she is grateful to the Artists Collective for helping him be the best he can be in any situation. If he returns to the street and deals drugs—which she hopes he won't—she knows that because of his training at the Collective, he will be the best he can be—the "man in the car" not "the man on the corner." She tells him, "Don't be the one on the corner. He's the one who gets killed."
>
> I think for a moment of parents I know anguishing over which college will admit their child. This mother with a son who can dance so beautifully is praying for his survival. She looks at me and says,
>
> "Of course you know he's my knee child."
>
> "Your knee child?"
>
> "Well, I have three sons."
>
> "So do I!"
>
> "Then you know that the oldest one is always walking around on his own exploring the world, and the baby is crawling on the floor. But that middle one stays close; he's the one on your knee."
>
> I know she is speaking of my middle child and I slide my chair closer.
>
> "You have to tell the brothers" (and this is the same term we use in our house whenever we speak of whatever two other boys are not the subject of conversation) "You have to tell the brothers that when you die, they have to take care of that knee child. Because it's going to be the hardest for him."

In so brief an encounter, we have forged a relationship. Nonetheless, an interview that has rendered both bonding and provocation finds very spare treatment in context in the Collective portrait:

The safe haven the Collective provides exists in a neighborhood that is perceived as far from safe. The Collective's Annual Report for 1992 reflects a recovery in enrollment that had fallen off in '91 because of "continued reports of drive-by shooting and other serious problems in the neighborhood." In '92 the report indicates, "While the neighborhood continues to be a 'high risk' area with drugs and crime, fewer drive-by shootings were reported."

The McLeans speak matter-of-factly about the realities of crime in the North End. Dollie McLean explains that the jazz sessions that had started in '75 had to be discontinued because they "had a little mugging and somebody took somebody's wallet." Decrying the drug empires through which "tons of cocaine" are brought into this country and thanks to which "heroin is back strong," Mr. McLean attributes blame to "the upper echelons of society" but says, "the little man on the bottom pays."

In comparison to the national blight, McLean asks with compassion: "The kid with the little $5 bottle of crack that they pick up over here in the North End . . . what did he do?" One local parent expresses her desire that the Collective will help her child to be "the best at whatever he does." She hopes her son will live an honest life; but even if he ends up dealing drugs, she says she tells him to be at the top—"Don't be the one on the corner. He's the one who gets killed."

The mother of a serious young dancer, she lives nearby and believes the habits her sixteen-year-old son has acquired in the safe haven of the Collective protect him wherever he goes. For her son, she explains, "This is it. He feels safe here . . . it is his safe haven. He loves to dance. He loves tap, modern, African— he's not so keen on the ballet—and he volunteers for Channel 26 (thanks to a Collective introduction) and he even directed a show." She believes that her son and his Collective friends, "dance their energy off." They are "not money oriented and that makes a big difference. You don't need $20, $30, $40, or $100 in your pocket. Give them a quarter or a soda and they're happy. Flashy cars and sneakers and leather jackets, no! He's looking at at least one year in college."

"They don't hang around clubs or bars; they don't smoke anything; they do fool around. Other than that, this is their place. It is a large part," she goes on, "of my son's itty bitty life." This North End mother believes that parents should get their children into the Collective "really early—in time to . . . save them from the personal things that would pull them into the street: 'Come on man, let's steal a car.'" Although Dollie McLean points out that "students are not turned away because they cannot pay," some community members perceive the Collective's safe haven as financially inaccessible. This mother says she knows people in the neighborhood who have "started to join, but couldn't afford it—not right now" [Davis et al., 1993, p. 24].

Co-Arts's relationship with the Collective continued long after the site visit. The Collective was one of the centers that implemented the working draft of our assessment plan and helped us to refine it (see Davis et. al., 1996). Although the portrait has long since been completed, each time we touch base, collaborators at the Collective receive us warmly and tell us of the latest developments with the same care with which they spoke into our tape recorders when we were visiting on site. Each year, I am honored by an invitation to the Yaboo ceremony in which youth are presented by their elders to the Hartford community. I was greatly saddened by the recent phone call in which Dollie McLean spoke to me in a voice that let me feel I was a member of the Collective family, "Oh and I have bad news to share. Our Derek has been arrested."

GUARDING THE RELATIONSHIP AFTER THE VISIT: CREATING THE FINAL PRODUCT

In the creation of the final product, the portraitist's relationship with the actors on the site takes on new dimensions. From the relationship forged in the co-construction of narrative and the back-and-forth communication of data collection and analysis, the portraitist now relates to the actors at the site as future readers of the portrayal. As we pointed out in Chapter Four, by clearly asserting her own perspective, the portraitist creates a space for the alternative views of any reader. In considering the specific readers who are the actors on the scene, the portraitist is mindful and protective. It is the actors who are most vulnerable to whatever distortion they may find in the image reflected in the portraitist's mirror.

In my representation of what I have learned from Mrs. Raymond, as seen in the preceding excerpt, I protect her identity. In spite of her great impression on me, I draw on her story only insofar as it informs the emergent themes and developing whole of the portrait. My changing impressions and our ultimate bonding are not usefully included in the final narrative—as they would be if Mrs. Raymond were the subject of the portrait. In creating the final portrait of the site, her voice becomes one of the many that are taken together and represented selectively throughout the narrative.

Nonetheless, the reader can sense our relationship, like others throughout the portrait, from the intimacy of the comments that have been shared and the circumspection with which they are presented. Indeed, overall, the reader can sense the depth of relationship between portraitist and actors on the site reflected not only in the intimacy of stories shared, but in the tone of personal descriptions and the care with which the aesthetic whole is woven together.

The actors at the centers Co-Arts visited also played a contained but nonetheless active role in the final writing of the portrait. This role that began in active reflection on site about our developing interpretation continued through a review of the last draft of the portrait. By the end of the week's visit, portraitists had at least a first-draft idea of the emergent themes that might frame the portrait. On the final day, a meeting was planned with the actor who had been key in orchestrating the site visit—usually the center's executive director—and the themes were reviewed together. Occasionally, the themes were shared with other actors on site as well. In this way, the co-constructive aspect of the portrait writing promised to be continued beyond the sharing of stories and collection of data into the writing of the final portrait.

When the final draft was complete, we sent it to the portrait site with a carefully worded letter that asked portrait subjects to review the draft thoroughly and let us know within two weeks whether there were any factual errors in the text. We reminded the actors that our hope was that they would find the portrait *authentic.* We explained that we meant that although we knew the portrayal would look very different if they had written it themselves, we hoped they would be able to read it and agree, "Yes, that is us."

By putting the constraints around factual errors, we tried to make clear to the actors that the portrait was a finished product—our interpretation was complete. Of course, as we expected, beyond several small factual errors that were gratefully corrected, constituents pointed out particular parts of direct quotes that they feared would be hurtful to constituents in ways we hadn't anticipated. While we did not change the wording of direct quotations (which had been scrupulously recorded) we were most often able to respond to these comments by omitting portions of a quotation and incorporating less charged but relevant comments within the sentence that introduced the quote.

The lessons this implementation chapter contains are clear. Portraitists need to prepare for site visits thoroughly, interact with the actors on the scene with dignity and care, and guard the relationships that are established throughout the writing of the final portraits. Opportunities for reciprocity can be found and should be exploited throughout the process of studying a site and framing a research portrait, the final gift of the portraitist. Informing every aspect of the portraiture process, the declaration of porous and protective boundaries in relationship is an exacting, challenging, and crucial enterprise on which the authenticity of the final portrait relies.

Artistic Refrain

Representing Rapport

Jessica Hoffmann Davis

The artist and teacher Nicolaides presents this hypothetical scenario:

> Imagine that a man from Mars or some planet totally different
> from ours is looking for the first time at a landscape on the
> earth. He sees what you see but he does not know what you
> know. Where he sees only a square white spot in the distance,
> you recognize a house having four walls within which are
> rooms and people. A cock's crow informs you that there is a
> barnyard behind the house. Your mouth puckers at the sight
> of a green persimmon which may look to him like luscious
> fruit or a stone.
>
> If you and the man from Mars sit down side by side to
> draw, the results will be vastly different. He will try to draw
> the strange things he sees, as far as he can, in terms of the
> things his senses have known during his life on Mars. You,
> whether consciously or not, will draw what you see in the
> light of your experience with those and similar things on earth.
> The results will be intelligible, the one to the other, only where
> the experiences happen to have been similar [1941, p. 6].

In his telling of this story of drawing what one sees, Nicolaides alludes to all
the features of portraiture that we have considered so far. We recognize context

in our understanding of the differences between Martian and earthly backdrops, and voice in the different interpretations that are shaped by knowledge and experience. But here we focus on *relationship* and consider this story as it addresses the inherent challenge of forging and representing outsider-insider rapport.

The image of the man from Mars (the outsider) portraying objects with which he has little or no familiarity is analogous to the situation in which the portraitist is forging relationships with individuals (insiders) whose experiences and environment may be entirely different from her own. How will the portrayal be intelligible if the experiential base of the portraitist does not include prior knowledge of the realities of the subject or actors on a site? Nicolaides suggests that it will not.

But conscientious preparation and the stance of supplicant learner can make a difference in the portraitist's purview. A preliminary review of replicas of earth-bound landscapes would help the Martian to see what the attending art student sees. Such preparation can also help forge an interpersonal relationship that can inform the vision and drawing of the Martian as surely as that of the earthly artist. The idea, for example, of a persimmon as a stone will expand the artist's understanding of the object as certainly as knowledge of the persimmon's acidity will ground the Martian's view. Empathetic rapport can forge relationships across improbable schisms.

Like the artist creating a work of art, the portraitist is also relating directly to the work itself. In the drawings of Happy by five-year-old Sydney and adult artist Amy (pp. 178–179), we see vivid examples of artists relating to their individual works. In representing Happy, Sydney drew a series of Jewish stars. These gratifying schemata, inverted overlapping triangles that miraculously present as stars, are a pleasure for Sydney to create. She explained, "This is Happy because I love to draw Jewish stars." Adult artist Amy created a still life that has been recognized by other artists as an "art school schematic" or formulaic representation. Amy explained as she created the drawing, "These objects make me very happy, very comfortable; they always give me a good result."

These remarkably similar descriptions of the drawing experience both represent the drawers' relationship with the activity of drawing and the understanding that that rapport is embedded in the meaning of the drawing. The actual experience of the artist joyfully constructing the portrayed objects contributes to the content of the drawing: the represented interpretation of Happy. And so it is with the portraitist's rapport with the subject. While the relationship may not be directly represented in the portrait, it is nonetheless imprinted on the portrayal, embodied in the carefulness with which descriptions of individuals are shaped and presented.

As five-year-old Taylor drew, he revealed his close connection with and personal imprint on the image in phrases such as "When I am happy my eyelashes always go up." Adult artist Seymour produced a drawing that from a distance is almost indistinguishable from Taylor's (see pp. 180–181). But on closer inspection, we see that there is no specific representational image in Seymour's drawing. Maintaining Taylor's shape of line and arrangement of form on the page, Seymour has portrayed the emotion of happiness exclusively through visual metaphor: uniting the thought of Happy with the upturned lines and balanced arrangement of space. Seymour is more distanced from his drawing; he is not apparently represented in the image. Instead, his presence is felt through the skillful manipulation of the medium of graphic symbolization. Here the artist retains the essence of the child's drawing and in reinterpreting it, redefines it.

What do these two drawings tell us about the relationship between the artists and the subject of happiness? Taylor may be more like the man from Mars drawing on a limited experiential base in representing the emotion. But Seymour has both breadth of experience and the ability to hold in his mind at one time the abstract thought of the emotion and his idea for representing it in nonobjective form.

Both Seymour and Taylor anticipate the needs of the perceiver of their work throughout their processes of construction. What will the viewer need to know in order to understand the interpretation? What Taylor invests in communication through line, form, and upturned eyelashes, Seymour invests in line and form alone. Seymour's perceiver has a different set of resources with which to construct an understanding of the drawing. But undoubtedly perceivers of both drawings will read them as Happy. Like artists, portraitists consider the needs of the reader in reinterpreting their work and thereby anticipate the relationship between reader and work and reader and portraitist as they create their representations.

Unlike personal relationships, which can be formed between portraitists and the physical actors on a site, the relationships between artists and abstract subjects do not hold the same ethical responsibility. In more literal artistic portraits, like the one that adorns the cover of this book, visual artists, like portraitists, balance the mandates of interpersonal rapport with those of aesthetic interpretation. Whatever liberties of representation may be taken will have human repercussions. Committed to doing no harm, portraitists carefully guard their relationships with the subjects of their portrayals. The reflection in the mirror that the portrait holds to experience may evoke difficult realizations.

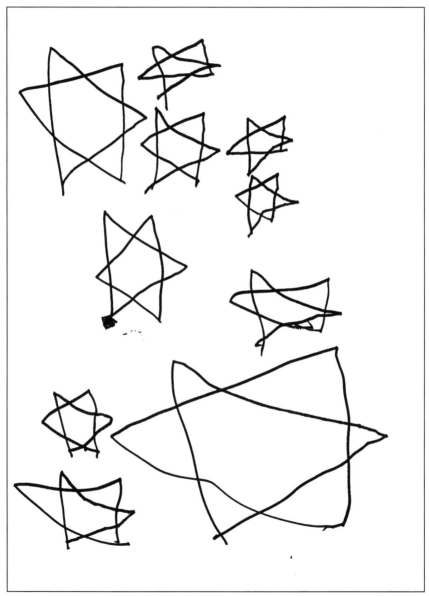

Five-year-old Sydney's drawing of Happy

Adult artist Amy's drawing of Happy

Five-year-old Taylor's drawing of Happy

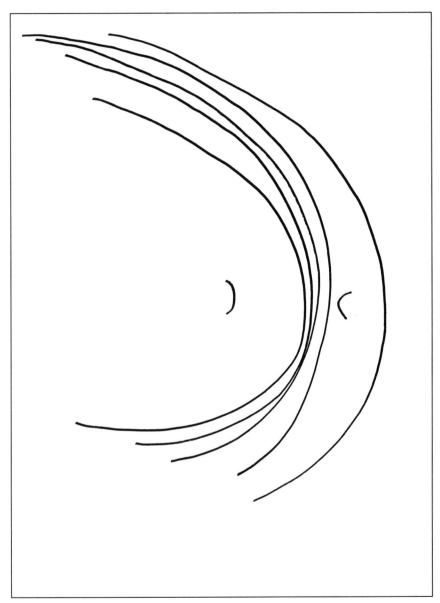

Adult artist Seymour's drawing of Happy

Buste au Fond Étoilé
7 April 1949

CHAPTER SIX

ON EMERGENT THEMES

Illumination

Searching for Patterns

Sara Lawrence-Lightfoot

The development of emergent themes reflects the portraitist's first efforts to bring interpretive insight, analytic scrutiny, and aesthetic order to the collection of data. This is an iterative *and* generative process; the themes emerge from the data and they give the data shape and form. The portraitist draws out the refrains and patterns and creates a thematic framework for the construction of the narrative. She gathers, organizes, and scrutinizes the data, searching for convergent threads, illuminating metaphors, and overarching symbols, and often constructing a coherence out of themes that the actors might experience as unrelated or incoherent. This is a disciplined, empirical process—of description, interpretation, analysis, and synthesis—and an aesthetic process of narrative development.

The portraitist comes to the field with an intellectual framework and set of guiding questions. The framework is usually the result of a review of the relevant literature, prior experience in similar settings, and a general knowledge of the field of inquiry. It also resonates with echoes of the researcher's autobiographical journey—those aspects of her own familial, cultural, developmental, and educational background that she can relate (either consciously or unconsciously) to the intellectual themes of the work. In Chapter Four we described these anticipatory frameworks that get expressed in the researcher's point of view, using the phrases "voice as preoccupation" and "voice as autobiography." We suggested that these voice modalities are embedded in the researcher's template; the intellectual and experiential structure is her point of reference and guides her angle of vision and her data collection.

This template may be fairly explicit and well-developed (like the "relevant dimensions" used by the *Safe Havens* researchers described in Chapter Four) or they may be more implicit and abstract (like the guiding preoccupations that informed my work in *The Good High School*). But whether the dimensions are explicit or implicit, formal or informal, they are part of the researcher's anticipatory schema. They are not, however, stated as (or meant to be) propositions to be proved or disproved. Unlike quantitative inquiry, where the researcher comes with specific hypotheses to be tested, discrete propositions to be proved or disproved, detailed interview questions, predetermined observational schedules, and a well-defined research plan, the portraitist enters the field with a clear intellectual framework and guiding research questions, but fully expects (and welcomes) the adaptation of both her intellectual agenda and her methods to fit the context and the people she is studying. She hopes to generate theory, not prove prior theoretical propositions. Her methodological plan and conceptual frame—independently constructed before entering the field—are only starting points, but aspects of both are immediately transformed and modified to match the realities of the setting. With the portraitist's first moves into the setting, the iterative process begins—a dynamic process of receptivity, negotiation, and accommodation that leads to more focused research questions and a more grounded research design.

Even though the portraitist anticipates changes in her research plan and is attentive to the cues in the field to which she must respond and adapt, it is important that she record her framework *before* she enters the field, identifying the intellectual, ideological, and autobiographical themes that will shape her view. The more conscious and explicit she can make this "voice of preoccupation" (and we suggest writing these reflections down in a form that encourages rumination, analysis, and critique), the more open she will be to what she encounters in the field. We see here a central paradox of this phase of the portraitist's work: the articulation of early presumptions does not inhibit or distort her clear vision; rather it is likely to make her lens more lucid, less encumbered by the shadows of bias. Making the anticipatory schema explicit (in the form of memos, journals, or self-reflective essays) allows for greater openness of mind.

In *The Good High School,* I recorded some of the anticipatory themes (developed more fully and specifically in memos to myself before embarking on the research) that guided my work in the field and that were modified by the complex and diverse realities I encountered when I visited the schools. The framework I brought to the research reflected a mix of my earlier research experiences, my interdisciplinary predisposition, my philosophical stance, my intellectual intrigues, and my own life story.

> I visited the schools with a commitment to holistic, complex, contextual descriptions of reality; with a belief that environments and processes should be examined from the outsider's more distant perspective and the insider's immediate, subjective view; that the truth lies in the integration of various perspectives rather than in the choice of one as dominant and "objective"; that I must always listen for the deviant voice as an important version of the truth (and as a useful indicator of what the culture or social group defines as normal), not disregard it as outside of the central pattern. I also believe, as did those artists who painted me, that portraits—and research—should be critical *and* generous, allowing subjects to reveal their many dimensions and strengths, but also attempting to pierce through the smooth and correct veneers [pp. 13–14].

I then traced the connections between my anticipatory template and some of the themes that resonated through the final portraits. "Given these empirical tendencies and value positions, it is not surprising that the portraits I have written move from the inside out, search out unspoken (often unrecognized) institutional and interpersonal conflicts, listen for minority voices and deviant views, and seek to capture the essences, rather than the visible symbols, of school life" (p. 14).

In *Safe Havens*, the Co-Arts research team was much more explicit about the "relevant dimensions" that initially framed their perspectives on community art centers and guided their collection of data: Teaching and Learning, Journey, Community, and Organization. These four dimensions would become the initial scaffold for perspective-taking and data collection. But even with this relatively predefined conceptual structure, the researchers were careful to remain open to the unexpected, alert to disconfirming evidence, and attentive to the contrasting and myriad ways in which these dimensions were represented, expressed, and named in the different community art centers that they examined in depth.

Once in the field, the portraitist begins by listening and observing, being open and receptive to all stimuli, acclimating herself to the environment, documenting her initial movements and first impressions, and noting what is familiar and what is surprising. The research stance evolves from quiet watchfulness—where the portraitist is mostly taking in stimuli and listening carefully—to the more purposeful activities of initiating relationships with actors, scheduling interviews, and developing a plan of action. With each stage of data collection, at the close of each day, the portraitist gathers, scrutinizes, and organizes the data, and tries to make sense of what she has witnessed.

Usually these daily reflections are documented in an "Impressionistic Record"—a ruminative, thoughtful piece that identifies emerging hypotheses, suggests interpretations, describes shifts in perspective, points to puzzles and dilemmas (methodological, conceptual, ethical) that need attention, and develops a plan of action for the next visit. In these Impressionistic Records we see the interplay between relevant dimensions and emergent themes, between our anticipatory schema and our developing insights drawn from our interpretive descriptions in the field. And Impressionistic Records allow us to become increasingly focused and discerning in our work with the discovery of patterns, the development and dialogue of ideas, and the convergence of phenomena. This ongoing dialectic—between data gathering and reflection, between description and analysis—begins in the very early stages of fieldwork (recording the researcher's acclimation to the setting) and lasts throughout the entire research process (until the writing of the final text). The emergent themes grow out of data gathering and synthesis, accompanied by generative reflection and interpretive insights.

Portraitists join with qualitative researchers of all varieties in emphasizing the flexibility of research design and the iterative process of data collection and thematic development. Miles and Huberman (1994), for example, describe the analytic work of identifying emerging themes (which they refer to as "coding") as at the core of the iterative process of qualitative research: "Coding is not just something you do to 'get the data ready' for analysis, but . . . something that drives ongoing data collection. It's a form of early (and continuing) analysis. It typically leads to a reshaping of your perspective and of your instrumentation for the next pass. At the same time, ongoing coding uncovers real or potential sources of bias, and surfaces incomplete or equivocal data that can be clarified next time out" (p. 65).

This ongoing coding, then, guides the researcher's activities. Any system of data organization and synthesis must be flexible enough to allow the researcher to shift gears and change direction as she moves from fieldwork to analysis and back to data collection. Miles and Huberman describe these "iterative cycles" that produce greater clarity and refinement of emergent themes: "The ultimate power of field research lies in the researcher's emerging map of what is happening and why. So any method that will force more differentiation and integration of that map, while remaining flexible, is a good idea. Coding, working through iterative cycles of induction and deduction to power the analysis, can accomplish these goals" (p. 65).

Marshall and Rossman (1989) also emphasize the adaptive, malleable research design that is key to qualitative inquiry. "Sound qualitative design protects the researcher's right to follow the compelling question, the nagging puzzle, that presents itself once in the setting" (p. 81). In their classic volume on qualitative inquiry, Glaser and Straus (1967) refer to this dialectical process—

of the researcher beginning to collect data while listening for emergent themes that will direct and shape the subsequent data gathering—as the "constant comparative method." They point out that this method, "which is like analytic induction in that the formal analysis begins early in the study and is nearly completed by the end of data collection" (Glaser and Straus, cited in Bogdan & Biklen, p. 72), is used typically in studies that seek to document social processes and relationships—the iterative adaptation of methodology and insight paralleling the dynamic quality of human interaction and experience.

Glaser and Straus's "constant comparative method" is very much like the dialectical work of the portraitist. Like the Impressionistic Records we suggest as the portraitist's daily tool of synthesis, reflection, and analysis, Glaser and Straus underscore the value of writing as a way to focus the analysis. The act of writing moves our thinking to a deeper level and connects field notes to conceptual ideas. Miles and Huberman (1994) suggest an analytic process—much like our Impressionistic Records—they call "memoing," in which the researcher writes ongoing memos to herself that trace the process of description and interpretation. "Memoing helps the analyst move easily from empirical data to a conceptual level, refining and expanding codes further, developing key categories and showing their relationships, and building towards a more integrated understanding of events, processes, and interactions in the case" (pp. 158–159).

Although thus far we have emphasized the flexibility of research design and the ongoing analytic work that interacts with (and guides) data collection in qualitative research, there is another stage of reflective scrutiny and retrospective analysis that follows the completion of fieldwork, when the researcher sits and sifts through interview transcripts, observational narratives, field notes, documents, and Impressionistic Records in search of patterns that will order and scaffold the narrative. This post–data collection analysis is less action-oriented and more ruminative than the day-to-day analysis of the data-gathering phase—less about preparing for the next day of purposeful and strategic data collection and more about deep contemplation and probing insight.

Goetz and LeCompte (1984) provide concrete advice for ethnographers searching for emerging patterns. They recommend a process of sorting, grouping, and classification that follows data collection and anticipates the construction of the narrative. "The notes are developed into a primitive outline or system of classification into which data are sorted initially. The outline begins with a search for regularities—things that happen frequently with groups of people. Patterns and regularities then are transformed into categories into which subsequent items are sorted. These categories or patterns are discovered from the data. They emerge in a rather systematic, if not totally conscious, application of the processes of theorizing" (p. 191).

Marshall and Rossman (1989) claim that this phase of the research process is the most ambitious and intellectually challenging, as the researcher tries to stay grounded in the authentic experiences of the actors while at the same time creating a coherent category system.

> Identifying salient themes, recurring ideas or language, and patterns of belief that link people and setting together is the most intellectually challenging phase of data analysis and one that can integrate the entire endeavor. . . . As categories of meaning emerge, the researcher searches for those that have internal convergence and external divergence (Guba, 1978). That is, the categories should be internally consistent but distinct from one another. Here the researcher does not search for the exhaustive and mutually exclusive categories of the statistician, but instead to identify the salient, grounded categories of meaning held by participants in the setting [p. 116].

Miles and Huberman (1994) offer a comprehensive explanation of the types and modes of data analysis that are appropriate for each stage of qualitative research. They identify three types of codes: descriptive, interpretive, and pattern. The first two are self-explanatory and typically are distinguished in the early stages of analytic work during the iterative process of memoing. Pattern codes are "inferential and explanatory" (p. 129), roughly analogous to the emergent themes that portraitists search out and create. Miles and Huberman suggest identifying pattern codes by looking for "recurrent phrases or common threads" (p. 149) and by observing, naming, and verifying patterns.

> Pattern codes are explanatory or inferential codes, ones that identify an emergent theme, configuration, or explanation. They pull together a lot of material into more meaningful and parsimonious units of analysis. They are a sort of meta-code. . . . *Pattern coding* is a way of grouping [summarizing segments of data] into a smaller number of sets, themes or constructs. For qualitative researchers, it's an analogue to the cluster-analytic and factor-analytic devices used in statistical analysis. . . . For the qualitative analyst, pattern coding has four important functions:
>
> 1. It reduces large amounts of data into a smaller number of analytic units.
> 2. It gets the researcher into analysis during data collection, so that later fieldwork can be more focused.
> 3. It helps the researcher elaborate a cognitive map, an evolving, more integrated schema for understanding local incidents and interactions.
> 4. For multicase studies, it lays the groundwork for cross-case analysis by surfacing common themes and directional purposes [p. 69].

Miles and Huberman, then, offer a clear and concise description of the phases and strategies of data analysis and the identification of categories. Their focus is on bringing discipline and rigor to the synthesis and analysis of data. Without contradicting the requirement of rigor, other researchers—working in the interpretive or hermeneutic tradition—resist the use of rigid, discrete codes and give less emphasis to the organization of data into analytic categories. They are more interested in discovering the nuanced connections among themes, in looking for subtle changes over time, and in maintaining the integrity and complexity of human thought, feeling, and action than in identifying broad categories of behavior.

In laying out the framework for what they call "voice-centered analysis," Gilligan and her colleagues (Gilligan, Brown, & Rogers, 1989) underscore the "interpretive" process of discerning patterns.

> Our *Reader's Guide* (Brown et al., 1987) is an interpretive model. As such it contrasts with coding manuals that are designed to teach coders to match key words or phrases or target sentences to a predetermined set of categories. . . .
>
> In designing our method, we sought to hold and represent the sense of tension that people often convey, and also to record the complexity of the narratives in order to capture the situational, the personal, and the cultural dimensions of psychic life, including language and voice, perspectives and visions, and the relationships between the reader's and the narrator's ways of seeing and speaking [pp. 95–96].

According to Gilligan, nuanced interpretive analysis requires that the researcher read and scrutinize an interview transcript four different times ("taking four soundings"). Each reading offers the researcher the opportunity of listening for a "different voice," from a different angle, and with an ear to the subtle meanings and complex perspectives. The multiple definitions of soundings—"measuring the depth or examining the body of water, making or giving forth sounds, and sound that is resonant and sonorous" (p. 108)—offer a metaphoric framework (an echo chamber) for listening to the narratives.

In his description of "radical empiricism," Michael Jackson (1989) also emphasizes the need to hear the cacophony of voices; attending to the myriad perspectives from different angles. Truth and validity, he suggests, never reside in a single voice, but always in the complex interplay of voices, the rich resonances of intellectual, emotional, aesthetic, and ethical currents. The researcher must set aside her need for control, order, and stability and submit to the complexity and instability of real lived experience.

> By turning from epistemology toward the everyday world of lived experience, the radical empiricist is inclined to judge the value of an idea, not just against antecedent experiences or the logical standards of scientific inquiry but also against the practical, ethical, emotional, and aesthetic demands of life (Dewey, 1980, pp. 136–138; James, 1978, pp. 30–40; Rorty, 1982, pp. 203–208; Whitehead, 1947, p. 226). This means that the traditional empiricist's hankering after order and control is to be seen as just one of many consoling illusions, one stratagem for making sense of an unstable world, not as an "accurate representation of reality" or a privileged insight into the way the world "really" works (Rorty, 1979, p. 10; 1982, p. 194) [p. 13].

Both Gilligan's and Jackson's emphasis on multiple soundings of the complex interplay of voices and perspectives and Miles and Huberman's emphasis on coding and categories point to a generative tension embraced by portraitists: the tension between organization and classification on one hand and maintaining the rich complexity of human experience on the other—the tension between developing discrete codes and searching for meaning, and the tension between the researcher's desire for control and coherence and the actors' reality of incoherence and instability. The portraitist does not try to resolve this tension by choosing one side over the other. Rather she works to maintain the tension and experience the dialectic between these two approaches to thematic development. Usually these resonant tensions ultimately get reflected in the portraitist's text where emergent themes (or the "meta-codes" of Miles and Huberman) both frame and scaffold the text, and the descriptive detail and empirical subtlety of the narrative allow for the expression of interwoven parts.

However qualitative researchers attempt to systematize and organize their data, they must always listen for the voices and perspectives that seem to fall outside, and diverge from, the emergent themes. Maxwell (1996), for example, underscores the value of attending to the perspective that is discrepant. Unlike quantitative researchers who isolate the outliers, the qualitative researcher makes use of the anomalies, learning important lessons by looking outside the trend. Maxwell argues that "the most serious threat to the theoretical validity of an account is not collecting or paying attention to discrepant data, or not considering alternative explanations or understandings of the phenomena you are studying" (p. 90).

Like Maxwell, Seidman cautions against ignoring the voices that deviate from the norm. As the researcher organizes transcript data into categories and searches for connections within and between categories, she must be vigilant in attending to the experiences and perspectives that do not fit the convergent patterns. "Some passages stand out because they contradict and seem decisively inconsistent with others. It is tempting to put those aside. These in particular, however, have to be kept in the foreground. The researcher has to try and understand their importance in the face of the other data he or she has gathered" (Miles and Huberman, cited in Seidman, 1991, p. 101).

In portraiture, we refer to this perspective that deviates from the norm as "the deviant voice," and we never stop listening *for* it, even as we become increasingly focused in our inquiry and certain in our analysis. The deviant voice is useful in drawing important contrasts with the norm; the divergence in perspective and the idiosyncratic stance helps us see the quality and contours of the convergent themes more clearly. The deviant voice is also useful in encouraging the skeptical, counterintuitive stance that the researcher must maintain throughout the course of the research. Incorporating this unusual perspective— the deviant voice—she may continue to scrutinize and challenge a facile consensus or find new ways of framing and understanding the dominant themes.

CONSTRUCTING EMERGENT THEMES

The portraitist draws out and constructs emergent themes using five modes of synthesis, convergence, and contrast. First, we listen for repetitive refrains that are spoken (or appear) frequently and persistently, forming a collective expression of commonly held views. Second, we listen for resonant metaphors, poetic and symbolic expressions that reveal the ways actors illuminate and experience their realities. Third, we listen for the themes expressed through cultural and institutional rituals that seem to be important to organizational continuity and coherence. Fourth, we use triangulation to weave together the threads of data converging from a variety of sources. And finally, we construct themes and reveal patterns among perspectives that are often experienced as contrasting and dissonant by the actors. Each of these modes for documenting emergent themes will be described and illustrated using passages selected from our texts.

Repetitive Refrains

The most easily recognizable emergent themes are the ones that are clearly and persistently articulated by the actors in the setting. The portraitist hears the same refrain over and over again, from a variety of people in a variety of settings. Actors give voice to this refrain through identifying it, naming it, and sometimes through actions and gestures. We also see it represented in signs and symbols in the environment. The refrains, audible and visible, proclaim: "This is who we are. This is what we believe. This is how we see ourselves." Sometimes the refrains are immediately apparent and the portraitist needs only to open her eyes—the colorful murals on the walls of a school building shout out the institutional values; the rules and rituals displayed in the classroom reflect the teacher's educational philosophy. At other times, the refrains are more measured or subtly expressed—through irony or innuendo—and the portraitist needs to listen more carefully and dig more deeply. But once she identifies the theme, the actors recognize its presence and confirm its importance.

In the following passage from *The Good High School,* I identify the repetitive refrains that were visible and audible in my visits to St. Paul's School in Concord, New Hampshire, an elite boarding school for the children of privileged families, and in my visit to George Washington Carver High in Atlanta, Georgia, a public school serving a largely poor, African American population. I was interested in the actors' views of what was important, what the inhabitants regarded as the predominant values and central issues. In both places, the teachers', administrators', and students' concerns were easily identifiable and convergent. They were spoken of by large numbers of people or pointed to by respondents who were best informed by virtue of their roles or positions. The abundance, tradition, and certainty of history were the signature themes at St. Paul's. At George Washington Carver, the collective message mightily resisted past legacies to forge a new, more promising identity.

> In St. Paul's . . . everyone made reference to the shaping and determining influences of history, the power and certainty of tradition, and the comforts they provide. The Rector spoke of it as he bid farewell to the Seniors and their parents on graduation day. Many of the students enjoyed the rituals, ceremony, and clarity attached to the historical traditions of daily chapel. Dressed in the modern casual garb of L.L. Bean and Calvin Klein, they crowded into assigned seats at morning chapel and experienced feelings of community and enlightenment in the Gothic structure. Certainty, abundance, and history permitted creativity and risk-taking, dramatically expressed in the pedagogy, classroom processes and curricula developed by teachers. It is not that there was no one who resisted the historical imperative or struggled against the classical, unquestioned institutional forms. Certainly there were voices who offered criticism and resistance. Yet even their hushed rage and muted frustration confirmed the strength of the phenomenon of rootedness and tradition.
>
> At George Washington Carver in Atlanta, there was an equally strong and identifiable contrary theme. The principal, with his passion, force, and energy, was fighting against historical imperatives and trying to force a new image. Everything he did was calculated to undo old perceptions, reverse entrenched

habits, and inculcate new behavioral and attitudinal forms.
The new image and the proud rhetoric preceded the resistant
institutional changes which lagged behind. Immediately, an
observer could recognize these themes. They were shouted out
by inspirational signs prominently displayed in the hall; they
were part of a slick slide show on Carver the principal wanted
me to watch *before* I visited the real place; they were part of
the harangue a loving and angry teacher gave to the graduating
seniors when he feared they would not live up to the image of
correctness, civility, and poise at the graduation ceremony
[pp. 14–15].

In the next illustration from a portrait of MollyOlga Neighborhood Art Classes
in *Safe Havens,* we see the overarching convergent theme—"constant struggle
and survival"—drawn forcefully and explicitly into the text of the piece. The
word *struggle* resounds several times in each paragraph and is referred to by all
the actors in their stories of the center's economic fragility, in their descriptions
of students haunted by poverty, neglect, and abuse, in their tale of the boy killed
in a drive-by shooting, and even in the images depicted on their canvases. Struggle is echoed in the teaching and learning, in the community building, and in
the institutional journey (that is, the "relevant dimensions" that the *Safe Havens*
researchers brought to the field). And struggle is seen as the bedrock of
resilience, the root of creativity, and the source of sustenance at MollyOlga.

It may be that the art center draws energy from its constant
struggle for survival. One adult student who grew up in the
Fruit Belt suggests that MollyOlga's constant struggle for money
might be "the best thing about it. They understand the reality
of things." A student who comes from outside the community
comments, "The fact that it's a struggling art school in an inner
city—I respect that they're here and it's free." Another adult
student believes that the struggle fuels the creativity of Molly-
Olga: "Escapism, pain, terror, fear, hunger. . . . There is a beauty
in us, in all of us, but when we are fat and happy and pretty
content, and well educated and our life is going to be provided
for and you've got a retirement fund, we don't allow that beauty
to come out."
A powerful abstract painting thick with pastels hangs in a
sort of memorial on the third-floor painting studio, an example
of an image that emerged from an inner struggle. The young
creator grew up in the Fruit Belt and used to come to MollyOlga
when he was a small child, and then came back when he was

in his early twenties. He wrote in his artist's statement for a 1987 exhibit, "Truly as I live, I am free when expressing the aliveness within me through Art. . . . My motivation now is to walk peacefully in an enthusiastic way, being truthful and honest to myself as an Artist. The future is shining on me." Five years later, as Molly talks about this student, her sadness is evident: "He had a very chaotic life, always, and he gradually just lost it, and . . . when you see him walking around, he just doesn't know anyone. . . . He's somebody I feel badly about . . . he's too far gone; he can't come back." She later explains that "his mind is so destroyed from drug use [he] can't bring himself back to reality."

Cutbacks in funding have clearly had an impact on Molly-Olga, but it is the loss of students' lives that is the hardest for Molly and Olga to accept. Within the past two years, four Molly-Olga students have been killed, two in drive-by shootings just around the corner. Even as she expresses her satisfaction with the services MollyOlga provides, Molly also expresses her sense of loss: "As far as the classes themselves, I'm pretty happy with how they're going. I think the thing that strikes me in relation to them is that so many of the kids have died recently." Duncan Bethel dedicates one of his paintings to those students who have not survived: "Thank you . . . Johnny S., Tony W., and Ricky M., former young artists at MollyOlga who died before they got a chance to grow up."

Tony W. was sixteen when he became a casualty of street violence. Olga tells a story that occurred when he was about eight years old:

"Tony was a very macho kid—short, bullish, always looking for a fight. . . . But one day . . . he was in the mood to work. . . . He called me over, 'How's this look? How's this look?' and he was doing a drawing in charcoals and browns—very sophisticated. . . . He just worked so hard, and at the end . . . I told him what a beautiful drawing he had done and how proud of him I was . . . and with my finger I made a star on his forehead. His mouth just opened up, his eyes went big, and he said, 'Can anybody else see it?' and I said, 'No, Tony. You know it's there and I know it's there, and that's what matters.' The next day, he came into painting class and he . . . comes close to me and says, 'Miss Olga, is it still there?' . . . and I said 'Yes, Tony.'"

The "star" that Tony earned stayed with him, a symbol of the sense of accomplishment accessed through art-making.

Just as MollyOlga is a constant in the community, the process
of making art and the resultant products become a constant and
lasting source of pride. Once that painting or sculpture or photograph is created, no one can take it away from the artist who
gave it life. Molly puts it simply: "Once they've done it, it's
always something that they've done."

MollyOlga's journey as a constant survivor in an inconsistent
context may in many ways be seen to parallel the growth of
a work of art. Regardless of how much planning goes into a
composition, a work of art is said to evolve, sometimes in
unexpected ways, over the course of its creation. Generative
mistakes and unanticipated developments may challenge the
artist to shift his or her original vision. Nonetheless, it would
be hard to contest that a work of art in progress reflects the
vision of its creator, which guides its evolution [pp. 61–63].

In *I've Known Rivers,* I refer to the overarching emergent themes I hear in each
of the storytellers' narratives as "life litanies." As I listen to their stories over a
year's time and witness the development of our deepening relationships, I begin
to recognize an insistent theme, a driving current that flows through each life journey. There may be a variety of ways in which this life litany gets expressed, yet
it offers coherence, purpose, and definition to the journey. Part of my challenge
as portraitist—in this case, as human archeologist—is to begin to identify this central emergent theme, to document the ways in which it is expressed, to try to
understand its origins and meanings, to interpret its symbols and metaphors, to
find ways of displaying it. This life litany, once revealed and traced, is a generative dimension of human experience. It is not like a worn-out story or a broken
record. Quite the opposite. It is a source of growth in work and identity.

In the following paragraph I reflect on the dominance and resonance of teaching in Katie Cannon's life story.

In my conversations with Katie Cannon, it became clear, almost
immediately, that teaching was her raison d'être. "Teaching,"
she exclaimed boldly, "is the fruit of my labor." Ever since she
was a young child, Katie wanted to be a teacher. She played
school with her siblings, relished being the teacher's pet and
surrogate, and saw teaching as precious, respectable, loving
work. Now a preacher, writer, researcher, and professor, Katie
still sees teaching as the central dimension in all her work. She
puts it at the top of her list of professional priorities; she works
harder on issues of pedagogy and curriculum than she does on
anything else; she is most happy when teaching blends theater,

inspiration, provocation, and intellectual challenge; and she believes that teaching is her primary vehicle for social criticism and activism. Throughout our weeks of intense conversation, teaching became the anchor to her professional identity, the mediating theme between her childhood origins and her greatly contrasting adult experiences. Uncovering it as her life litany allowed Katie to see it revealed in its many guises throughout her development. It also allowed her to see its shaping influence in the way she told and interpreted her story [p. 613].

Resonant Metaphors

The portraitist is often able to identify emergent themes in the metaphors, symbols, and vernacular of the actors. These words or phrases resonate with meaning and symbolism, sometimes representing the central core of institutional culture or the dominant dimension of a life story. The metaphors—spare like poetry—embrace and express a large arc of human experience. The portraitist needs to listen hard for these metaphors and search for the symbols, always trying to decipher their meaning in a particular context and questioning actors about their origins. Like life litanies, resonant metaphors are not only expressive of the central themes and values of human experience, they are also generative. They embody values and perspectives *and* they give them shape and meaning.

In this short excerpt from the portrait of the Manchester Craftsmen's Guild, cited earlier in a different context, founder Bill Strickland offers a radiant metaphor—"a place in the sun"—that lights the vision of the Guild, illuminates the values, and shines down (for free) on all the students who walk through the door. Davis and her colleagues do not have to search far for this metaphor; Strickland generously hands it to them—a gift to light their way.

> The Manchester Craftsmen's Guild is also not disconnected from the business and educational opportunities glowingly mounted on Pittsburgh's new profile. The Guild offers free classes in ceramics and photography to Pittsburgh Public High School students who are considered "at-risk." Its mission is to engage high school students in learning through the arts in order to help them enroll in institutions of higher education. Symbolically, the Guild's archways open to the world beyond the North Side. Bill Strickland believes that Manchester Craftsmen's Guild offers an environment in which each student can begin to find his or her place in the sun. . . .
>
> And *a place in the sun* is a theme that radiates throughout the inner workings of the Manchester Craftsmen's Guild [p. 83].

In the following passage from *I've Known Rivers,* Cheryle Wills, a glamorous and successful businesswoman from a prominent upper-middle-class family, names the metaphor that shapes her life's commitments and give them value. She speaks about using her abundant resources—inherited and self-generated— to "give forward" (not "give back") to the African American community; to help others less fortunate, to help them help themselves. "Giving forward"—a kind of purposeful tithing—is a generative gesture, an act of charity and creativity. Cheryle returns time and time again to this metaphor as a way of examining and explaining her vision and her actions. The metaphor is woven through the texture of her life and embroidered into the text of her portrait.

> Cheryle Wills often refers to the obligation and responsibility that come with having lived a life of privilege. The nourishment of a loving family and good friends "are gifts you can never give back . . . all I can do is give forward . . . I memorialize my forbears by giving of myself." Cheryle's parents, the Andersons—who lived a comfortable and elegant existence— came from families who had been middle-class in the Negro community for generations. Her mother came from a long line of dignified women who carried their beauty and status like "royalty." They were proud of their blackness. As Cheryle puts it, "We are arrogant about being black." Not only did this black arrogance challenge white entitlement, it also signaled their deep identification with the black community, even when their education, status, and light skin gave them access to the white world. This lineage brought with it a sense of noblesse oblige. Because Cheryle's forebears had been blessed with a secure and plentiful life, they felt obliged to give much back to the community. Cheryle frequently paraphrases the Bible passage "to those to whom much has been given, much is expected" as she talks about the way her maternal great-uncle started the first NAACP in Jefferson City, Missouri and the way her parents always worked to "feed the hungry and clothe the poor."
>
> But it was a member of her second husband's family who served as Cheryle's most powerful symbol of "giving forward." Senior—the man who named Cheryle Duchess because of the royalty he saw in her—became her most influential mentor. Also coming from a very prominent, light-skinned family, in Cleveland, Senior ("who could have passed for white, but never did") stood on the boundary between the black and white worlds. He was "the one" black person chosen by the white folks—the one who had "access to white conversation,"

the one whom they respected and trusted. The white establishment would go to Senior when they needed something from the black community, or when they wanted to assuage their guilt, or when they needed someone to make the cultural translations or interpret the black political scene. As Katie Cannon would say, the whites in Cleveland made Senior an "honorary white person," a role he accepted only because he knew someone had to play it if the black community was going to survive. Senior's access to the white power brokers provided critical information and resources to the city's black folks.

A powerful leader, Senior built a funeral home into "Cleveland's most beloved institution." The House of Wills was a place of refuge for those journeyers from the Deep South who needed to establish their identities and plant new roots. It was the first place blacks would come for help when the city stopped picking up their garbage or their electricity got turned off. The building itself was an ornate architectural masterpiece that offered high tea, music, and culture free to people whom the downtown hotels refused to serve. It was a generous place of employment where, "if they hung around long enough," young men could find a job, get trained, and build a long career. And it was a thriving, innovative business that made the Wills family prosperous and powerful. Cheryle studied Senior's genius—the way he combined service and entrepreneurship, the way he mixed high style with basic needs, the way he connected art and politics. His fluency in making the translations across racial lines and his dexterity in joining business and altruism became etched in Cheryle's mind and heart, and became central to the way she chose to live out her own version of noblesse oblige.

Even in the early months of working in the funeral home Cheryle experienced the opportunity to "give forward." Her office, on the first floor just as one came in the front door, was the first place people would arrive when they were seeking help. She remembers the parade of poor folks—many of them illiterate, many of them recent migrants from the rural South—who walked through the doors. Cheryle recalls their dignity and their hopefulness despite the despair and poverty that filled their lives. "This was the first time I'd actually known black folks, poor black folks, and I was amazed by their dignity and optimism." Many who came to her office would have no birth certificate, no Social Security number, no identity, and Cheryle would patiently help them patch together the meager remnants of their desolate history. Then she would fill out the appropriate forms and negotiate the bureaucratic mazes until their identities were legally assured. This was all done without fee ("Senior better not hear that any of us charged folks for these services"). The effort of completing the correct forms and making a few telephone calls were more than paid for by "their undying gratitude." "They would say to me," recalls Cheryle, "'you've given me back my whole life.'" In that moment, the twenty-three-year-old Duchess felt the deepest satisfaction, the chance to balance the scales between her privilege and their needs, fulfilling some of the duties of her fortunate station [pp. 587–589].

Institutional and Cultural Rituals

Just as we may discover emergent themes in the metaphors and symbols expressed by actors in the setting, so too may we see them expressed through the rituals and ceremonies that punctuate the life of a community or institution. Rituals—often displayed through art, music, drama, and dance—are aesthetic and ceremonial reflections of an organization's purpose. We witness the ritual and we see values revealed, priorities named, and stories told that symbolize the institution's culture. Rituals are not only an aesthetic, ceremonial expression of institutional values, they are also opportunities for building community, for celebrating roots and traditions, for underscoring continuity and coherence. When the portraitist participates in and observes ceremonial events, then, she must examine the emergent themes that might be embedded in the rituals, visible signs and reflections of the organization's purpose and coherence, artistic expressions of community life.

In the following illustration from the portrait of St. Paul's School, we are introduced to the symbolic importance of chapel services. The significance and centrality of chapel—as community ritual—is documented in several spheres. First, we know from the daily calendar that mandatory chapel services happen four times a week; the theme emerges from the routine, structured activities of teachers and students. Second, we read an excerpt from the school catalogue, where the importance of chapel is described and its relationship to spirituality and community is made explicit; the theme is found in the organization's official public documents. Third, we are given the portraitist's account of attending chapel. Through her observation of the ritual she is able to make connections to other dimensions of the school culture and community where the emergent themes are also embedded.

Chapel is the most precious moment in the day. It binds the community together. The five hundred students from the third through sixth forms and the eighty faculty of St. Paul's come together at 8:00 four mornings a week. There is time for peace and reflection, for beautiful music and poetic words. Streams of sunlight filter through the magnificent stained glass windows, shining down on all inside. They seem like the enlightened people, the chosen ones. There is the connection between mind and soul, body and spirit, the sacred and the secular. The baroque organ with pure and clear sound is "one of the best in New England." It fills the space with rich, reverberating sounds. The organ playing is impeccable.

Chapel services are an expression of unity, fellowship, and a commitment to Christian traditions at St. Paul's. As a church school, it has had a long-time association with the Episcopal Church, and the rituals and structure of the Episcopal ceremony still form the basis of morning chapel services. However, the denominational ties are no longer deeply ingrained. The school catalogue stresses the relationship between spiritual commitment and community life:

"Chapel services, studies in religion, and our common life in Christian fellowship are expressions of the unity and fundamental faith of St. Paul's School. . . . The school supports the beliefs of each faith, encouraging students to recognize the strength and loyalty of the commitments of their families. The school recognizes that all its members should discover the meaning of the Christian tradition in their own lives through free inquiry, and the experience of community life in that tradition."

The beautiful and old architectural lines of the chapel are in contrast to the ruffled and contemporary people sitting in the long, carved pews. Dressed in typical adolescent garb—rustic chic—the students' faces are still and attentive. Some slump over in weariness, some eyes are half-closed, but most seem to be captured by the ritual. When fellow students make music, they receive full attention and generous applause. The day I visit, the service is an all-musical program of Bach. The first piece is played well by a trio of flute, harpsichord, and violin. It is a slow movement that requires sustained and disciplined tones. Occasionally the violin is clumsy in technique and flat in tone, but that is the only evidence of this being an amateur performance. The second piece, which is the first movement of Bach's Third Brandenburg Concerto, begins energetically, but quickly degenerates. The students, led by a faculty conductor, barely struggle through the difficult string variations, but no one winces at the grating sounds. There is strong applause for the ambitious willingness of the students to do less than well in public. I am also impressed by the sustained elegance with which this musical disaster is carried off. This seems the ultimate in certainty and style. There is no embarrassment, a full acceptance of the efforts made, and the expectation of applause.

The faculty sit in the upper pews, also in assigned seats. Chapel is a compulsory community event for faculty as well as students. Along with the formal evening meals, Chapel is considered one of the important rituals that symbolizes community and fellowship, emphasizes discipline and ceremony, and reflects a sense of continuity between past and present. Looking down the row of faculty, the dominance of whiteness and maleness becomes immediately apparent. Most are wearing tweedy jackets and ties, and the unusual ones stick out—the blond and pregnant history teacher; the bearded, tall Jewish head of the English department; the casually dressed dance teacher with a head full of irreverent ringlets. It is not that there is no diversity within the faculty, it is that their sameness is exaggerated in this setting as they sit lined up in the back pews of Chapel.

It is also in Chapel that one experiences the impressive orchestration of the school. All seems to flow so smoothly and evenly, almost effortlessly. Behind this smooth scene is the hard, disciplined work of many. "Chapel Notes" for the week tell what music will be played, what hymns sung, and what lessons will be read. A faculty member is assigned to regulate the acoustics system just in front of her pew to ensure the right volume for each microphone. Notes are delivered to the rector well in advance of the "Morning Reports." The rector arrives the day I am there and opens an elegant note from the senior class. The script is like calligraphy, the image above the writing shows a bird in flight, and the message inside combines poetry and allusions to scripture and prayer. The senior class has decided that this sunny day will be their senior-cut day and they are off to the beach in rented buses. Their absence is no surprise to anyone. Their actions are certainly not devious or even assertive. This is part of the anticipated ritual. The person sitting next to me whispers, "Of course the rector was informed about this well in advance." It is beautifully orchestrated—the anticipated "surprise" event, the ceremonial note to the rector, the announcement to the assembled people, and the restrained approval of everyone.

The supreme orchestration of events and people at St. Paul's reflects, I think, the abundance and privilege of the school. In order to be able to anticipate and coordinate life in this way, one must be able to foresee a future that is relatively certain. Years of experience rooted in tradition seem to guide the present. Some things seem to fall into place without conscious effort. It has always been that way. History has cast a form on things. In his concluding remarks on graduation day, the rector underscores the mark of tradition and history, "This ceremony has become traditional, and therefore mandatory" [pp. 223–226].

Triangulation

The passage about St. Paul's anticipates the portraitist's drawing of themes through *triangulation*. Using triangulation, the researcher employs various strategies and tools of data collection, looking for the points of convergence among them. Emergent themes arise out of this layering of data, when different lenses frame similar findings. For example, we see the triangulation of data from a variety of sources in a passage that examines institutional diversity from the portrait on Brookline High School. In the first paragraph we hear about the importance of diversity at Brookline High through the words of four different people. Here the emergent theme arises out of the diversity of voices: the voices of the headmaster, a black faculty member, a Catholic sophomore, and a new arrival. The theme resonates across the school's different constituencies.

Second, we are given factual evidence—data derived from enrollment and personnel information. We get a racial and ethnic breakdown for students, faculty, and administrators, and we are alerted to the intragroup differences (and struggles) between the indigenous middle-class black students and the interlopers from the METCO program.

The third data source comes from classroom observations. We have heard people voice their different perspectives, we have reviewed the numbers—now we see the action. But even here we gain a binocular perspective through the inclusion of the actual observational record that is set off from the interpretive text of the portraitist. All of these sources echo the emergent theme of *Rich Diversity*—an institutional goal, a deeply held value, a source of perspective and practice.

No matter who you talk to about Brookline High School,
the first thing mentioned is the diversity of the student body.
Faculty, students, and administrators seem to want to correct
the outdated, anachronistic images of the school that portray an
elite suburban enclave. Bob McCarthy, the school's headmaster,

says enthusiastically, "People used to say diversity was a weakness. Now we're saying diversity is a strength. This is an important shift in orientation for faculty, students, and the community." A prominent black faculty member echoes McCarthy's optimism, "Brookline is a special place. I've never seen a better mixture of kids. You've got a little United Nations." A thoughtful, pretty sophomore who sits next to me in history class tells about the enlivening quality of diversity, "I went to a strict Catholic elementary school where everyone was the same, very protected and very sterile. When I first came to this school I felt afraid of all the different types of kids. But now I feel *challenged* by all the different groups and much less afraid." Even those who assert the great advantages of a multiethnic school admit the tensions and conflicts among the groups. Says one new arrival to the school, "This is a very cliquish, very separatist place . . . I don't know where to break into the circle . . . For every friend I make, there is an enemy."

There are 2,100 students in Brookline High School, with 20 administrators, 150 teachers, and 40 adults in other professional capacities (guidance counselors, social workers, career counselors, and so on). Thirty percent of the student body is minority, the largest proportion being Asian (including Chinese, Japanese, Korean, Indian, and Iranian in significant numbers). Twelve percent of the student body are black. Half of those come from Boston's METCO Program (Metropolitan Council for Educational Opportunity) and half are indigenous to Brookline. Class divides this group. Most of the METCO students come from working-class backgrounds, and their Brookline peers tend to be offspring of professional, upper-middle-class parents. Says Bob McCarthy, "Historically they have been pressured into behaving as a group," despite their differences in background and experience. Another observer who is close to both groups claims that the divisions between METCO and Brookline blacks are unfortunate but inevitable. "Brookline blacks *naturally* take on the feelings, attitudes, and ways of the kids they've grown up with. I call it elitism. It never flares out in the open. There are no fights between them . . . but it bothers me. Maybe I am at fault. Maybe I want black folks to be *too* close."

Forty percent of the students are Jewish, largely from upper-middle-class families. The Jewish population in the school is declining as parents grow worried about the increasing diversity and what they perceive to be lowering standards. McCarthy claims that there has been a noticeable migration of Jewish families to the more distant and protected suburbs of Newton, Lincoln, and Concord. For the most part, the elementary schools in Brookline still enjoy a superior reputation and continue to attract the offspring of high-powered, academic-minded citizens. But the high school no longer has its old appeal as an elite school. Parents who have the resources and who are concerned about status and standards have begun to search out private schools for their adolescents, or move to more homogeneous towns.

The remaining 30 percent of the population reflects a mixture of white students from a variety of ethnic and social class backgrounds. The one visible and identifiable subgroup of students from this last category is Irish Catholic and working-class. Known as the "Point" kids because they are from the High Point section of Brookline, they are long-time residents of the town. Most of the parents were students at Brookline High; many of their mothers work as secretaries in the school, and their fathers "keep the town running" as policemen, firemen, sanitation workers, and mailmen. The Point kids are 10 percent of the student population and have a reputation as tough kids. "Historically they have battled with whatever group is lowest on the totem pole," says McCarthy. Their current competitors are the black METCO students whom they claim receive more attention and resources than they do. They view the black kids as advantaged interlopers and often take out their feelings of deprivation and rage on this group. A teacher who has worked closely with the Point kids for a decade offers a different analysis of their hostility. "They feel this school really *belongs* to them. . . . They have always felt resentful of the upper-middle-class Jewish kids whose image forms the public stereotype of the school. But the Irish kids feel the privileged Jewish kids are unavailable to receive their hostility—in some sense they are invulnerable—so they take out their anger on black kids."

The diversity of the student population is additionally heightened by the presence of numerous language groups. One hundred and ninety students, about 10 percent of the population, speak English as a second language; they represent more than fifty-five languages, originated in twenty-five countries. Some of these students speak very little English and have great difficulty communicating with their teachers and peers. An increasing number of Russian Jews, recently emigrated from their homeland, speak no English and require special attention and expertise. A three-year, federally funded bilingual program, called Project Welcome, seeks to reach out to the new arrivals, offering support and guidance.

Beyond the special programs for foreign students, the school curriculum seeks to be adaptive to their needs. "U.S. History for Foreign Students" is a good example of a social studies course offered for new arrivals with limited proficiency in English.

The teacher is a woman in her mid-thirties. Her wavy red hair hangs nearly to her waist. A hunk of hair is gathered on top of her head in a coiled braid. Her pale skin is lightly freckled and her eyes sparkle light brown. The classroom is arranged so that all the chairs form a circle. Meredith, as she introduces herself to me and is called by the students, refreshes the students' memories concerning the day's lesson. "Today we'll hear from the Committee on Leadership." It seems the class has divided into six committees. Each committee must report back to the entire class and all the students must reach a consensus before proceeding to the next committee report. The idea behind this course is shared by two teachers, both of whom are in the classroom. Although Meredith is teaching, Robert Hall, her co-teacher, is in the room observing the action.

Meredith asks Kay, a Korean girl, to sit front and center of the group to give the Committee on Leadership report. Meredith smiles at Kay, leaning down toward her, and coaxes her to begin reading. She speaks gently and with warmth and soon Kay begins to read from her report. Meredith writes Kay's points on the board. Kay comes to a word which she tries to read and just shakes her head. Smiling, she looks into her lap, shaking her head back and forth. Meredith moves quickly to her side and reads the words quietly to Kay. As she moves back to the blackboard she says, "It's all right, Kay, you're doing fine." Kay's smooth oval face is framed by black hair that falls in soft, sculpted waves to her shoulders. Her lips frame the words before she speaks them in a soft, tentative voice.

Another student walks into the room and stops to talk in Spanish to two other students sitting on the edge of the circle. Meredith moves toward him, motioning him to sit down. While this is going on, Kay is trying to read point number four. The other student settled, Meredith walks over to Kay and apologizes. "Kay, I'm sorry. I missed that. What was number four?"

All points on the board, Meredith says, "I think I understand Kay's points. Let me repeat them." She checks with Kay when she is unsure. The committee has developed seven recommendations. Meredith says to the class, "What questions do you have?" Silence in the room. "Does everyone agree that we need a leader?"

One boy questions why only the representatives of the six committees get to choose the leader. Meredith is listening intently to him. She leans gently over Kay. "Kay, do you think you can explain your committee's reason?" Kay just shakes her head, her faint smile looking more fixed. Meredith turns back to the student. "Norris, why don't you develop your reasons for another way of selecting a leader?" The room is silent. She asks, "Does everyone understand the issue? No? Let me draw a diagram." Most of the students face the board and appear to listen.

There are four Venezuelan students in the room. I am able to locate them by their orientation to one another in the room. One of the two girls asks a question. "Can one of the representatives be a leader too?" Kay says "No." "Why not?" questions Sophia. "Just tell me why not." Kay begins to respond, but stumbles on a word. She seems to shrivel in her chair. She shakes her head back and forth. Meredith moves close to her. "Kay, just take a deep breath. It's hard, I know."

One of the Ethiopian students offers yet another alternative. Meredith works hard to keep the choices in front of the students by writing them into her diagram. She watches the students' faces carefully and moves quickly around the room, touching students gently.

Lugo points to the diagram saying, "I don't understand very much. Will you explain?" The request "Will you explain?" is one that Meredith uses a lot to encourage students to amplify their responses. The students seem to have picked up the question and use it in their questions to her and to each other. Meredith speaks clearly, slowly, and patiently. She leans forward urging words out of the students.

"We need some more opinions from some other people. Lenora, what do you think? Would you please give me your reasons? This is not just a vote, I'm looking for your opinions."

A second Ethiopian student, a tall, thin young man, speaks very softly. Meredith is by his side in a moment. She asks him to speak louder for all to hear. "I can't," he murmurs. Meredith urges, "Speak to Sophia across the room." Meredith leans down, "I know you speak quietly, you always do." She smiles fully on him, "Okay, you speak to me and I'll shout it out for you."

There is no talking among the students. They shift in their chairs so that there is an occasional creak. One of the Venezuelan girls exchanges flirtatious glances with Lugo on the other side of the room. Lenora is dressed in pink—pink sweat pants, pink socks, pink sneakers, and a pink shirt under a pastel blue sweater. Her makeup is dramatic and she is singing to herself, keeping time with her head. Meredith barely touches her shoulder, "Lenora?" Lenora stops her rhythmic motion.

As class breaks, the Venezuelan students speak in Spanish to one another and the Chinese, Korean, and Ethiopian students likewise seek each other out for a few moments of easy conversation. For Meredith, it has been an energetic session. She has moved among the students, watching them carefully, helping them to frame their words, assisting them in whatever ways she could. In a later conversation, she turns the same full, warm smile on me and says, "I can't help it. I get a kick out of the students. I like them" [pp. 159–162].

Revealing Patterns

In the Brookline High illustration the portraitist discovers the convergent themes as she listens to a variety of voices, observes the pedagogy and the actors in classrooms, consults the enrollment data, and reviews the internal and external school documents. From all angles, at all levels, in every tongue, the school's inhabitants speak about "diversity" as a central theme: about the challenges, rewards, and tensions that are a part of weaving this theme into everyday life; about the inevitable dissonance between the rhetoric and the realization, between the vision and the implementation. The researcher documents the convergence of perspectives from various sources; she hears the harmony of their voices.

But sometimes the convergent themes do not emerge through triangulation of data sources. The consensus is not clear; the story is more scattered. In quantitative research, the scattered data points would mean that the investigator would have no story to tell. In qualitative research, on the other hand, the divergent and dissonant views are themselves a story. The portraitist attends to the lack of consensus, trying to make sense out of the dissonance, often trying to discern the underlying patterns. She asks, Is there a coherence underneath this seeming chaos? Is there a line of reasoning, a logic, a reasonable explanation for why these perspectives seem divergent? We see the portraitist's hand as she constructs a theme that will explain the dissonance, that will bring order to the chaos.

When the researcher makes the connections and discovers the order, it is likely that the patterns will not be immediately recognizable to the actors. After all, the chaos and incoherence that they are experiencing may have to do with their place in the middle of the action. With some distance and some dispassion, the researcher may be able to see the pattern that eludes the actors' view. She can see the forest; they can only see the trees.

In the following excerpt from *The Good High School*, I contrast the obvious repetitive refrains that were immediately clear and visible at St. Paul's School and George Washington Carver (referred to earlier in this chapter) with the more scattered story I heard at Highland Park High School. At Highland Park, I traced the connections and searched for the order among the diverse strains.

> In Highland Park . . . teachers, students, administrators, and
> counselors spoke about the tough competition, rigid hierarchies,
> and enormous stress experienced by students. There were
> obviously different perspectives concerning these phenomena.
> The more successful and rewarded students were less critical
> of the brutal competition, but they always feared losing their
> lofty status and worried about slipping down the steep pyramid.
> The low status, non-achieving students were more likely to
> be critical of the competition, seek rewards outside of school,
> and find ways of punishing the achievers. The broad range
> of students in the middle often felt lost and without identity
> or voice. The creative and analytic task of portraiture lies in
> exploring and describing these competing and dissonant per-
> spectives, searching for their connections to other phenomena,
> and selecting the primary pieces of the story line for display
> [p. 15].

Oftentimes the emergent themes—arising out of scattered pieces—mark the interpretive reflections of the portraitist. Hearing the stories and witnessing the action, then reflecting on their meaning and relationship to one another, the researcher begins to see the patterns. In the following excerpt from Katie Cannon's portrait, I reflect on Katie's reflections and illuminate a life theme that was not at first apparent to either of us. With drama and passion Katie tells the tale of stalking her teacher with a knife—a hidden tale that she has repressed for more than twenty-five years. Katie is shocked by its reappearance during our interviews, surprised by her urgent need to tell it, and amazed by what she discovers—about her pain and her rage—when she finally releases the story. The theme emerges through our dual reflections: Katie reflecting on her own story (making connections she has never made before) and my reflecting on her reflections (identifying and naming the patterns I see).

> Katie leans forward, her voice rapid and as intense as ever. She
> was the tenth-grade class president at the George Washington
> Carver High School, and together with a few classmates was

planning the culminating event of the year, a class trip. They were sitting in a cluster in the classroom having an energetic, spirited conversation, "laughing, talking, planning." Miss Boulware came from across the hall and began to complain loudly about all the noise the group was making. With a shrill voice, she berated them, told them they were "acting like fools." Katie and her friends were surprised by her harsh tones and accusations. Although they had been enthusiastic and occasionally loud in their planning, they were not being disruptive or raucous. When their homeroom teacher, Mrs. Martin, came back, Miss Boulware reported the group's transgressions and Mrs. Martin felt compelled to punish them. She "had thought she could trust them"; she had expected them to act responsibly and they had disappointed her. For their sins, they each received "five licks on our hands" (with a ruler) and her words of recrimination.

Katie was outraged, seething with anger at the injustice. Suddenly, the fury inside her erupted like a volcano. She said to her friends angrily, brutally, "If I had a knife, I'd kill her." Her classmates were stunned by her statement. James Torrence decided to test her sincerity. He reached in his pocket and pulled out a pocket knife. "Here is the knife," he challenged. "I couldn't back down. I just couldn't reverse myself. I was just shaking with anger," recalls Katie, her voice still ringing with rage. She strode across the hall with the knife in her hand and said to the people gathered, "I'm looking for Miss Boulware." The answer came back, "She's not here." So Katie walked out, slowly. She left Miss Boulware's classroom, but she did not leave her anger behind. Now her voice is shaking—"She was not there to kill but I would have staked my life on it . . . as long as there was any energy left in me, I was going to kill her. She had violated me . . . I was humiliated."

Katie walked back across the hall to the classroom where her expectant peers looked at her with new eyes of awe and apprehension. "My whole image among my colleagues had changed. No more Goody Two-Shoes." The anger did not subside. "I could feel the quaking, the shaking . . . I could feel how close I was to altering my life forever." During the next class period, in Mr. Thompson's Algebra II class, Miss Boulware strode in. "I understand Katie Cannon's been looking for me." To which the whole class chorused back, "Oooh." In silence, head bowed, Katie followed Miss Boulware out of the class. Standing outside against the concrete wall under the fire escape, the teacher confronted her. "Do you have something to say to me?" Katie "said the Lord's Prayer over and over again" to herself, trying not to unleash her anger and remaining steadfastly silent. For two years after, every time Katie would see Miss Boulware, she would stare at her in hateful, blunt silence. In the hall, on the lunch line, in the library, their eyes would lock in mutual enmity.

By day's end the grapevine had carried this story to every corner of the school. "Katie Cannon was looking for Miss Boulware with a knife. She was ready to stab the life right out of her." "Everyone was buzzing about it. It was the hum of the school." And Sister Sara just couldn't wait to carry the news home to their mother. She couldn't wait to watch Katie receive their mother's wrath. As the time drew closer for Katie to go home, she felt a wave of panic more serious than any she had experienced the whole day. "All the fear of mother had come down on me." She knew her mother's outrage would be much worse than anyone else's, that she would have to endure terrible humiliation once she got home. And she was infuriated with Sara's obvious pleasure over the anticipated pain. "This was going to be worse than going to prison," thought Katie as she headed home on the school bus. As soon as they landed at the door, Sara told Corine Cannon the terrible tale and paused long enough to wait for the fire-works. But none came. No fireworks. No screaming. No humiliation. Only a simple and strange directive to Katie, quietly spoken: "I want you to go and clean the living room," said Mrs. Cannon.

Relief is written all over Katie's face as she relives this treacherous moment. "For the very first time in my life, my mother came through!" Katie still has no clue about why she responded as she did. It was completely, shockingly uncharacteristic of her mother who was not shy about berating her children. She never spared them her anger. But here she was telling Katie to clean the living room, the one room in the house that never even got dirty. "We have a poor working-class living room. You know, one of those rooms with plastic all over every-thing, a room that is never used . . . nothing at all to clean!" Her mother's words felt like a blessed gift. "To me, it felt like *paradise,* that living room. . . . Nothing to dust, nothing to do. I thought it was the most *beautiful* space, heavenly." Cannon stayed in her new-found asylum feeling deeply relieved and grateful to be spared her mother's wrath. But even more shocking than *not* getting punished was the way the event got buried forever. "It was never mentioned again." Not by anyone—her mother, her sisters, the kids at school, her teachers. It vanished, erased from the local lore. "It was very strange that there was no mention of it. . . . That is probably the reason I forgot to tell you about it last time." For some reason it is still a forbidden tale in Katie's hometown.

The image of Katie stalking her teacher with a knife haunts me. It brings home to me the rage that she harbors, the anger that coexists with her laughter. Both her rage and her laughter are expressed with exuberance and intensity and often seem to explode at the same moment. Katie knows the knife was not just meant for Miss Boulware. "It was a *life rage.* I could feel all the anger, all the energy drain right out of me . . . I felt exhausted." It was the response to all the years of accumulated abuses: "all the violation, all the humiliation, all the Jim Crow!" Katie also knows that "the prisons are filled with fifteen-year-old black girls" who have suffered the same abuses—stoically, silently—and then in a moment of electric irrationality, have committed a crime that will keep them incarcerated for the rest of their lives. "One moment they're talking to their friends on the phone or dancing, doing their teenage thing . . . and the next moment they're killers." Ordinary girls who have endured extraordinary pain, who finally can't take it any more, who suddenly go out of control, do violence to the nearest victim, and who are finally themselves victimized for life. Katie knows their reality. She has suffered like them. She too, except for the grace of God, might have lived her life incarcerated in a prison cell [pp. 56–58].

In summary, the portraitist enters the setting with a perspective, a framework, and a guiding set of questions that are the result of her previous experience, her reviews of the literature, and her conceptual and disciplinary knowledge. *Before* she embarks on data collection, she tries to articulate the contours of this framework, discern her anticipatory schema, and register her preoccupations. This is an early self-reflective, self-critical exercise that increases her consciousness about the lens she brings to the field and allows her to open her eyes (as well as her mind and her heart) to record the reality she encounters.

Once in the field, the portraitist engages in an iterative process of data collection, interpretation, and analysis. Each day in the field is followed by reflection and critique as the researcher works to reconcile what she is observing and documenting with her anticipatory framework. She writes an Impressionistic Record that allows her to record emerging hypotheses, develop more discerning questions, become more focused in her inquiry, and chart a course of action for the next day.

The interpretive and analytic process, then, begins immediately and threads its way through data collection until it becomes the central activity of synthesizing, sorting, and organizing data after the researcher leaves the field. The portraitist works to develop a process and a structure for categorizing the data, for tracing the patterns, for capturing and constructing the themes—all the while trying to preserve the nuance and complexity of real lived experience, and always remaining attentive to the "deviant voice."

The emergent themes are rendered using five modes of analysis. The first (and most common) identifies the visible and audible refrains spoken and enacted by actors over and over again in various contexts. Emergent themes are also heard in the resonant metaphors voiced by the actors, capturing in a few words a wide angle of experience and deep meanings shared by many. These metaphors are often embroidered into the rituals and ceremonies that symbolize—through art, music, dance, poetry—what the institution values. The portraitist also discovers emergent themes through triangulating data from a variety of sources and underscoring the points of convergence. But patterns do not always develop out of convergence; they must also be discerned through reflecting on the dissonant strains, through discovering the order in the chaos, through finding the coherence in what often seems inchoate and scattered to the actors in the setting.

Implementation

Naming Convergence

Jessica Hoffmann Davis

W hen I collected drawings from Maxine, the painter whose flowers grace Chapter Three's artistic refrain section, she expressed a great interest in the cognitive approach that fueled my study of the drawings of artists and children. Maxine listened attentively as I explained my particular perspective, and then drew me in close to speak frankly from one artist to another: "I love what you are doing, Jessica," she said, "but never forget: art is magic."

In this respect, the methodology of portraiture and the artistic process are very similar. In disassembling the whole to lay the process bare, the magic or integrity of portraiture's flow may seem challenged. The tensions that Lawrence-Lightfoot identifies in our illumination section between the hard edges of classification and the complex blur of human experience are reminiscent of the conflict Maxine identifies between a view of art as a self-conscious process of thought instead of a mysterious result of emotional inspiration. But just as the magic of art is sufficiently stable to survive and inform a cognitive approach, so too can the unity of portraiture withstand and guide an analysis of the methodology's component parts.

Naming convergence within a complex and diversified whole may seem to be a reductive activity. But the identification of emergent themes does not reduce the complexity of the whole; it merely makes complexity more comprehensible. Indeed the recognition of emergent themes serves as surely to identify important disjunctures as to clarify the ways in which the parts of the whole fit together. Methods for naming convergence differ among researchers and between individual and group researchers. Lawrence-Lightfoot's approach as an individual and as the innovator of the process is described in our illumination section. In this section, we address the implementation of emergent themes as a process of identification and application developed and operationalized by a group of researchers.

Although our approach can be used as well by the individual researcher, it is more codified than what has been introduced so far and may beg rewriting by individual voice as interpretation. As artists and researchers who appreciate the positive impact of constraints on creativity, our team was patient with and grateful for the structure. We were certain that a framework would offer consistency to our diverse portrayals, and serve to highlight and not obscure the numerous differences among sites. Our structured group approach—derived from and consistent with Lawrence-Lightfoot's individual approach—should prove to be of equal use to others.

Lawrence-Lightfoot has identified the components of the process of identifying emergent themes as listening for repetitive refrains and resonant metaphors, exploring and discovering cultural and institutional rituals, triangulating data from a variety of sources, and attending to dissonant threads. These mutually informative strands of the process are implemented throughout the stages of the portraiture methodology: from preparation for the site visit through the data collection to the final writing of the portrait. Throughout these three stages, the portraitist simultaneously discovers in process and imposes on product the burgeoning structure of emergent themes.

The ongoing dialectic between process and product assures that the discovery of themes throughout the process of data collection and analysis informs and is informed by the imposition of themes on the product—the interpretation represented in the final portrayal. With regard to the identification and application of emergent themes, the question that portraitists must repeatedly ask of process is Do the identified emergent themes resonate throughout the actors' language and institutional culture and do they illuminate dissonant threads? And the question that portraitists must repeatedly ask of the product is Do the emergent themes that I have identified adequately scaffold my interpretation and resonate throughout the dimensions that I recognize as relevant?

PRE–SITE VISIT AND ON-SITE IMPLEMENTATION OF EMERGENT THEMES

Beyond the benefits discussed in earlier chapters, a careful pre–site visit review of documents pertinent to an institution may provide portraitists with preliminary ideas for the themes that will emerge as unifying threads throughout a diversified and complex entity. This preparation not only serves to suggest possible themes early on, but also helps to prepare the portraitist for the on-site activity of *listening for* emergent themes.

Repetitive refrains recur in the specific language that insiders use when representing the site to outsiders—when describing, for example, what makes the site special or the details of its educational philosophy. As mentioned previously, the expression "Oasis on Clark Street" not only resonated through the content of constituents' descriptions of the Artists Collective, it also showed up in various promotional materials and even served as the topic and title of an original musical production. We found that information in the publicity materials and year-end reports that the Collective shared with us prior to our site visit.

Similarly, at Boulevard Arts Center in Chicago, the expression "main alternative" (to the economic and social pressures of a poor urban community) appeared in the center's descriptive materials. After researchers found frequent reference to the term in the content of resonant stories and in the actual language of various actors on the site, *Main Alternative* was chosen as a theme in our early portrait of Boulevard (see Davis et al., 1996). In the course materials shared by Manchester Craftsmen's Guild, researchers took special note of "Life Skills Courses," which primed the portraitists' palette for the discovery of a related theme. That theme, designated by frequent conversational reference and reinforced by the core educational philosophy, was *Winning the Right to Be Heard.*

On site, the portraitist listens for repetitive refrains in literal statements uttered by the actors and as recurring themes evoked throughout the text of repeated stories. At Manchester Craftsmen's Guild, much of the curriculum is devoted to helping at-risk students learn to speak a language that will "take them where they want to go," which at the Guild is a quite clear destination: college. Students have opportunities to show their artistic productions in photography or ceramics to groups of individuals who ask questions about the creation of the work. Responding to these questions, students transcend the everyday linguistic codes they share with peers and acquire an additional vocabulary for self-expression. The Guild's emphasis on learning new ways to speak as a vehicle for personal advancement lends thematic content (the appearance in institutional rituals) to the literally repeated refrain (in numerous conversations with a variety of actors): *Winning the Right to Be Heard.*

Researchers' day-to-day process of listening for emergent themes functions as a sort of on-site hypothesis finding and testing. At the end of the day, portraitists review field notes, log observations while they are fresh in their minds, and begin to reflect on the emergence of possible themes. At the end of one of my first days on site at the Artists Collective, I devoted a portion of my notes to the potential themes I had considered throughout the day. I began to enter evidence for the various possible themes (recorded in block capitals):

Artists Collective notes   1/8/92 10 P.M.

- ENVIRONMENT: DM describes it as a "positive place" where people care—deal with issues of grooming, self-presentation, heritage . . . as part of the arts learning. Students learn to acknowledge each other: "simple things." Students "behave quite differently" at center than they do at school.

- SAFE HAVEN: View of tests—Christmas test party is "something to see"—students "munching away" but they're testing. Signing in and out in response to parental needs (called to find out when kids had left). Separated from outside world: Kids and other visitors are buzzed in. BUT it's a real environment—comments on artist's life.

- HOME: JM used to go into students' homes and introduce himself to parents—what's missing is community outreach person to make those kinds of connections. "Family organization." Dollie as "controlling person" (self-described) matriarch? Cheryl is "everyone's mother"; entire families attend center; center itself constitutes tight family—stories repeated throughout the day like family tales—*are there people who are not members of family?*—DM talked about student who's having trouble now because father recently left: "We've watched her grow up here." DM has had to "train people to be conscious" of children's pain and needs but also to know when to draw the line. When students have developed to a point where they "need something else," teachers need to learn that they "gotta let that kid go." Even the tough kids who never quite "make it" at the center remain attached (Duane) and protective of teachers and staff. "This place has become those children's home."

- GROWTH/EVOLUTION/DEVELOPMENT

Of the center: "First trying this, then the next thing . . . have to be clever" (for example, martial artists as security because SIDA grants wouldn't cover it). Started as drum and drill team with African percussion. Started out with everything free—that didn't work; now everyone required to pay $10 registration fee, scholarships available—no one turned away—learn through experience.

Of the students: When students grow up and advance, DM says they have to learn to "let that kid go"—see that they "need something else"; (like children—hard to see them grow up but need to let it happen)—some kids let recognition "go to their heads" because they "don't understand what the growth is." Chant/rap in music class: "Can you imagine what Hartford would be without the Artists Collective and you and me? There's music, dancing, martial arts, and drama—all the things I need to tighten up my Karma. I need this education to help me grow, and not only do I like it but it's good for my soul. AC (2, 3) AC and me! (2, 3, 4) AC! (2, 3) AC and me!"

Of the teacher: Young teachers from JM's program do their "finishing" at the Collective; teachers learn from one another—"through Aca Lee Thompson being here, Cheryl has grown."

Dollie's own growth: Special order clerk, jewelry clerk, doctor's laboratory "that was the final piece . . . the finishing."

- INTERCULTURALISM

  Drummer's comment: most of the performers in the youth orchestra are "non-Black"—reversal.

  white faculty at Weaver High is "intimidated" by Yaboo.

  "Black Christmas" song.

- GETTING HIGH: comments on feeling backstage at performance.

Working as a team, two researchers bring their respective growing lists of possible themes to table at the end of each day and review each other's discoveries. Those potential emergent themes that occur to both researchers hold greater weight in the developing interpretation than those that seem more idiosyncratic. Researchers identify the most promising themes (*hypothesis finding*) and, in their different courses of action on the subsequent day on site, listen for those themes in their respective observations (*hypothesis testing*).

Regarding the potential themes proposed in my preliminary list, portraitists listening *for* these themes would consider whether they heard much from the various voices and sources on site about the *environment* at the Collective. Is *getting high* an expression that recurs in the language of the actors on the scene? Quite often, a potential theme is discarded by the second day of listening for it. Both my potential themes of *environment* and *getting high* were rejected early on. More frequently, particular concepts and phrases that are initially proposed are subsumed by the emergence of other, more clearly descriptive and resonant themes.

The relevant dimensions identified by the portraitist provide a structure for reflecting on themes. Noting the distinction, *themes* reside in and emerge from the site; *relevant dimensions* (or at least a working slate of them) are brought into the site. Relevant dimensions are embodied in the expertise and lens of the portraitist; emergent themes are embodied in the language and culture of the subject or site. Both frameworks serve to organize knowledge, information, and understanding, and both themes and dimensions are negotiated by the researcher. The relevant dimensions organize what is known about the larger field or domain of which the subject or site is representative; the emergent themes organize what becomes known about the particular site or subject.

Relevant dimensions can be seen as describing "areas of mattering"; emergent themes can be seen as describing "instances of mattering." In *Safe Havens* and *The Good High School,* the relevant dimensions are the areas and aspects within and across which goodness or effectiveness occur. The emergent themes name and frame the particular instances of goodness or effectiveness. In the context of the *Safe Havens* work, themes like those already mentioned—the *Main Alternative* at Boulevard or *Winning the Right to Be Heard* at Manchester Craftsmen's Guild—organize particular institutional constructions within and across the Co-Arts dimensions. Depending on the particular theme, it will resonate differently and more or less vividly throughout the four dimensions.

Implementing our relevant dimensions in our developing interpretation on site, Co-Arts researchers actually tested potential themes across dimensions. For example, considering the notion of the term *Safe Haven,* does it represent community members' attitudes toward the Artists Collective (*Community*)? Does *Safe Haven* play out in the Collective's educational curriculum (*Teaching and Learning*)? Is it a factor in plans for the future (*Journey*)? Does it appear in conversation about or the actual organizational structure of the Collective (*Administration*)?

While some emergent themes will necessarily have more resonance within one dimension than another, resonance *across* dimensions suggests authenticity—the likelihood that a theme is indicative of the whole of the institution and not just a part. The test for resonance across all dimensions identifies various potential emergent themes as more or less apt for naming and representing convergence throughout an institution.

The final themes selected for the Artists Collective were *Safe Haven, Family,* and the *Process of Being Somebody,* threaded throughout with the notion of *Rites of Passage.* Looking again at my excerpted notes, we see that the seeds of each of these themes had been planted early on. *Safe Haven,* a term used repeatedly by students, parents, and staff, was proposed from the start, and in the end, the notion of *Environment,* a researcher term infrequently heard at the Collective, was subsumed by that theme. The potential theme of *Home* developed into the theme of *Family*—the "Collective Family" was a repeated refrain—and the notion of *Growth and Development* grew into the *Process of Being Somebody* and of course, *Rites of Passage.*

Portraitists must be diligent in their attempt to name convergence with the language of insiders. That connection serves the objective of authenticity not only because it provides a link with which the actor as audience can make sense of the interpretation, but also because it tests the mettle of the hypothesized theme. If the portraitist cannot find a name for the theme within the language of the actors on the site, it is more likely that the theme is being imposed from outside in than emerging from inside out.

In co-constructing the portrait on site, portraitists can turn to the actors for help in affirming and naming themes. As mentioned in the chapter on relationship, Co-Arts researchers would meet with key actors on the scene at the end of their visits and review their current ideas for names and meanings of themes. We would ask our hosts whether the themes we were considering sounded apt to them. In response to our queries, center directors were quick to nod approvingly or to ask for clarification.

When we shared the possible emergent theme of *Life as a Performance Art* (a researcher-imposed phrase) with Jackie McLean, cofounder of the Artists Collective, he seemed puzzled. When I began to explain what we meant by that term—the seriousness with which students' behavior was regarded within the performing arts environment of the Collective and the habits of discipline and self-respect instilled therein—he nodded vigorously, "Oh, you mean, the process of being somebody." Through this exchange, a familiar expression (we had heard it frequently on site) among insiders and an observed governing structure came together in the theme the *Process of Being Somebody.*

From the very first assertion of potential themes, portraitists must address the question of what does not fit and begin to listen for what Lawrence-Lightfoot has called the deviant voice. Note that in my excerpted notes, under the potential theme of *Home,* the question is immediately posed: "Are there people who are not members of the family?" Having a particular theme proposed helps focus the portraitist's listening not only for what is convergent, but also for what is divergent. Because of the proposed theme of *Home* or *Family,* I was particularly attentive to those voices expressing alternative views—for example, the mother who complained that the scheduling of classes at the Collective in the early evening cut into her family time at home.

In the final portrait, I included selected "deviant" voices of individual families that feel estranged from the Collective. One such voice was cited in our chapter on relationship: the single-parent mother who wanted to present her daughter in the Yaboo ceremony. That mother met resistance in her challenge to Collective family traditions of male family members presenting novitiates.

As mentioned early on (and illustrated in Chapter Three), Co-Arts researchers consistently began their portraits with sections on context that ended with an introduction to the emergent themes. In this format, the final themes were presented as the framework for both the underlying interpretation of the site and the discernible presentation of the portrait as an aesthetic whole. This approach is evident in the following contextual introduction to the Manchester Craftsmen's Guild:

> And *A Place in the Sun* is a theme that radiates throughout
> the inner workings of the Manchester Craftsmen's Guild.
> Two graceful brick archways on either side of the reception-
> ist's desk lead to the Guild and Bidwell administrative offices
> and to the main instruction and performance facilities of the

Guild. The administrative offices have the light-colored wall-to-wall carpeting, secretarial front line, and filing cabinets of an elegant and well-organized executive office. The door to Strickland's office is encrusted with yellow, dark blue, red, green, and purple shards of glass hinting at the glass-making history of Pittsburgh.

One of the archways in the lobby opens to a hallway lined by the photography and ceramics studios and the Guild's gallery, a square room inset with large circular glass windows. Through the circles of glass are visible the oversized black and white portraits on display that were taken by a photographer who taught Guild students during a summer program. The enlarged faces of men, streaked with emulsion by the artist, stare at one another from the beige walls. In the middle of the polished hardwood floor, a white podium rises to offer a dried flower arrangement to the still elegance of the room. At the end of the building behind the gallery, a deep turquoise curtain swathes the arched entrance to the "acoustically perfect" Music Hall, which was officially opened in 1986. The elegant concert hall setting is where students from a weekly drama class deliver monologues and acknowledged jazz masters perform.

At the Guild, in this carefully designed setting, at-risk students are not only taught how to develop photographs or throw pots but are also empowered to believe that they can be successful. Bill Winston, the Arts Education Coordinator, teaches these students that *"Winning the Right to Be Heard"* is a crucial strategy for successfully negotiating the world of higher education and professional careers. This concept, introduced by Winston, emerges as another resonant theme at the Guild. It is explained in an introductory handout to the Guild's "Life Skills Training Program":

"Manchester Craftsmen's Guild uses this concept to further advance the personal expression and cultural and personal insight of its at-risk culturally diverse students. This process then opens doors of educational opportunity and, ultimately, employment security, through attitude adjustment and heightened self-esteem using the successes achieved in the field of performing and visual arts."

The strategy of winning the right to be heard helps students to chart their own course to their place in the sun. Winston explains that students have to learn to speak up in class, to speak out, to use language that will be heard and understood.

He says that at the Guild students are given an "understanding of how different systems work" in education or business and how to interpret and respond to different professional and interpersonal cultural styles.

Winning the right to be heard builds on the notion that relationships with others are an important ingredient in personal success. Reflected in the aesthetic interplay of disparate physical elements in the architectural environment, *Relationship* is an apparent and central theme in all that the Guild teaches and embodies. Relationship is understood from a one-on-one basis between individuals to the broader concept on an institutional level. Relationship as mentorship is at the heart of the Guild's structure in its role in Strickland's own development and in his mission of providing others with similar opportunities.

Relationships prioritized at the Guild include those between and among teachers, parents, students, celebrities, foundations, and other institutions. Relationship as collaboration is reflected in the origins and name "Manchester Craftsmen's Guild" and the collaborative efforts of the group that put it all together in what Strickland calls the center's "humble beginning" on the North Side's Buena Vista Street.

Today, the Guild relies on collaboration with the Pittsburgh Public School System to facilitate and advance its programs. Most of the students who come to the center arrive on school buses provided by the Pittsburgh Public High Schools. Artists-in-Residence from the Guild teach ceramics and photography to high school students in the schools and thereby publicize the Guild-based programs. The relationship between these visiting artists and school students contributes to the makeup of the Guild population. Assistant Executive Director Nancy Brown remarks, "The Artists-in-Residence in the schools are such active recruiters and that sort of mentoring relationship begins there." For example, she says, "We have artists that attract minority students."

When not in classes, students from the Guild can be seen sitting on the polished wooden benches in the hallways or around the tables in the cafeteria that is just off the entrance lobby. Adult Bidwell students in white jackets and chef's hats sit in groups and Guild teenagers chat or pore over school books. The large open cafeteria has rows of skylights in its high ceiling. Hanging in the hallway just outside, an abstract metal sculpture is a creative reminder of the metallic image of the city.

The design and materials of the building seem appropriate to the disciplines taught at the Guild. Strickland comments that the materials used in the building—the "color of clay" that is "fired earth"—warm the physical space. As a ceramic artist who was "in clay" all his life, Strickland has "an emotional connection with the building."

These three Themes—A Place in the Sun, Winning the Right to Be Heard, and Relationship—are three prongs of a carefully thought-out plan, a specific mission that is supported by a purposefully designed environment. A place in the sun is obtained through winning the right to be heard which is a life skill passed on from mentor to student. Strickland proclaims, "This place is very clearly defined and if anybody's unclear about it all they have to do is ask me, and I'll remind them how clearly defined this place is. You've got to have that. If you start fooling around with people's lives, you really have to know what you're doing." The brick walls reinforce the solidity and pragmatism of the Guild, the circular windows magnify the lenses and apertures of photography and illuminate the ceramic sculptures, and the warm quilts bring associations of home and nurturing [Davis et al., 1993, pp. 83–85].

IMPLEMENTATION OF EMERGENT THEMES IN POST–SITE VISIT ANALYSIS AND WRITING OF THE FINAL PORTRAIT

After the site visit, portraitists face the challenge of making sense of compilations of data and structuring the final aesthetic whole. At this juncture in the work, identified emergent themes actually serve as vehicles for coding transcriptions and classifying various sources of data. Reading through transcriptions and field notes, Co-Arts researchers sorted and coded their data by theme. Stories and quotations that reflected the theme of Family, for example, were cut and pasted into a designated "Family" file, and so forth for the other themes. Dissonant threads—what Lawrence-Lightfoot calls deviant voices—were also coded by theme (in terms of which the dissonance was clear). In this way, the emergent themes not only alerted researchers to deviant voices, but also provided a tangible structure for keeping track of dissonance.

Written documents collected before and during site visits, such as promotional materials, curricular guidelines, mission statements, and annual reports were also reviewed, coded, and filed by theme. Using colored markers, researchers would identify passages or illustrations that offered evidence of coherence or suggestions of dissonance.

Even in the writing stage, portraitists are open to changes in their plans that unexpected discoveries will suggest. In consultations with other researchers on the team, group portraitists can find sounding boards for their developing ideas and seek colleagues' input in naming emergent themes. As mentioned previously, one change that is frequently made is in the wording of the title of the theme. The deeper exploration of actors' language, afforded through coding transcriptions and other data collected on site, will sometimes reveal that an expression spoken by insiders describes a governing theme more accurately than the phrase researchers initially selected, thus rooting the theme from inside out.

A review of the introductions to the three themes in the portrait of the Manchester Craftsmen's Guild points to the resonance of emergent themes across relevant dimensions and illustrates the ways in which themes embrace repetitive refrains, engage resonant metaphors, incorporate cultural and institutional rituals, and draw on the triangulation of data from a variety of sources.

As discussed earlier, *A Place in the Sun* is a metaphor taken directly from the language of Executive Director Bill Strickland. The theme incorporates the luminescence of facilities at the Guild (*Administration*), the Guild's educational objectives (*Teaching and Learning*), and the Guild and its director's pilgrimage from anonymity to recognition (*Journey*), which helps the organization achieve its overarching mission to serve at-risk youth (*Community*). *Winning the Right to Be Heard* is a repetitive refrain among the actors at the Guild and a metaphor for the strategies for success (institutional rituals) that are taught to students.

Finally *Relationship* addresses the key component of teaching and learning and administrative collaboration at the Guild: the understanding of mentorship as the most powerful ingredient in the Guild's approach to educating its students. In introducing emergent themes, Co-Arts researchers highlighted the interrelationship of emergent themes as reflecting the cohesion of the whole. As evident in the Guild selection, the naming of themes points not only to the individual surface strands of color gracing the tapestry of an institution but also to the underlying warp of the fabric and the continuity and discontinuity of the overall weave.

In the introduction to the portrait of MollyOlga Neighborhood Art Classes, the theme of *Constant Survival* is drawn from the underlying struggle of the center (*Journey*), the theme of *Model of the Professional Artist* from the descriptive language and curricular content of the teaching and learning at the center (*Teaching And Learning*), and the theme of *Realistic Accessibility*, a term used repeatedly by director Molly Bethol, from the admissions policies and overall philosophical mission of the center (*Administration*). Furthermore, each of these themes plays out across all four dimensions.

The unusually neat organization of the MollyOlga portrait's themes (each deriving from a separate dimension) and their tidily structured interrelationships (evidence of each dimension within each theme) offer structural resonance to the carefully ordered institution in which every single student has a record stored on an index card and artists literally work on ascending floors: beginners on the first, intermediates on the second, and advanced on the third.

Additionally, these themes incorporate and emerge from repetitive refrains, resonant metaphors, institutional rituals, and triangulated data from a variety of sources. In introducing the themes in the portrait's *outside in,* the portraitist also provides the reader with contextual information that is richly informative. The remainder of the portrait develops the themes thus introduced and fills out the skeletal structure presented in this opening section. But, serving almost as an abstract or a précis for the portrait as a whole, this contextual section on its own would tell the reader a great deal about the site:

> The solidity of this building—the cold cement stairs, stone foundation, and durable brick structure—provides a metaphor for the constancy that MollyOlga represents in this neighborhood. It has survived the arson and violence for which this community is known, and it has also survived adversity of a different sort. Despite rampant funding cuts in arts programs throughout New York and this country as a whole, MollyOlga continues to offer classes in painting, photography, drawing, and clay to children and adults, free of charge. *Constant Survival* emerges as a theme at this community art center.
>
> Beyond a red door that is kept locked at all times, the interior space of the center is itself a work of art. Sunflower yellow walls and ceilings vibrate under fluorescent lights and provide a vivid backdrop for the ordered display of children's art. Pieces labeled with title, name, and age of creator are hung from floor to ceiling in white rectangular mats. In the work of the youngest children, primary colors dominate the tempera paint and chalk compositions. The older children have mixed and employ more subtle hues: ochers, viridian greens, burnt umbers. There is no evidence of assigned projects in the work displayed on the walls—no variations on themes such as "my family" and "what I did this summer" as are sometimes apparent in children's art rooms. The diverse images include animals, human figures, interiors, outdoor scenes, and purely abstract forms. Among all these paintings, it is rare to find one where more than a little bare newsprint is visible. Among these two-dimensional pieces, three columns of shiny clay sculptures hang in the first floor rooms.

The winding stairwell leading to the second and third floors is replete with visual images of a different kind. Acrylic and oil paintings and black and white photographs, labeled with titles and artists' names, cover the stairwell wall and fill the second-floor hallway. The third-floor painting studio, reserved only for the most proficient students, has eaves, nooks, and corners typical of an attic, but every inch of empty space is covered with art. The upper floors of MollyOlga feel privileged: a removed place for the more advanced artists.

It is on the third floor that Molly Bethel, the founder and director of this community art school, keeps her works on paper in a large leather portfolio behind a locked door. Each piece is separated from the others by carefully placed sheets of tissue paper. Molly looks at her pastel paintings from behind large shaded glasses that shield pale blue eyes. Her long white hair is pulled back in a low ponytail and she wears a paint-splattered wrap-around smock over jeans and boots. Now that her children are grown, Molly has just recently begun to exhibit her own work again in addition to directing and teaching at MollyOlga. Between the sheets of tissue paper lie vivid abstract renditions of stones made of layered lines and shapes painted in pastel.

Olga Aleksiewicz Lownie carries in samples of her work wrapped in dark green plastic bags. She has cropped auburn hair with straight bangs that hit her arched eyebrows and frame bright, dark brown eyes. Olga speaks with the tiniest hint of an accent reflective of her birth and early years in Eastern Europe. Wire earrings, strung with colored glass beads and bent into human forms, end in spirals that dangle to her shoulders. She wears an oversized shirt smeared with dried clay over black corduroy trousers. Olga unwraps richly colored oil paintings, reminiscent of Bonnard, and opens an ordinary egg carton to reveal a dozen eggs intricately decorated in the Ukrainian tradition.

With the exception of the most advanced students who have established styles of their own, the students at MollyOlga never see the work of their mentors. "They have to do their own," Molly explains, "so nobody sees [our work] until they're real secure in what they're doing themselves." The artist's perspective that Molly and Olga bring to their own work is what shapes the basic philosophy and pedagogy of MollyOlga Neighborhood Art Classes. *The Model of the Professional Artist* is a second theme that guides the education provided at this place where art making for students of all ages is taken seriously.

Molly explains that the ongoing exhibition of art in the entry, hallways, and classrooms at MollyOlga sets a tone such that "the minute somebody walks in the building, they see that there's art all over the place . . . and it's matted; it's treated with respect." During a visit to a MollyOlga exhibit at an African American and Native American art gallery in downtown Buffalo, a four-year-old student at MollyOlga is at ease with the large oil paintings on display. When asked, "Do you think that someday your paintings might be on the walls?" her immediate response is, "My paintings are on the walls." Back at MollyOlga, they hang in a perpetual art show that is very much like this professional exhibition.

The ongoing art exhibit at MollyOlga includes selected works by every student at the art school. The annual opening is a festive event for which community members and "people from all over . . . from all walks of life" line up at the door to view the art and enjoy a live band. Throughout the year, Molly and Olga ask children to save those paintings or drawings that represent their "biggest accomplishments." Before the exhibition, Molly and Olga review the body of work collected from each child and choose which pieces will hang—usually two per child. For MollyOlga students, like professional artists, exhibition becomes "something to work toward." This one remains hanging throughout the year.

The teaching staff at MollyOlga, made up primarily of professional working artists, is racially diverse. In addition to being director, Molly teaches drawing and painting classes to children and adults. Olga is the center's treasurer as well as a teacher of children in painting and clay. Like Molly and Olga, photography teacher Barbi Lare and clay teacher Sally Danforth are white. The three instructors, or assistant teachers, are individuals of color. Curtis Robinson, who works in children's painting and clay, and Dorothy Harold in children's clay, are black. Lenore Bethel, who works in photography and painting for children and adults, is biracial. All three instructors started as "teen assistants," growing up in the Fruit Belt community, learning art at MollyOlga.

Describing the staff in terms of the color of their skin, Lenore points out, is an outsider activity. She explains, "Everyone in the building is the same. We are all artists and teachers. Only outsiders tend to make a distinction of color." Molly says that it makes her "angry . . . to be simply dismissed by the color of my skin." Her commitment to the community in which she lives and works speaks to a different reality. She points out that she has been living in the neighborhood since 1959 and working in the neighborhood since 1956: "I've got a drug house next door to me. Come on." Furthermore, as a spouse in an interracial marriage, she says she is a member of the "smallest minority": "There are fewer interracial marriages than there are whites and blacks" she says, "and both sides look at interracial marriages sideways." When teaching young children to mix skin color, Molly demonstrates to them that "all colors of skin have brown and white in them—it's just a variance of proportion."

Just as all classes are literally *free* (of charge) at MollyOlga, the center is committed to creating an environment where students are *free* to pursue their own artistic visions. This freedom, both literal and figurative, is fundamental to a third theme that characterizes the MollyOlga experience. *Realistic Accessibility,* a phrase coined by Molly, is considered to be a "tremendously important" concept that guides this center's understanding of educational effectiveness. Molly and Olga assert that the opportunity to learn in the arts should be accessible to everybody "*not* depending on whether they can afford to pay for it."

With an understanding of how seemingly minor factors such as financial aid forms and parental permission slips can present insurmountable barriers, Molly and Olga make sure that the center's claim of accessibility is real by eliminating these bureaucratic obstacles. Children and adults who want to do art can and do literally come in off the street, and the program allows them to join classes at any time during the year. The center also cultivates an "attitudinal accessibility"—an atmosphere where nontraditional learners as well as degreed artists are comfortable to create. Like line, form, and color, which are building blocks for an artist's composition, these three themes—constant survival, the model of the professional artist, and realistic accessibility—are the elements out of which this portrait of MollyOlga is constructed [Davis et al., 1993, pp. 52–56].

Portraitists understand that the identification of emergent themes, like all the methodological features of portraiture, depends on the particular voices of the portraitists and the tenure of the relationships developed with actors on the site. The emergent themes identified in a specific portrait are not the only themes that resonate throughout an individual site or story. Nonetheless, if well chosen, the selected emergent themes will be truthful in terms of the subject they help portray.

There is a certain truth about works of art that makes the representations they contain not just depiction but valid expression of human experience. There is also a validity in the interpretation that a research portrait represents that tells the reader not just about an individual or a site but about more general human experience. The emergent themes organize that experience and make it comprehensible to the actors on the site who are encountering it first hand as well as to the readers of the portrait who reinterpret the experience through their reading.

Emergent themes also provide opportunities for readers to discuss the stories of vast and complex individuals or sites in terms of other individuals and sites. This function of emergent themes is particularly useful to portraitists looking across a field of institutions through the individualized portrayals of a few representative sites. In the end of *The Good High School,* Lawrence-Lightfoot was able to look across the portraits she had created and, through a comparison of the emergent themes of each site, derive a view of the principles of goodness provided by the collection of portraits. Following her lead, in the end of *Safe Havens,* I compare the themes of each portrait and derive therefrom some markers of educational effectiveness in the field of community art centers.

In the excerpts from portraits included in this section, we see evidence of themes as repetitive refrains (such as *Realistic Accessibility* and *Winning the Right to Be Heard*) resounding throughout the language and actions of actors on site. We see resonant metaphors such as *A Place in the Sun* and *Constant Survival,* which reveal the ways in which actors experience their realities. We also see emergent themes as institutional rituals important to organizational continuity such as *Winning the Right to Be Heard.* In the identification and confirmation of all these themes (hypothesis finding and testing), we see the triangulation of data from interview transcripts, observed on-site activities, and an assortment of written materials.

The methodological steps that lead to the construction of these themes begin before and persist throughout the collection of data on site to the writing of the final portrait. Summarizing the process in end-of-day on-site reflection and, if applicable, in consultation with fellow researchers, portraitists record their developing ideas and evidence for emergent themes and consider their aptness. Reflecting in this way at regular junctures throughout the site visit allows the portraitist to maintain an ongoing rapport with the process (the collection of data) and with the product (the portrait) that will, like the developing interpretation, be organized around emergent themes.

In daily on-site observations, interactions, and interviews, listening for proposed themes, ever open to those yet to be discovered and to dissonant threads more evident in light of the evolving structure, portraitists test the mettle of hypothesized themes in structuring the developing interpretation and the final portrait. As themes appear to be more salient, researchers explore their viability within and across identified relevant dimensions. During the site visit and at its conclusion, portraitists engage the actors in reflecting on developing themes, and in naming convergence. After the site visit, in the ongoing analysis of data, emergent themes are implemented in a new way, as structures for coding and triangulating data from a number of sources. But even in this stage of data analysis, the portraitist remains skeptical, ready to change, if necessary, the content or naming of convergence.

Finally, in the writing of the portrait, the emergent themes are used to structure the aesthetic whole. While individual researchers may vary the details of the configuration that organizes their portraits, groups of researchers may be better served by agreed-upon schemata that afford some recognizable measure of consistency across their work. In either situation, the presentation of emergent themes and the interrelationships among them illuminates the structure of both the site and the portrait—the parts of the interpretation and their necessity to a view of the whole.

Artistic Refrain

Defining Forms

Jessica Hoffmann Davis

Emergent themes occur within and across the stories, language, and rituals of subjects and sites. Naming convergence, emergent themes clarify the ways in which parts of the whole fit together and make tangible the intangibles through which insiders experience their realities. The portraitist's job of identifying the emergent themes that structure interpretation is akin to the artist's efforts at grasping the essential traits that define forms and thereby make objects visible. Arnheim describes the activity and its function:

> To make an object visible means to grasp its essential traits; one
> can depict neither a state of peace nor a foreign landscape nor
> a god without working out its character in terms offered by the
> image. And when Paul Klee writes in his diary: "I create pour
> ne pas pleurer: that is the first and last reason," it is evident
> that Klee's drawings and paintings could serve so great an artist
> and so intelligent a human being as an alternate to weeping
> only by clarifying for him what there was to weep about and
> how one could live with, and in spite of this state of affairs
> [1969, p. 254].

Looking within and across the drawings of emotions by artists and children, emergent themes can be noted that have been recognized as clarifying and resonant by numerous individuals. For example, consider five-year-old Sydney's and adult artist Joan's drawings of Sad (pp. 234–235). The emergent theme presented in these drawings (and apparent in a number of other artist portrayals) is tears—dripping tears cascading down the page.

Tears represent both a literal repetitive refrain and a resonant metaphor, uniting the image of declining weighted shapes with the thought of weeping and the subject of the portrayal: sadness. These three origins for the metaphor—in linear construction, physical association, and referential meaning—are akin to the notion of triangulation of data through which emergent themes in research portraits gain their authenticity.

Turning to the emergent themes within the drawings of Sad by twelve-year-old artist Benjamin and adult artist Amy (pp. 236–237), we see a different sort of resonant theme: one that is associated with cultural rituals and ceremonies. In both these drawings (as in other artist portrayals) the unbounded emotion of sadness converges in the physical image of figures, seated in chairs, with their heads bowed.

These powerfully clear interpretations of sadness demonstrate the potential of particular activities to represent more general understandings. The artist's theme of sitting in chair with head bowed is not unlike the portraitist's theme of *Winning the Right to Be Heard* or the *Process of Being Somebody*. Like these portrait themes in which sitewide rituals converge in one resonant refrain, more general physical displays of sadness converge in a simple but profound association.

These are the powers of images that Klee describes: the potential of works of art to organize what seems chaotic and to contain in comprehensible structures what is otherwise beyond comprehending. Importantly, the naming of convergence does not diminish complexity. The viewer perceiving Sydney and Joan's thematic interpretations of sadness through tears or Ben and Amy's seated figures understands that the apparently simple portrayals represent a complex emotion.

Indeed the simplicity of the theme leaves ample room for intricate associations that might otherwise be lost in the process of unpacking less well-structured representations. The identification of emergent themes in research portraits helps to make clear even the dissonant threads that lend clarifying contrast to the coherence of portraitists' interpretations.

Just as artists judge the objects they portray with a selective vision that sorts out the essential features that will make the meanings of their drawings visible, portraitists listen selectively for potential themes through which broad understandings will converge into manageable structures. And just as portraitists feel the tension between the need to organize and classify and the integrity of complex and contradictory experience, so too do artists need to balance the constraints of their medium and the boundlessness of human experience.

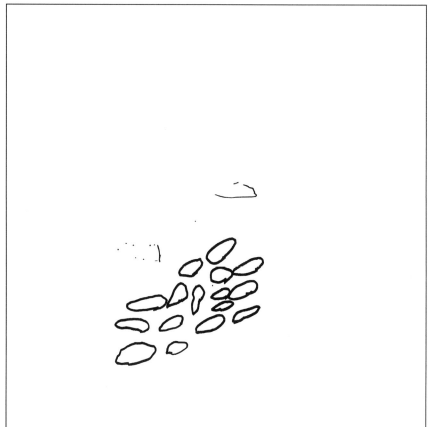

Five-year-old Sydney's drawing of Sad

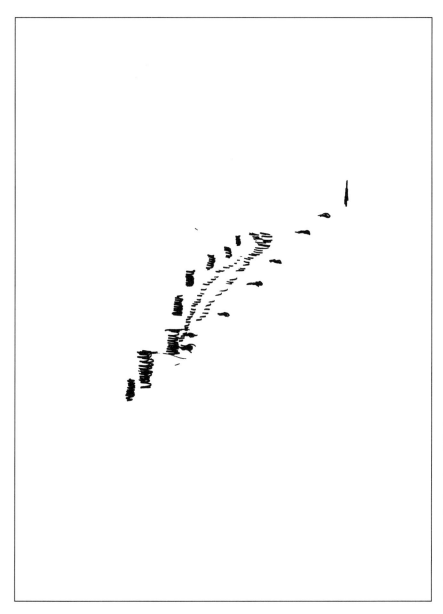

Adult artist Joan's drawing of Sad

Twelve-year-old Benjamin's drawing of Sad

Adult artist Amy's drawing of Sad

The naming of convergence by identifying emergent themes has been described as a delicate and complicated process that ironically results in hearty simplification. But artists and scholars who study art recognize that children achieve such triumphs of representation with apparent and understandable ease. Rudolf Arnheim explains the facility as an attribute of children's developmental status: "If one wishes to trace visual thinking in the images of art, one must look for well-structured shapes and relations which characterize concepts and their applications. They are readily found in work done at early levels of mental development, for example, in the drawings of children. This is so because the young mind operates with elementary forms, which are easily distinguished from the complexity of the objects they depict" (1969, p. 255).

The artist Paul Gauguin, like many other artists, saw the child's facility as the artist's objective:

> In one of his letters from Tahiti, Gauguin had written that he felt he had to go back beyond the horses of the Parthenon, back to the rocking horse of his childhood. It is easy to smile at this preoccupation of modern artists with the simple and childlike, and yet it should not be hard to understand it. For artists feel that this directness and simplicity is the one thing that cannot be learnt. Every other trick of the trade can be acquired. Every effect becomes easy to imitate after it has been shown that it can be done. Many artists feel that the museums and exhibitions are full of works of such amazing facility and skill that nothing is gained by continuing along these lines; that they are in danger of losing their souls and becoming slick manufacturers of paintings or sculptures unless they become as little children [Gombrich, 1984, p. 468].

While portraitists may be less inclined than contemporary artists to emulate the work of children, in selecting emergent themes they reach for the souls of the subjects or sites that they portray. In daring to name convergence they provide essential clarity and elevate their portrayals from the sphere of individual scenario to the realm of more universal human experience.

Figure Stylisée 1st state
21 November 1948

CHAPTER SEVEN

ON AESTHETIC WHOLE

Illumination

Shaping the Story

Sara Lawrence-Lightfoot

In the last four chapters we have explored context, voice, relationship, and emergent themes, offering descriptions of their contours, purpose, and expression—in the field and in the text. Although we examined each element separately—as if they were discrete and nonoverlapping—our discussions pointed to the interactions among them: the way, for example, relationships are created and sustained in (as well as shaped by) a particular context, or the way the researcher's voice interprets and constructs the emergent themes.

Just as we dealt with each element separately, so as to discern it more clearly and examine it more deeply, we now turn to the ways in which each element is a part of a larger whole—the *aesthetic whole*. In this chapter we stitch the pieces together to create a whole cloth, recognizing that the gestalt is much more than the sum of its parts. How do we construct the whole? How do we give it structure, form, and coherence? How do we make judgments about the composition? What should be included and excluded? How much should our decisions and choices be guided by empirical considerations? How much by aesthetic sensibilities?

In developing the aesthetic whole we come face to face with the tensions inherent in blending art and science, analysis and narrative, description and interpretation, structure and texture. We are reminded of the dual motivations guiding portraiture: to inform and inspire, to document and transform, to speak to the head and to the heart. How do we create a document that is both authentic and evocative, coded and colorful?

In the opening chapter of *The Good High School*, I speak about the portraitist's search for patterns, her documentation of what is important, her choices about emphasis and inclusion, her selection of the pieces—of different colors and textures—that will be stitched together to create the portrait.

> The portraitist's search has the qualities of an investigation.
> It is determined, uncompromising, and increasingly focused.
> All of one's senses are used to decipher what is important and
> the quality of things. Decisions are made about what must be
> left out in order to pursue what one thinks are central and criti-
> cal properties. The piecing together of the portrait has elements
> of puzzle building and quilt making. How does one fit the
> jagged, uneven pieces together? When the pieces are in place,
> what designs appear? A tapestry emerges, a textured piece with
> shapes and colors that create moments of interest and empha-
> sis. Detailed stories are told in order to illuminate more general
> phenomena; a subtle nuance of voice or posture reveals a criti-
> cal attitude. What evolves is a piece of writing that conveys the
> tone, style, and tempo of the school environment as well as its
> more static structures and behavioral processes. Words are
> chosen that try to create sensations and evoke visions for the
> reader. It is a palpable form, highly textured—what Jerome
> Bruner has referred to as "life writing" [p. 16].

Very few social science researchers have tried to seriously describe the process of creating the gestalt. Nor have they offered clear strategies for constructing the aesthetic whole. Chapter Six demonstrates the variety of ways that qualitative researchers have focused, ordered, and classified their data around emergent themes, revealing the ongoing iterative process that occurs between the collection of grounded data and the generation of theory. But researchers have given less attention to articulating the process of moving from selecting the threads (the emergent themes) to weaving the tapestry (the portrait). This is understandable. The act of creating the gestalt is a less codified and delineated activity than the identification and naming of emergent themes. It is both systematic and creative, structured and organic, disciplined and intuitive.

In their volume on ethnography, Goetz and LeCompte (1984) offer a rare glimpse of the researcher organizing data, defining categories, and developing the complex whole. They speak of the ethnographer as puzzle builder assembling the pieces into a coherent pattern within the frame.

> Once a researcher has established the categories within which
> the data are organized and has sorted all bits of data into rele-
> vant categories, the ethnography as a portrayal of a complex

> whole phenomenon begins to emerge. The process is analogous
> to assembling a jigsaw puzzle. The edge pieces are located first
> and assembled to provide a frame of reference. Then attention
> is devoted to those more striking aspects of the puzzle picture
> that can be identified readily from the mass of puzzle pieces
> and assembled separately. Next, having stolen some surrepti-
> tious glances at the picture on the box, the puzzle worker places
> the assembled parts in their general position within the frame
> and, finally, locates and adds the connecting pieces until no
> holes remain [pp. 191–192].

The puzzle building that Goetz and LeCompte describe is related to the development of a "credible" and "believable" story. When we speak about creating
a believable story, we inevitably must consider the whole—not just the pieces
of the puzzle but the assemblage. Maxwell (1996) refers to this standard of credibility, this effort to construct a trustworthy narrative, as "validity." Objectivity
is not the standard for validity as it is in quantitative research. Validity is a complex construct in qualitative inquiry; it reflects the synthesis of several rigorous
methodological themes. Maxwell speaks of it holistically as "the correctness or
credibility of a description, conclusion, explanation, interpretation, or other sort
of account" (p. 87). He explains: "The use of the term 'validity' does not imply
the existence of an objective truth to which any account can be compared. However, the idea of objective truth isn't essential to a theory of validity that does
what most researchers want it to do, which is to give them some grounds for
distinguishing accounts that are credible from those that are not. Nor are you
required to attain some ultimate truth in order for your study to be useful and
believable" (p. 87).

Like Goetz and LeCompte, Eisner (1985) emphasizes the researcher's goal of
finding corroboration among the pieces of the puzzle and underscores
Maxwell's concern with "creating a whole" that is believable. He argues that
validity hinges on two processes, "structural corroboration" and "referential
adequacy." The first he likens to the systematic logic and the development of a
credible argument that is the work of a lawyer seeking to build a strong case.
"Structural corroboration is a process of gathering data or information and using
it to establish links that eventually create a whole that is supported by the bits
of evidence that constitute it. Evidence is structurally corroborative when pieces
of evidence validate each other, the story holds up, the pieces fit, it makes sense,
the facts are consistent" (p. 241).

Miles and Huberman, however, worry about the parallel Eisner draws with
the lawyer's work, and warn of the danger inherent in the researcher creating
a logical, plausible story—in Goetz and LeCompte's words, "connecting pieces
until no holes remain" (1994, p. 192). "Plausibility," they argue, "is the opiate

of the intellectual. If an emerging account makes good logical sense and fits well with other independently derived analyses with the same universe, you lock onto it and begin to make a stronger case for it" (p. 264). The story begins to take on a life of its own. In the effort to avoid succumbing to this intellectual's opiate, Miles and Huberman identify three probable sources of researcher bias that should be heeded in order to resist the seductions of plausibility.

1. *Holistic fallacy:* interpreting events as more patterned and congruent than they really are, lopping off the many loose ends of which social life is made.

2. *Elite bias:* overweighting data from articulate, well-informed, usually high status informants and underrepresenting data from less articulate, lower-status ones.

3. *Going native:* losing your perspective . . . being coopted into the perceptions and explanations of local informants [p. 263].

The first two of these three seductions are important in the researcher's construction of the puzzle (the third is more relevant to the gathering of data and the building of relationships). She must be careful not to force incoherent data into a falsely smooth coherence, and she must be careful not to give powerful people undue prominence in the narrative or mistake articulateness for knowledge or wisdom.

Eisner's second process, *referential adequacy,* begins to address some of Miles and Huberman's warnings and is a helpful counterpoint to his suggestion of "structural corroboration." "Referential adequacy" refers to the researcher's "testing the criticism against the phenomena it seeks to describe, interpret, and evaluate . . . the empirical check of critical disclosure" (p. 244). Referential adequacy depends, in part, on the expertise of the researcher, and on her familiarity with the setting being studied. Discerning critical observations can only come from someone who has a deep understanding of the environment and is able to perceive the subtle and complex changes that a less sophisticated researcher would never notice.

In creating the aesthetic whole, then, we work to construct a credible story—putting pieces together to create a logical coherence, but being careful not to impose a facile consistency or a simplistic logic that will misrepresent the complex reality we are documenting. In the process, we ask questions that are deceptive in their simplicity—that seek the response of the actors in the field and the audience who reads our work. When Miles and Huberman speak about validity as "truth value," for example, they ask, "Do the findings of the study make sense? Are they credible to the people we study, and to our readers? Do we have an authentic portrait of what we were looking at?" (p. 278). Kidder (1982, p. 56, cited in Lather, 1991) uses the term "face validity" to describe the "click of recognition" that one feels in reading the narrative—a "yes, of course" response instead of a "yes, but" response.

In constructing the aesthetic whole, the portraitist seeks a portrayal that is believable, that makes sense, that causes that "click of recognition." We refer to this "yes, of course" experience as *resonance,* and we see the standard as one of authenticity. The portraitist hopes to develop a rich portrayal that will have resonance (in different ways, from different perspectives) with three audiences: with the actors who will see themselves reflected in the story, with the readers who will see no reason to disbelieve it, and with the portraitist herself, whose deep knowledge of the setting and self-critical stance allow her to see the "truth value" in her work.

WEAVING THE PORTRAIT, WEAVING THE TALE

How does the portraitist achieve resonance? How do we construct a portrait—an aesthetic whole—that resounds with authenticity? Goetz and LeCompte speak of arranging the pieces of a puzzle. We might think of stitching together a colorful quilt. My favorite metaphor refers to weaving a tapestry because the image allows for various configurations of color, texture, and design, as well as a clear structure of overlapping threads (the warp and the weft). The metaphor also embraces other powerful images related to portraiture: the interweaving or combining of elements into a complex whole (weaving the incidents into a story), or contriving something complex or elaborate (weaving a tale), or interlacing strands or strips of material (weaving a basket), or spinning (a web). The weaving metaphor, then, reflects the elements of structure, texture, color, design, and the images of spinning a tale, telling a story, shaping a narrative.

The portraitist constructs the aesthetic whole—weaves the tapestry—while attending to four dimensions: the first is the conception, which refers to the development of the overarching story; second is the structure, which refers to the sequencing and layering of emergent themes that scaffold the story; third is the form, which reflects the movement of the narrative, the spinning of the tale; and last is the cohesion, which speaks about the unity and integrity of the piece. I will describe each of these dimensions in this chapter, illuminating their aesthetic and empirical properties.

Conception

When the portraitist begins to shape the whole, she must identify the overarching story. Out of the torrent of data, the flow of perspectives and perceptions from the actors, the portraitist draws the emergent themes and organizes the multifarious threads of individual and collective experience. Once identified and articulated, the conception both embraces and shapes the development of the narrative. Writers and literary critics speak about the conception of their work as the first tool for ordering the material. Madden (1980), for example, argues that a writer needs a conception to move from raw materials to the whole, and he speaks about the discovery of conception as merging intellectual insight with emotional resonance. "An intuitive fusion of emotion and idea produce a conception. A conception is a total, gestalt-like grasp of the story that enables the author to control the development of a situation, the characters, theme, plot, style, and technique, so that in the end they cohere, as in a single charged image. The concept orders, interprets, and gives form to the raw material of the story and infuses it with vision and meaning" (p. 104).

Like the novelist, the portraitist searches for the overarching vision, the embracing gestalt that will give the narrative focus and meaning. She recognizes that this conception must reflect the weight of empirical evidence, the infusion of emotional meaning, and the aesthetic of narrative development. Usually the portrait's conception grows out of the dominance of an emergent theme (often "the repetitive refrain" referred to in Chapter Six) that reveals itself in many forms, through diverse voices, in a variety of settings. For example, in the portrait of St. Paul's School, the conception that gives order and focus to the piece is the theme of "abundance, tradition, and certainty." It is the most powerful refrain; it is expressed through ritual and rhetoric, through pedagogy and ceremony, through ecology and architecture. In my first movements into the lush landscape of St. Paul's, I speak about the abundance (of land, lakes, buildings), the tradition (of the classic architecture, the chapel service, the baroque organ, the formal dining, the rector's announcements), and the certainty (of the long history, the rich endowment, and the students' futures). These themes resonate through the narrative, expressed in explicit statements by teachers and students, subtle nuances of behavior, paragraphs in the school catalogue, and illustrative and evocative stories.

Even when there are references to people's experiences, backgrounds, or perspectives that do *not* seem to fit the dominant conception, we recognize that the contrasting image does not detract from the conception, but actually underscores its centrality and power. For example, at the close of the St. Paul's piece, I introduce the story of Lester Brown, one of two African Americans on the faculty (and a graduate of St. Paul's himself) whose own life history offers a vivid contrast to the dominant themes of the institution and to the experiences and backgrounds of his colleagues and students. Growing up in a poor black community in Philadelphia, surviving the isolation of his token black presence in a predominantly white public school, living a reality so distant from the privilege and protection of St. Paul's, Lester tells a story of courage, ambivalence, and estrangement that (strategically placed at the end of the portrait) illuminates and enhances the prevailing conception of abundance and tradition at St. Paul's.

The conception of the portrait, then, is expressed through repetition, reflection, reiteration (of themes, stories, illustrations) but it is also underscored through contrast, through listening for the deviant voice.

The final section of the St. Paul's piece is titled *"Between Two Worlds: A Minority Perspective"* and it opens with a reference to the portrait's prominent conception—of tradition and abundance.

> The majority of students at St. Paul's come from families of affluence and privilege. They exude the casual certainty and demeanor of entitlement that reflects their upper-middle-class status. Many already have the savoir-faire and cosmopolitan style of people much beyond their years. Their Calvin Klein T-shirts, Gloria Vanderbilt jeans, L.L. Bean jackets, and the Nikon cameras dangling from their necks show restrained opulence. Their sophistication is accompanied by an open friendliness. Every student I spoke to willingly and sponta-neously responded to my questions. Some approached me with generous words of welcome and eagerly told of their experiences at St. Paul's. Their stories of life at the school were uniformly positive. They praised the rector, their teachers, the academic program, and the school's rituals and ceremonies. Mostly, they echoed the rector's words of "loving and caring." There were the typical and expectable complaints about dress codes and dormitory rules, but surprising praise for the food. For most students, St. Paul's is an inspiring and demanding place where they feel challenged and rewarded [pp. 240–241].

Later on in this section on the minority view, we meet Lester Brown and hear about his early school experience in West Philadelphia, his easy transition to St. Paul's in the late 1960s, and his successful experience there. The account blends his strong commitment to the black struggle and his appreciation of, and affiliation with, the St. Paul's community.

> I was eager to learn about the history and experience of blacks at St. Paul's and turned to Lester Brown, one of two black fac-ulty and the new assistant dean of admissions. Brown's perspec-tive reveals an intriguing blend of historical recollections and contemporary views.
>
> A student at St. Paul's from 1969 to 1973, Brown graduated with an engineering degree from the University of Pennsylvania and returned to his alma mater for his first job. Lester Brown was born and raised in West Philadelphia and calls himself a "Philadelphia boy." He went to school not in the familiar black

territory of West Philly, but in Kensington, a working-class Irish Catholic neighborhood where he experienced open hostility toward blacks. It was a fiery, dangerous time. He rode the elevated street cars and buses on his hour-and-a-half trek to school. His walk from the streetcar to the school sometimes had to be protected by police and national guardsmen. Because Kensington was a magnet school with special resources and a more academic climate, Brown decided to become "a sacrificial lamb." He soon discovered that the white kids inside were friendly and good, while the white kids outside were hateful. "It was not a matter of race, but of how you behaved that counted." He and two other buddies of his from West Phila-delphia were discovered and "adopted" by a generous Jewish woman—a volunteer in the school who offered them "cultural enrichment," friendship, guidance, and support. Brown called her "my fairy Godmother." Everything she touched magically turned into something good. It would happen invisibly. "We didn't know how things happened. Suddenly, everything would come together." So it was with Brown's coming to St. Paul's. When he was about to go on to high school, this woman asked him about his plans. He had thought of going to Central High School, a Philadelphia public school with a good reputation, but she said, "You know, Lester, there are other options you should consider." Without much effort, he and his two friends found themselves spread apart in fancy private schools, far away from family.

Brown remembers the transition to St. Paul's as immediate and easy. His experience with "good whites" in the Kensington School made him not prejudge or stereotype his white peers at St. Paul's. When Brown arrived in 1969, a strong, cohesive group of black students provided solace, support, and a source of identity for individual blacks. (Brown remembers there being forty-five blacks in the school as compared to twenty-three eleven years later.) A strong group consciousness permitted individuals to move forcefully out into the sea of whiteness and not feel overwhelmed or confused. Brown remembers the leader of the group, a strong, articulate, political figure, who gained respect and some measure of fear from faculty and students. He was not considered radical, but he was disciplined and outspoken, and everyone knew he was serious.

Blacks were a clear presence on the campus in the early seventies. "Believe it or not, we even had a Third World room— a space we could make our own, decorate the way we wanted to, a place to gather." The energy and vitality of this cohesive black group infected the campus spirit. Aretha Franklin's and Ray Charles's sounds could be heard across the manicured lawns; poetry readings portrayed black voices; and parties were dominated by a black spirit. "We were so sure of ourselves, we invited the *whites* in!" The irony of their success as a strong and dynamic force on the campus is that it led to their own demise and failure. Soon there was little differentiation between whites and blacks. The boundaries that had helped them establish their identity and made them strong enough to reach out eroded, fading into blurred distinctions [pp. 242–243].

Finally, we hear about the contrasts between Lester Brown's experience at St. Paul's ten years earlier and the weakened and invisible status of today's black students. Although many come from backgrounds similar to Lester's, their experience is vastly different. Their feelings of rootlessness, isolation, and ambivalence, of being caught between two worlds, sadden Lester and bring the portrait to a poignant conclusion. The rootlessness of the African American students amplifies the rootedness of the privileged ones. Here the portrait's central conception is underscored through irony and contrast.

Most black students come from working-class urban backgrounds in New York, Chicago, and Boston. When they come to St. Paul's, they are overwhelmed by the abundance and plenty that surrounds them. At first, nothing is taken for granted. "They appreciate the green grass and woods; they appreciate the gym floor; they appreciate the room accommodations." It takes them almost a year to make the major cultural shift, cross the class and ethnic boundaries, and begin to feel comfortable. At the same time, they are required to make a difficult academic leap. Courses at St. Paul's demand a kind of thinking they may have never experienced in their prior schooling. "They've never had to think before." They are expected to be questioning and articulate, and their academic skills are not as practiced or sophisticated as those of their peers. The dual demands of cultural assimilation and academic competence bear down on them with great force. It is amazing that they hang in, survive the onslaughts, and return the next year ready to face the challenges.

But where does this lead? Most likely, a prestigious college career will follow. Next fall, Cheryl will go to Amherst. Others have gone to Harvard, Yale, Princeton, and Williams. Stephen, the only black boy in the sixth form, will not go immediately on to college. He'll travel to Spain with no clear plans, no job lined up, and no facility in Spanish. His career plans seem to be distantly related to his travels. He hopes one day to enter the foreign service, and he wants "to get Spanish under his belt." He seems apologetic about his vagueness, adrift and alone in the school.

Stephen and Cheryl will be sad when school ends and they will have to return to New York and Chicago for the summer. "We have no friends at home," they say. Away from their family and friends for four years, they are strangers at home, feel distant and awkward in their old neighborhoods, and will miss returning to the now-safe environment of St. Paul's. Their profound connection to the school, and their sense of disconnection and alienation from home, seem to be related to what Lester Brown describes as the "breeding of arrogance." He fears that successful accommodation by blacks to St. Paul's means that they are likely to leave as "different people" with well-socialized feelings of entitlement and superiority borrowed from peers, from faculty, and from a culture that inevitably separates them from their own people and, perhaps, from themselves. The naturally smiling and open face of Lester Brown grimaces at the thought. He, too, feels implicated and guilty about his participation in this process of cultural and personal transformation [pp. 244–245].

In portraits of individuals, we usually see the conception that shapes the aesthetic whole expressed in the person's "life litany." In the preceding chapter, we referred to teaching as the central, generative force in Katie Cannon's life. Throughout our interviews, she says—many times—"teaching is the fruit of my labor" and we witness her love of, and commitment to, teaching in her early family experiences when she played school with her sisters, in her nursery school years when she loved arriving at school early to prepare the classroom for her classmates, in her determination to become the teacher's "pet" and surrogate, in the energy she devotes to her "fierce" pedagogy and to mentoring her graduate students. I title Katie's piece *The Fruit of My Labor*; a profound expression of the power of teaching in her life, a declaration about the emotional energy she gives to it, and a metaphor for the nourishment she gets from it.

Structure

If conception expresses the overarching vision of the aesthetic whole (the tapestry), then the structure represents the warp and weft of the weaving. The structure serves as a scaffold for the narrative—the themes that give the piece a frame, a stability, and an organization. Again, the novelist's view of narrative structure is helpful here. In explaining his view of structural cohesion, Lodge (1992) writes, "The structure of a narrative is like the framework of girders that holds up a modern high-rise building: you can't see it, but it determines the edifice's shape and character" (p. 216). In portraits, the girders are usually not hidden very well. They are most often visible as bold subheadings that reflect the emergent themes—sometimes as the punch line of stories, or as metaphors that thread their way through the piece.

In the Co-Arts research, a group process, the girders were explicit in the design of each of the Community Art Center portraits. The "relevant dimensions" identified before the researchers visited their portrait sites (that is, teaching and learning, community, journey, and so on), became the warp of the tapestry; the "emergent themes," expressed and documented in each of the art centers, became the weft. These cross-cutting threads gave a common structure to the *Safe Haven* pieces, providing a unifying framework for the collaborative work of a group of researchers.

The narrative structure implemented by a group of portraitists seeking consistency across portrayals may also be useful to novice researchers who, in balancing the many parts of the portraiture process, need scaffolding to construct a coherent whole. In general, the girders tend to be less obvious in texts composed by individuals who are more practiced and sophisticated in the methods of portraiture. But even when the girders are more muted, they still serve as a scaffold for the writer and as important—though implicit—markers for the reader. Whether the girders are obvious or subtle, however, there is always a strong relationship between the conception of the piece and the structure of its elements. As the portraitist builds the structure she is both guided by the conception and responsive to the emergence of the larger pattern. Once again, the St. Paul's piece offers a clear example of the relationship between conception and structure. We note the overarching conception of "tradition and privilege" and we see it reflected in (and shaped by) the "emergent themes" suggested by the subtitles: *"The Aesthetics and Comforts of Abundance"* (which speaks about the beauty and gentility of the rich environment), *"A Binding Together"* (which refers to the safety and unity of the St. Paul's community and the rituals that affirm its continuity), *"The Inquiring Spirit"* (which describes the intellectual confidence, ambition, and creativity of students who have lived lives of educational privilege), and *"Unimpeachable Power"* (which documents the rector's assumed and unchallenged positional authority in the community). Each subtitle builds structure and offers clarity to the conception of the portrait.

Form

If we think of structure as the scaffold and the girders of the portrait as providing a frame for the narrative, then we think of form as the currents that wash across the structure. Structure might be thought of as formalistic, even mechanical, whereas form is seen as organic and fluid. Madden (1980) refers to form as a kind of "mysterious phenomenon" that captures emotion and movement. He says, "Form . . . follow[s] the gestalt-making mental process, the convolution of emotions rather than the mechanics of episodes, while simultaneously growing, through various techniques toward an organic whole" (p. 183). Madden sees the crucial interaction of form and structure; both together "generate energy, life, emotion, and they shape meaning" (p. 183).

For the portraitist, form is the texture of intellect, emotion, and aesthetics that supports, illuminates, and animates the structural elements. Standing alone, the scaffold is stark, bare, unwelcoming—unconvincing in its abstraction. But form—expressed in stories, examples, illustrations, illusions, ironies—gives life and movement to the narrative, providing complexity, subtlety, and nuance to the text, and offering the reader opportunities for feeling identified and drawn into the piece.

In the following excerpt from Katie Cannon's portrait we see the "convolution of emotions" embedded in the story of Katie's relationship to, and total identification with, the gentle ladies who were her first teachers. She admires everything about them: their commitment, their professionalism, their discipline, the rhythm of their lives. She loves to be in their midst, hang out in their house, play with their things, and watch their moves and gestures. It is in the texture—the detail, nuance, and emotion—of this excerpt that we see the form that animates the structure.

> Katie started school at three years old at a school created by Lutherans, "the only place in the county where blacks could go to preschool." In this region, at this time (1953), it was not considered "natural" to send your children to preschool. "It was a very progressive thing to do . . . people worried that kids would be distorted" by this early education that took them away from their family. But Katie's mother—who believed in the power of education and was fiercely determined in her effort to send all her children through school—resisted the local disapproval and sent Katie and her older sister Sara off to the Lutheran school. "It was a hardship [for the family] at fourteen dollars a month for each of us," says Katie appreciatively. At 6 A.M., the two girls would be dropped off by their mother or Cousin Waddell at one of their teachers' homes, Mrs. Skinner's or Miss Lindsay's. The teacher would just be rising when they arrived and the little girls would have to occupy themselves quietly in the living room while the teacher washed up, dressed, and had her breakfast. Katie would sit and look at "the same book over and over again" or she would play with her miniature

animals. Even though they had to be quiet and stay out of the way, Katie loved the feeling of being in the teachers' homes, glimpsing the private lives of these admired mentors, watching the sequence and order of their daily preparation.

When Mrs. Skinner or Miss Lindsay had finished breakfast, they would be on their way to Mount Calvary Lutheran School where they would arrive well before any of the other children. Katie relished this time of day. "Opening up the school. It was almost like you lived there. I felt ownership of the space." The quiet morning hours would be suddenly shattered by the arrival of the other small children and Katie would energetically and enthusiastically join the activity. School was a place of excitement, accomplishment, and reward. "Education was always my life-giving source," she says simply. Katie would get so deeply involved in the school day that she would usually forget to go to the bathroom. By the time they reached the point in their daily schedule when the teachers and children bowed their heads to recite the Lord's Prayer, Katie would—as if on cue—proceed to wet her pants. "It was the first time in the day when I would pause long enough to realize I needed to go to the bathroom. My bladder was full, but I had been so involved in the action in the classroom that I wouldn't even notice. I'd wet my pants every time!" So Katie and her teacher worked out a system where she would ritualistically rise to go to the bathroom as soon as she heard the opening words, "Our Father, who art in heaven. . . . " "I was the only one to get permission to go to the bathroom during the Lord's Prayer," remembers Katie proudly.

She still seems to appreciate the place of "special privilege" she had with the teachers, a privilege she worked hard for and earned. It was the perfect match: the teachers who wanted order, civility, quiet, and poise from these rural black children and Katie who loved rules, structure, engagement, attention, and control [pp. 34–36].

Coherence

Finally, the aesthetic whole emerges through the development of *coherence*—when there is an orderly, logical, and aesthetically consistent relation of parts, when all the pieces fall into place and we can see the pattern clearly. To achieve this unity, the portraitist must have identified the overarching vision for the piece (conception), underscored the emergent themes creating a scaffold for the narrative (structure), and given insight, aesthetic, and emotion to the structure through the texture of stories, illustrations, and examples (form). In addition to conception, structure, and form, the portraitist shapes the aesthetic whole by developing narrative coherence, which includes the framing and sequencing of events and experiences and the articulation of a clear and consistent voice and perspective.

The most classic form of narrative unity is having a beginning, middle, and end to a story. The narrative holds together because there is a building of experiences, emotions, and behaviors that allows the reader an increasing knowledge and understanding of the scene and a growing relationship to the actors. The careful sequencing of events also permits the reader to make informed interpretations of the experiences in the tale. Although narrative coherence depends on the sequencing and unfolding of events, it is also achieved through repetitions of images, patterns, and refrains. The writer works to create a balance and rhythm between new, developing material and familiar and repetitive refrains. In speaking about creating a unified whole, Madden writes that "the repetition of motifs, situations, character relationships contributes to the effect of *unity*. . . . In all novels, some principle of integration is at work, striving for structural, thematic, symbolic, spacial, temporal unity" (1980, p. 182).

In the opening paragraphs of Toni Schiesler's portrait in *I've Known Rivers,* for example, she touches—briefly and poignantly—on the central and powerful pieces of her life story. The fleeting, evocative images flash on the screen, catching the reader's attention and imagination. Toni races through the stories of her poverty and homelessness—her sister lost to a secret adoption and the anguish contained in that secret; her love of learning and her early intoxication with reading; her mother's generosity, guilt, and violent rage; and the power and beauty of her mother's voice, her only inheritance. Each of these themes is documented and explored throughout the portrait, offering the reader the chance for growing insight and developing interpretations.

> At our first, exploratory meeting, Toni begins to tell me her story in quick vignettes, as if to let me know some of the variety, range, and change in her life. I pick up the pieces, not pursuing any in depth, satisfied that this is not our last conversation. (There is something about her that feels deeply familiar, pleasantly undefended, plainspoken and eager; something about her that seems poised, ready, accessible for this project.) I hear a little about her childhood in New Haven: she is the only daughter of a hard-working, determined domestic who decided very early that Toni was "a special child" whose gifts needed to be recognized, supported, and nurtured. Mother and daughter were poor, struggling and living in the projects, but Toni remembers an abundance of adventures—free concerts in the parks,

trips to the library, touring on the public city bus, where Toni learned precociously to read by deciphering letters from the advertisements above the seats. "I remember learning to read on the bus, riding with my mother. I *loved* to read. I read everything I could get my hands on." Her memories are of a mother who "when she could manage it, gave her *all*."

These early loving images are diluted (or at least questioned) by her mother's frequent apology, "I'm sorry I wasn't a good mother," and by Toni's knowledge that her mother "didn't want children" and "didn't want to have her." Confusion mixed with sadness seems to sweep across Toni's face as she tells the story of visiting her mother last Sunday. ("I see her every Sunday. She is in a nursing home in Wilmington. She had a stroke.") Her mother at almost eighty-three years old has been diminished by the stroke; her speech is now labored and her thinking a bit confused. On Sunday her mother repeated the troubling words Toni had heard many times before: "You know I *never* liked children." This declaration feels so at odds with her daughter's experience. Toni wants to understand her mother's words, but at the same time she doesn't want to hear them. She quickly provides a response: "Why do you say that, Mom . . . because of the way *he* treated you?" "Yes," replies her mother in simple assent. I listen and try to understand this puzzling scenario: a mother who "gave her all"; who planned wonderful "free adventures"; who saw her only daughter as a gifted, special person; but who didn't like children and didn't want Toni to come into the world. Nor was Toni the only child; she had a sister two years younger. "But we got separated when we were young and she was adopted by another woman. Now that the other woman is deceased, we have rediscovered one another . . . and there is infrequent contact. So growing up I was really the only child." I see a sadness in her eyes as she races quickly through this story.

Other memories of her mother make Toni smile warmly, make her glow. Toni's mother was a singer with "a beautiful contralto voice" who had once sung with a big band (when the star performer got sick suddenly) and who sang on the radio (one of those programs where you called in requests). Toni remembers sitting on her grandmother's knees by the radio listening to her mother sing, loving the mellow, soothing voice. She aches in knowing that her mother had wonderful talents but was unable to make it as a musician "because of the circumstances." She reminds me of Alice Walker's essay *"In Search of Our Mother's Garden,"* and with tears in her eyes says, "That moves me so much because it is my mother's story of unfulfilled dreams . . . of the world not letting her make it, not letting her realize her potential." The image of her mother as singer seems to be the proudest childhood picture that Toni has—one that expresses creativity and beauty; one that gives her mother significance against the dark, poor landscape of New Haven. She promises herself that she will pursue the history of her mother's musical past. "I want to find out the name of the big band leader she worked with, how she got the job at the radio station. . . . " Her voice trails off, holding onto these vestiges of pleasure and expressiveness in her mother's impoverished life. "You see we were on and off welfare . . . my mother did day work in people's homes . . . we were poor" [pp. 197–199].

The powerful refrains of poverty, ambition, secrets, rage, and voice thread their way through the piece, reflected in vivid stories, illustrations, and allusions, until we return full circle at the end of the portrait to the poignant metaphor of "voice as legacy." We have journeyed a great distance and returned to the same place. Though I presented this excerpt in Chapter Four, it is well worth rereading here:

It is hard to know how to give shape to our final session, how to give words to the sadness we both feel. I am haunted by Toni's bereft feeling that her mother has left her so little. I remember that one of the most precious legacies left by her mother has been her wonderful voice. Toni has said repeatedly, *"My mother's power was in her voice."* She meant this in two ways, I think. First, she has always known her mother as outspoken, forceful in her candor, frightening in her honesty. Her mother possessed the voice of power, clarity, and confrontation. "My mother always said what she thought. She was *not* like me. She was not worried about other people's feelings." Perhaps Toni's struggle to "find her voice" is part of her determination to feel more identified with her mother, to draw on some of her mother's fight and power. But she is also thinking of her mother's beautiful singing, soothing, comforting—an expression of her artistry. Toni lives with both legacies. As we search for closure, I long to hear Toni's own voice. "Will you sing for me, Toni?" I ask. "In all this time, I've never heard you sing" [p. 285].

Speaking of voice, narrative coherence also depends on the clarity and consistency of the researcher's voice. The portrait is woven together through the sequencing of events and the repetition of refrains, but also through the lucidity and constancy of the narrator's voice and perspective. The portraitist establishes her voice and perspective early in her research in the field, and tries to echo the dynamics and contours of voice in the text. For example, in *The Good High School* portraits, my voice moves within a relatively narrow range from "voice as witness" to "voice as interpretation" (see Chapter Six), from "thin" to "thick" description, from documentation to interpretation. My perch on the boundaries of these school environments shapes my voice in these portraits: a voice that observes, analyzes, and offers insight; a voice that seeks to examine and understand but rarely a voice that is in dialogue with the actors' voices. This is similar to the "narrative distance" assumed by the Co-Arts researchers as they shape their group voice. They settle on a voice of descriptive interpretation and they hold that sound, rhythm, and texture throughout the *Safe Havens* pieces, creating a coherence within and across the portraits.

On the other hand, in *I've Known Rivers,* my voice is more audible, dynamic, and interactive, reflecting the intensity and depth of my relationships with the storytellers and my purpose in telling two intertwined stories: one that traces their life journeys and the other that chronicles our developing relationships. In these portraits my voice is bigger and warmer compared to the more muted, cooler tones of *The Good High School* and *Safe Havens.* But in all three volumes, the voices are designed to be clear and consistent, reflecting the researcher's perspective in the field, her relationships with the actors, and her efforts to bring coherence and unity to the narrative.

To summarize, in creating the aesthetic whole we blend empirical choices and aesthetic sensibilities; we seek to capture insight and emotion; we want to develop a narrative that both informs and inspires. We have described four processes that must be synthesized in constructing the aesthetic whole. First, the portraitist must identify the conception, the overarching gestalt, the big story that will frame, focus, and energize the narrative. Next she must build the scaffold that structures the narrative—cross-cutting girders that will bind the work together, and interlacing threads that will reveal the design of the weaving. These girders—often identified by the subheadings of the portrait—reflect the emergent themes that have been documented in the research. The portraitist creates the form—the flow of the narrative—that washes over the structure and gives the piece texture, nuance, and emotion. It is the flesh on the bones of piece. Finally, unity is developed through the aesthetic sequencing of events (the beginning, middle, and end of the story) along with the rhythmic repetition of images, insights, and metaphors—blending change and constancy, new developments and old refrains. Throughout, the portraitist's voice must be clear and consistent, reflecting her perch and perspective in the field, her relationship with the actors, and the aesthetic contours and emotional range of the narrative.

When all these empirical and literary themes come together, the aesthetic whole possesses resonance. The portrait seems credible and believable. The researcher experiences the resonance in the synergy of context, voice, relationships, and emergent themes. The actors sense the resonance in seeing their images and experiences mirrored in the narrative. The images are rarely the ones they are used to seeing; they are often not very appealing or flattering. Sometimes they are shocking. But after the shock wears off, the actors sense the resonance in the essence of their being that gets revealed and in the patterns that the researcher has discovered amid the incoherence of their lives. And the reader experiences the resonance in the portrait that seems to hold together and make sense. "Yes, of course," they murmur as they feel moments of insight, identification, and recognition.

When all these resonances—the researcher's, the actors', the audience's—echo through the piece, we speak of the portrait as achieving authenticity. When these forces—empirical and aesthetic—come together, the work seems both deeply grounded in space and time and timeless. It feels like the portrait painted of me by the artist when I was in my mid-twenties (see Chapter One)—a portrait that was not particularly appealing but was deeply familiar; a portrait that did not look like me, but captured my essence; a portrait that marked a moment in time, but felt timeless. In this still silent painted woman, I could see my grandmother and my mother, and anticipate the way my children (as yet unborn) would one day see me. T. S. Eliot (1920) speaks about going beyond the frames of time in literary portraiture, as well:

> It is part of [a literary critic's] business to see literature
> steadily and to see it whole; and this is eminently to see
> it *not* as consecrated by time, but to see it beyond time.

Implementation

Composing the Narrative

Jessica Hoffmann Davis

In addressing the last and most comprehensive feature of portraiture, the aesthetic whole, we return to the place we began and to a view of the entire endeavor. The portraitist as artist is constructing and communicating her understanding for the reconstruction and reinterpretation of the reader. This communicative expression of understanding relies on the creation of a unified whole. Without unity, without the parts fitting together into an intelligible articulation, there is no communication—no understanding to be shared or found.

As Lawrence-Lightfoot explains in the illumination section of this chapter, resonance (a term we have used throughout our discussions) after all is manifest as recognition—as "yes, of course." The "yes, but" response affirms a fragmented view of parts: "This part is true; this other is not." The overall "yes, of course" is a holistic response, the recognition of a portrayal that taken in all at once—appreciated in its entirety—rings true.

The aesthetic whole of the portrait is framed by the portraitist's "overarching vision." The view of the whole encountered all at once is considered to be greater than the sum of its constituent parts. The challenge of implementation lies in the task of composing the narrative—assembling the various parts into one unified, coherent representation. What the portraitist comprehends as the whole of the interpretation must be rendered comprehensible for the reader. In order to achieve this rendering of an intelligible whole, the portraitist must thoughtfully delineate and organize the separate parts, and then weave them together into a pattern so carefully unified that the conjoining seams are invisible.

At every juncture, the portraitist is balancing three areas of judgment: aesthetic and empirical concerns, the separate parts of the overarching interpretation, and the various features of the methodology through which the interpretation has been attained. Three broad concerns—questions of "how to"—underscore the numerous queries that have been raised and fuel the portraitist's process of composing the narrative: how to fit together what is included, how to decide what to exclude, and how to know when the whole is unified. Our discussion in this section is structured around these three central issues of implementation.

In our discussion of each of these concerns, we consider the aesthetic and empirical decisions at hand, the salient parts of the interpretation, and the role of the various features of the methodology of portraiture that have been addressed separately throughout this volume: context, voice, relationship, and emergent themes. Weaving these elements of process together in our discussion, we not only address the integration of parts of a research portrait, we also reassemble a unified view of the fluid and cohesive methodology of portraiture that we have so far purposefully disassembled.

As it is with the implementation of every feature discussed so far, the composition of the aesthetic whole is an activity that does not wait to begin after the data has been collected. The consideration of the whole informs and fuels the portraitist's process of data collection and analysis and the reciprocal process of creating the final product: the research portrait. The question that portraitists must continuously ask of process is, How does the interpretation that I am mounting make sense of (lend coherence to) the various parts of my experience of the subject or site? And the question that portraitists must continuously ask of product is How true to my overall vision of the whole is the representation I have constructed in the final portrait?

FITTING TOGETHER WHAT IS INCLUDED

When Picasso said, "I painted all my life like Raphael so that one day I could paint again like a child," he voiced a sentiment that many artists, writers, and experts in various domains embrace: "You learn the rules so that one day you can have the freedom to break them." As a teenager, at the same time that I was studying iambic pentameter and the Shakespearean sonnet, I was discovering the poetry of e. e. cummings. In response to an assignment to write a fourteen-line sonnet with rhyme pattern structured after Shakespeare's, I created a visual display of words in keeping with cummings's spare lower-case spread that I so admired. My English teacher's response to my breaking of the rules was clear and terse. "Unlike you," she explained, "e. e. cummings knows how to write a sonnet in Shakespearean form."

Although my English teacher's pedagogical approach may be disputable, her underlying thinking is certainly applicable to the intent and content of this volume. If the methodology of portraiture is more than a graceful compilation of random reflections, personal views, and interactions with individuals and sites, there must be an underlying structure that can be learned by novices, adapted with experience, and defied with expertise. Throughout these pages, we have delineated such underlying structures and principles as they have been created, developed, and practiced by individuals and groups applying the methodology over time.

In the construction of the individual research portrait there is a similar need for underlying structure to guide the development of a cohesive whole even as the structure provides constraints that can be powerfully challenged. A research group's quest for consistency is best served by an agreed-upon schema for the creation of the overarching aesthetic whole of all portraits. Researchers can use this schema to guide their efforts in composing the narrative and to serve as a standard against which variation might be employed in response to aesthetic and empirical considerations.

Returning to our quilting metaphor, researchers working as a group develop a pattern for their tapestries and proceed synchronously in their selecting and sorting of fabric shapes, even as they rearrange their placement and alter their stitch to fit individual circumstances and settings. Project Co-Arts's pattern or skeletal framework was called a "generic outline." It delineated a plan of action in which each portrait began, as we have discussed and demonstrated, with an opening section that accomplished two objectives: to introduce the site in terms of its context or setting, and to introduce the emergent themes as entities in themselves and in relationship to each other.

The generic outline then called for individual sections, one for each emergent theme, giving evidence of the resonance (and dissonance) of the theme in terms of or with regard to each of our identified relevant dimensions. Presenting each theme section as a more linear construction than portraitists could or would want to achieve, the generic outline specified the following pattern:

Theme 1
    a. Relevant Dimension 1
       i.   evidence
       ii. evidence
       iii. evidence
       iv. dissonance
    b. Relevant Dimension 2
       i.   evidence

    ii. evidence
    iii. evidence
    iv. dissonance
   c. Relevant Dimension 3 (and so on. . . .)
  Theme 2 (and so on. . . .)
  Conclusion

The last item of the outline called for a brief retrospective holistic view that might be accomplished explicitly through the portraitist's reflection or implicitly through a story that seemed both emblematic and integrative.

Portraitists working as a group may want to meet and structure similar outlines for the construction of their final portraits, implementing fewer or more and obviously different relevant dimensions. As we did, they may use their outlines more as structures for selecting and coordinating what will be included than as fixed writing plans that order the presentation of portions of the narrative. Co-Arts portraitists did not, for example, include stories that evidenced each dimension in separate and sequential order as might be suggested by the outline. Instead, researchers used the outline only to ensure that they included stories exemplifying the resonance of themes across dimensions and that they balanced their examples of evidence thoughtfully throughout the text.

The generic outline provides portraitists with a schema with which to assemble and begin to organize the parts of the whole. Applying such a schema will help portraitists ensure that all parts of the whole are in place and, at least in terms of content, in structural proportion to one another. Depending on requirements of length, a group of portraitists may want to limit the number of emergent themes. Because different emergent themes resonate more or less audibly throughout particular relevant dimensions, some sections will be broader in their focus than others. Also, deviant threads or dissonance may be prevalent in some sections and not in others, or in terms of one relevant dimension and not others.

In sum, a generic structure addresses the issue of what should be included and how to give the parts of the whole coherence. From an empirical standpoint, the schema requires evidence. Specifically, the format calls for examples of thematic claims, and notably more than one example, as well as examples of dissonant strains made more apparent by virtue of the assertion of each theme. The structure's call for empirical evidence across as well as within numerous dimensions sets the stage for resonance across parts of the whole ("yes, of course") rather than in just one part or another ("yes, but").

The schema also provides a basic structure for aesthetic considerations. In his immortal text, *The Poetics*, the philosopher Aristotle explains the classic narrative or plot structure of beginning, middle, and end alluded to in our illumination section: "A whole is that which has a beginning, a middle, and an end. A beginning is that which does not itself follow anything by causal necessity, but after which something naturally is or comes to be. An end, on the contrary, is that which itself naturally follows some other thing, either by necessity, or as a rule, but has nothing following it. A middle is that which follows something as some other thing follows it. A well constructed plot therefore must neither begin nor end at haphazard, but conform to these principles" (1951 ed., p. 31).

This fundamental diagnosis of the parts of the whole raises important aesthetic considerations, which the portraitist can address in terms of the generic structure. Where will the narrative begin? As the generic structure suggests, the narrative begins with an introduction of physical location and of the themes that will organize both the structure of the narrative and the content of the interpretation that is being voiced.

Which theme will come first? Applying Aristotle's standard, the portraitist will begin with the theme that need not follow anything—the theme that can most artfully begin the presentation without relying on aspects of the content of other themes. Which theme will be next? The one that builds most sensibly on the opening thematic structure and simultaneously sets the stage for the theme that follows it. And the last theme? Of course, the one that will most gracefully build on the threads of earlier themes and knot the remaining threads with some finality, without calling for further edification from other themes.

These aesthetic considerations, balanced by the empirical requirements, are also engaged in concert with the various methodological activities of the portraiture process. The methodological issues raised for each feature guide reflection on the aesthetic whole. Accordingly, portraitists can scrutinize the whole, asking:

- Has contextual information been included as clarifying introduction to and edifying backdrop throughout the portrait?
- Has voice been sufficiently revealed and modulated so that it will inform but not distort the interpretation presented in the portrait?
- Have relationships been respected and faith kept with the actors on the scene throughout the shaping of the final whole?
- Do the identified emergent themes resonate throughout the language and culture of the actors on the site and do they adequately scaffold the interpretation presented in the portrait?

These methodological questions—heralded throughout our implementation sections—arise in consideration of the integrated whole of the final portrait as surely as they warrant consideration throughout the process of compiling and coordinating data.

Aristotle warns poets of the haphazard, which is a common pitfall in the attempts of novice portraitists. A moving representation of a relationship forged on site is not illuminating as a fragmented encounter haphazardly attached to an arbitrary theme. Scattered observations—no matter how carefully described—are only relevant to the whole when the portraitist applies the quilter's needle and thread. The portraitist needs to assemble the respective parts of the interpretation and to justify the inclusion of each separate entity in terms of its relation (even as a dissonant refrain) to the developing whole.

While a schema may serve as a guide for a novice, a launching pad for an expert, and a unifying structure across the work for a group of portraitists, it can never be the definitive factor in constructing the aesthetic whole. Empirical evidence can no more be altered to fit a pattern than the aesthetic whims of the portraitist can be allowed to rewrite the stories of the actors on site. A schematic structure serves only to organize the coordination of the components of the whole, not to determine the size and shapes of constituent parts.

Indeed the overall "gestalt" of the subject or site determines the portraitist's composition of the aesthetic whole. Aesthetic resonance is achieved when the structure of the portrait is commensurate with the portraitist's interpretation of the subject or site. For example, with MollyOlga Neighborhood Arts Class's fastidiously ordered environment, aesthetic resonance is achieved by shaping a carefully ordered portrayal organized tightly around separate and sequential themes.

The subject or site itself, then, as it is perceived and understood by the portraitist, is the governing force in the construction of the aesthetic whole. Patterns or substructures, like the generic outline, are there to be adapted in response to the portraitist's interpretation of the overall gestalt. Portraitists' ongoing considerations of the structural requirements of the final portrait assure that a view of the whole is guiding the development of each unfolding part. The weaving together of the parts of the whole exemplifies the ongoing portraiture dialectic between process and product. It is out of this continuous weaving that the aesthetic whole is created—not from a tying of strands initiated and resolved at the end of the portraiture process.

DECIDING WHAT TO EXCLUDE

As we have indicated, empirical considerations of resonance govern the portraitist's decision of what to exclude from as well as what to include in the narrative. For example, when deciding whether to include a given story, portraitists need to ask, Is the story I am considering representative of others I have heard, or noteworthy in its deviance from the majority of voices on site?

We can liken resonance to the silken threads spun by a spider, and the resultant web to the aesthetic whole. It is because portraitists find and represent resonance that it is there to be discovered by the readers. The reader's "yes, of course" response acknowledges the thread of the familiar carefully spun throughout a well-structured and perceivable web. In likening her work to that of the spider woman, Lawrence-Lightfoot describes this process of finding and applying resonance to the construction of the whole.

Once the pattern of the web begins to be established, aesthetic concerns take hold and the test for empirical resonance is not the only measure of inclusion. Not every resonant story will be included in the particular whole that is being spun—the unique interpretation that is accruing. Neither will every viable emergent theme be used in a particular portrayal. In order for the various parts to cohere, they must make sense in relation to one another. Accordingly, the test for aesthetic *coherence* becomes a governing factor. Empirical resonance alone will not guarantee a final product that can be apprehended all at once; aesthetic coherence is what assures a unified, comprehensible whole. Portraitists must prioritize the integrity of the whole that is being structured by selected emergent themes and attend to it in their decisions of what particular evidence and dissonance will be included or excluded.

Along these lines, Co-Arts portraitists came to realize that, with the bulk of data that was collected, many different portraits could be constructed for each site. And each possible portrait would embrace a somewhat different set of themes. Consider the early potential theme of *Getting High* (included in my excerpted notes in Chapter Six), which was eventually rejected for use in our portrait of the Artists Collective. This theme is a good example of one that might easily be used in a different portrayal of the center. Evidence for the theme could be found in the natural high that students experience in performance (*Teaching and Learning*); the getting high from drugs that is the nemesis of the North End (*Community*); the getting high that contributed to founder Jackie McLean's troubling history with drugs and ultimate recovery (*Journey*) and the McLeans' personal commitment to offering students an alternative way to get high through music training and performance (*Administration*). There was much evidence for this resonant theme, many stories that congealed around it, and clear confirmation of its nomenclature in the language and culture of constituents.

But *Getting High* did not prove viable in the portraitist's aesthetic judgment of its potential to lend coherence to the whole. Coherence is the aesthetic achievement artfully described by Aristotle in the discussion of the essential relationship among the beginning, middle, and end of the narrative. Specifically, when considering whether to include or exclude a theme like *Getting High*, portraitists can ask, What will the inclusion of this theme add to the whole that is not already apparent from the themes I have selected? How does that theme relate to and inform the other themes that I have chosen? In response to such aesthetic considerations, the theme of getting high was excluded from the final portrait of the Artists Collective.

The implications of exclusion on the basis of aesthetic concerns like *coherence* differ from those grounded on empirical considerations such as *resonance*.

Exclusion on empirical grounds—that is, for lack of resonance within constituents' language or culture or lack of corroboration through a triangulation of data, suggests that a potential emergent theme is not of demonstrable merit for inclusion in any portrayal of the subject or site. Exclusion on the aesthetic grounds of coherence suggests that a potential emergent theme is not essential to the construction of the particular interpretation represented in the portrait, but may be suitable for inclusion in another portrayal.

Decisions of what not to include in the final whole play out differently across the different features of portraiture. But with regard to each feature, the decisions incorporate both empirical considerations such as resonance and aesthetic considerations such as coherence. In terms of *context,* information that proves to be extraneous (lack of coherence) or ambiguous (lack of resonance) should be excluded. In terms of *voice,* the self-indulgently autobiographical (lack of resonance) that detracts from the developing interpretation (lack of coherence) warrants exclusion. Honoring *relationship* through process and product, information that betrays the actors' trust (no matter how resonant or coherent) does not find its way into the final portrayal. Finally, in selecting *emergent themes,* themes that do not play out within or across relevant dimensions (lack of resonance), thereby not uniting threads across the interpretation (lack of coherence), do not find their way into the growing structure.

DETERMINING WHEN THE WHOLE IS UNIFIED

The discussion of the aesthetic whole illuminates the separate and contiguous roles played by the various parts of the methodology of portraiture. If we extend our quilting metaphor: *context* functions as the underlying cloth on which the design is sewn, *emergent themes* are revealed as the shapes that will be joined together, *voice* is seen as selecting the pattern into which they will fit and joining the seams that hold them, and *relationship* is viewed as imbuing the *aesthetic whole* of the finished quilt with symbolic meaning.

The question of when a work of art is finished, when things are *right,* is an issue of great interest to developing artists and students of the artistic process. How does the portraitist know that the portrayal is complete—a unified whole that fills the empirical requirements of sufficiency (sufficient resonance to achieve authenticity) and the aesthetic requirements of unity (sufficient coherence to produce an aesthetic whole)? Again evoking Aristotle, the whole is unified or truly "one" when "the structural union of the parts [is] such that, if any one of them is displaced or removed, the whole will be disjointed and disturbed" (1951 ed., p. 35).

This view of the union of parts provides another test that can be implemented in reviewing the developing narrative: the test for *necessity.* Portraitists can literally review the parts of the narrative and consider what if anything is dispensable. If there are dispensable parts of the whole, unity has not yet been achieved. Readers of the portrait will not be able to apprehend the portrayal all at once and respond to overall resonance if unnecessary sections create imbalance in the final product.

Practically, of course, it is helpful for portraitists to have at least some idea at the start of their work of the approximate length of their final portrayals. Thirty- to fifty-page portraits like those found in *The Good High School* or in *Safe Havens* contain different versions of unity than the portraits in *I've Known Rivers*, which are two to three times as long. Of course, longer pieces allow for the development and interrelation of more emergent themes. But portraitists should never include more themes than can be explored in depth or any themes that lack either resonance within their respective contexts or significance to the particular aesthetic whole.

Longer portraits obviously also leave room for more stories, but portraitists should never include stories just for the sake of their inclusion or stories that are not resonant or notable in their dissonance. The size of the tapestry will make a difference in what is contained, but the structures and principles that guide the composition and weaving persist throughout the endeavor. In sum, the importance of a unified structure guided by the underlying principles of resonance, coherence, and necessity of the parts to the whole will apply regardless of the length of the research portrait.

In reviewing the narrative to ascertain whether unity has been achieved, portraitists can follow the lead of visual artists, who may consider their work as a composite of separate parts and negotiate balance in terms of the size or weight of each part. Psychologist Rudolf Arnheim (1966) describes the principles of balance in these terms. Regarding a drawing, for example, one can consider the borders of the page as the boundaries of the aesthetic space. Within that space, one can imagine the imposition of "compositional schemata" or grids that divide the space into separate sections. Considering a vertical line or axis breaking the space in half crossed by a horizontal line dividing it into four sections, Arnheim explains balance as occurring within and across these four quadrants.

Symmetrical balance is achieved when shapes of equal size or weight are distributed side to side or top to bottom around the vertical and horizontal axes imposed on the space. Asymmetrical balance is achieved when, for example, a large dense shape in a lower right quadrant is balanced by a smaller shape in the higher left quadrant. This works because things higher on the vertical axis—that is, further away or resisting the pull of gravity—appear heavier. However it is achieved, a balanced composition is unified, and a unified composition achieves clarity of expression—what we have been calling resonance, evoking the "yes, of course" response.

The generic outline can be conceptualized as a sort of grid—a narrative equivalent to Arnheim's compositional schema. Considering the designation of parts of the whole as apportioned in the generic outline, the portraitist could also consider the achievement of symmetrical or asymmetrical balance within the narrative. For symmetrical balance the question might be, Has equal attention been given to every theme, creating a sense of balance among the interrelated parts? For asymmetrical balance, the portraitist might ask, Has one theme been the dominant one, achieving balance through juxtaposition with and resonance throughout other themes?

The resonance of the themes of *Safe Haven, Family,* and the *Process of Being Somebody,* for example, can be seen lending ballast to the presentation of the overarching theme of *Rites of Passage* in the following excerpt from the Artists Collective portrait.

> Will the Collective achieve its own rite of passage into its own adulthood as "The Showplace of Albany Avenue," a "new arts and cultural center" that will accommodate the arts training programs, a resource library, a recording studio, and a multi-use performing arts theater? The sort of place, the Collective's accountant explains, where "Jesse Jackson would come talk"?
>
> The Collective has raised $4.2 million of the $7 million necessary to move into the new location. Founding catalyst Tony Keller is concerned that the remainder of the final funding may be hard to achieve, concerned "that it is such a struggle to move it from the present site to the dream house." Keller regrets the resistance with which some constituents within the community have met the Collective: "Those that have a deep sense of loyalty [to the Collective] are those that have been touched by it." He expresses "disappointment . . . that it has never become as much as a city institution that is absorbed by the supportive structure."
>
> Keller explains, "Some of the reasons go back to the New York City vs. Hartford" tension and the funding "power elite's ability to overlook an effort that does not seem to be 'coming out of the community.'" Jackie McLean recognizes the tension within the community and voices their sentiment: "'Who do they think they are coming in here to help us? We coulda' done it!'" He says, "When I get them all together, I say, 'Why didn't you do it? You didn't do it, so stop talking about it. We did it.'"
>
> But the resistance runs high enough to make the fund-raising struggle for the move to the new space extremely hard. Jackie McLean says of his wife, "She is tired now of the fight . . . and

what we are hoping will happen is that this decade in the '90s that we'll meet some younger people and that is why I am trying to develop all these guys [Hartt students] 'cause they work here and at the Collective to instill in them the same morals and methods and ideas that we have." As Dollie McLean puts it, "I mean we've been doing this now since 1970. That's a long time. I mean it's to the point where sometimes—I just said to my husband yesterday, I said, 'You know, it really gets discouraging when you have to keep convincing.' I'm always convincing, justifying, almost feeling sometimes that maybe we're doing something wrong . . . rather than bringing something that's really a wealth to this community and to our entire community. It's a struggle. It should not be a struggle to do something like this. It should not be a struggle. My energy shouldn't have to be spent going to a thousand meetings just to find people and paper and questions. You know what I mean? Particularly after we have the longevity that we have."

But this is the vision that the McLeans and constituents at the Collective share: that the Oasis on Clark Street will get to serve as safe haven for a greater share of the African American population in the greater Hartford area. The new site is on Albany Avenue and Woodland Street, still in the North End, but Dollie McLean says, "It's a more traveled thoroughfare, same problems though, same problems exist. But I think people would quicker come there."

Jackie McLean explains, "And this building that we are putting up is the final step in the dream and also a place where families could come and interact and that is what Yaboo is all about . . . and once the mothers and fathers get into this with the kids—this whole beautiful thing . . . and with that goes pride for the community—pick that piece of paper up; don't throw glass bottles down the street . . . all of those things exist in the North End of Hartford" [Davis et al., 1993, pp. 48–49].

Beyond the balancing of themes, portraitists will want to review portraits with an eye to the overall balance of descriptive details. For example, has the physical presence of actors on the scene been equivalently described? The portraitist may choose to give detailed physical descriptions of a few key characters and mention only a few characteristics of others. But if this is done with no sense of consistency or balance, the reader may be left with a distorted visual image—an awareness of the director's countenance but no sense of the actors around her. A close physical description of one child may or may not be suggestive of his or her class of peers. These are aesthetic decisions the portraitist must make in balancing the parts of the aesthetic whole.

Within the structure of the generic outline—the narrational schema—in terms of the evidence called for under each section or theme, the portraitist can make judgments in terms of balance. For example, with an eye to balance, the portraitist can consider whether evidence has been equitably distributed throughout the portrait or if some themes are presented with more resonance than others. Such incidents of imbalance can set the reader up for a "yes, but" response to the whole.

In reviewing the parts of the whole with an eye to unity, the portraitist needs to consider consistency and coherence within the individual parts as well as in terms of their relation to one another. Such careful analysis of the separate forms allows a progression to the view of the whole. Beginning with micro questions such as those concerning the distribution of contextual details or physical descriptions, the portraitist can move to larger questions of balance, such as the relative amount of evidence offered for different emergent themes.

From looking within themes, the portraitist can then consider the relationship among themes and the balance of the thematic structures that scaffold the portrayal. From considering the relationship among parts of the whole, the portraitist can progress to scrutiny of the whole and ask of the parts that have been considered, Would the displacement of any of these disturb the continuity of the whole piece? If the answer to that definitive question is yes, then the portraitist can be reassured that unity has been achieved and the final portrait is ready to be comprehended as a balanced and resonant aesthetic whole.

The final piece of the structure suggested in the generic outline calls for the tying together of threads: a conclusion that retrospectively incorporates the various parts of the whole. In our conclusion to the portrait of MollyOlga, we mention by name the portrait's central themes: *Constant Survival, Model of the Professional Artist,* and *Realistic Accessibility:*

> Olga reports that at Jammin' for MollyOlga, which occurred just weeks after the Los Angeles riots, "many people whom I didn't know . . . commented that 'isn't it nice that we can all be together.'"
>
> At this fundraiser, as at MollyOlga itself, people of diverse ethnic, economic, and experiential backgrounds come together and "the common denominator is that everybody is here to do art." In Molly and Olga's view of the artist's model, which guides the efforts of this art center, to "do art" seriously is to make it "an integral part of your life." Molly articulates the question that she has asked herself since she first began offering art classes in her kitchen to neighborhood children: "So how do

you go about making [art] practical, workable, and functional?"
How can art be made "realistically accessible" to nontraditional
populations so that it may become a constant part of peoples'
ways of living? In the words of a third-floor painter, MollyOlga
is based on an unwavering belief in the "value of the experience
of making things."

There are artists at MollyOlga who talk about bringing their
artistry elsewhere—setting up studios or makeshift darkrooms
in their homes so that the creative process is literally accessible
to them even when they are not at MollyOlga. Others may never
again pick up a paintbrush or piece of colored chalk, and art
making may fall away from the process of their daily lives. But
for the period of time that students are at MollyOlga, whether it
is one day or decades, they are artists. Although Molly and Olga
never claim that the spirit of the artist always goes beyond those
yellow walls, one wonders whether the artist's perspective
MollyOlga has invested in its students will not in itself prove
to be a constant survivor [Davis et al., 1993, pp. 79–80].

Lawrence-Lightfoot employs a similar technique of resolution in the conclusion of her portrait of Milton Academy. Indeed, the titles throughout that portrait suggest a schema similar to the generic outline. The portrait, titled *"Milton
Academy, Breaking New Ground: Humanism and Achievement,"* begins with a
description of context moving from outside in called *City Backdrop.* Each subsequent section points to different manifestations of the overarching theme of
Tradition and Changes. In the conclusion, titled *The Critical Edge,* Lawrence-
Lightfoot ties the strings of the weave into a provocative final knotting:

The dialogue, charged and spirited, reflected the vivid tensions
of value and morality at Milton: the tensions between feminine
and masculine perspectives, between historical and contemporary views, between achievement and nurturance, between
nature and technology. These opposing themes, always to be
struggled with and never to be resolved, create the energy and
vitality of Milton, but also the persistent feelings of incomplete-
ness and unease.

I remember again the first words uttered by the teacher with
the furrowed brow during my initial visit to speak at Milton: "I
think of my work as play . . . a great adventure," and I recognize the pleasure of his discomfort. Education as adventure will
never feel complete or wholly satisfying. There will always be
the gnawing imperfections. And then I remember seeing Janet

Malcolm's *Psychoanalysis: The Impossible Profession* on Milton's library shelf and recall the quotation that begins her book.

"It almost looks as if analysis were the third of those 'impossible' professions in which one can be sure beforehand of achieving unsatisfying results. The other two, which have been known much longer, are education and government" [Sigmund Freud, *Analysis Terminable and Interminable* (1937)] [Lawrence-Lightfoot, 1983, p. 305].

Despite the similarities, the balancing act that portraitists perform in constructing narrative differs greatly from the challenge confronting visual artists. Both portraitists and artists deal with layers of action, foreground and backdrop, central and peripheral forms. The aesthetic space confronting both visual artist and portraitist has planes and edges as well as shadows and depth. But the portraitist's narrative plane is ultimately linear and has a beginning, a middle, and an end.

In the quest for unity, the portraitist attends to *resonance,* which designates particular stories and convergent themes as pertinent parts of the whole. The portraitist attends as well to *coherence,* through which the various parts gain meaning from their relationship to each other. And ultimately, the portraitist attends to *necessity* or the indispensability of any designated part to the aesthetic whole.

Unity is expressed in the methodology of portraiture as surely as in the research portrait. Just as the close attention to each separate part of the portrait is obscured from the reader through the invisibility of seams, so too is the methodology of portraiture, which we have so closely studied part by part, in the end a seamless endeavor. Enriched by carefully constructed *context,* expressed through thoughtfully modulated *voice,* informed by cautiously guarded *relationships,* and organized into scrupulously selected *themes,* the research portrait is the result of a seamless synthesis of rigorous procedures that unite in an expressive *aesthetic whole.* Just as the portrait (product) is perceived as one unified whole, so too is the methodology of portraiture (process) performed as a unified endeavor.

Artistic Refrain

Achieving Balance

Jessica Hoffmann Davis

The drawings of Happy by five-year-old David and professional artist Henry (pp. 276–277) demonstrate symmetrical balance according to Arnheim's description: in a symmetrical composition, forms are balanced from side to side and top to bottom around the center of the drawing.

The drawing of Alone by artist Carol (p. 278), like the drawing of Sad by artist Linda (p. 279), demonstrates asymmetrical balance: an uneven distribution of form around the center of the drawing. Notably, none of these portrayals adheres to the schema of symmetrical or asymmetrical balance with the single purpose of following those respective plans.

The artist teacher Nicolaides is clear on the danger of following rules for the sake of adhering to a plan:

> You do not start with the rules of composition. You start with the gesture which gives the design. It is wrong to make a plan first and then fill the plan with activity. The activity should come first. One sees murals in which workers are about to hit each other over the head with their pickaxes instead of hitting the earth. In such paintings the plan came first. The plan should grow out of the activity, out of what is happening. The pattern grows out of a concrete and actual condition.
>
> No matter how interesting the mechanics of composition are, they lead you to nothing. You can cold-bloodedly create a

Five-year-old David's drawing of Happy

Adult artist Henry's drawing of Happy

Adult artist Carol's drawing of Alone

Adult artist Linda's drawing of Sad

> composition with which there is no apparent fault, but what of
> it? Diagrams without a real objective search are meaningless,
> and that search must be touched by the thing called the creative
> impulse, which is willing at all times seemingly to destroy the
> rules. When you become self-conscious about rules, they
> impose limitations upon you [1941, p. 151].

In all four drawings, the rules of symmetrical and asymmetrical balance serve the artist's intentions; the artist does not self-consciously follow the rules for their own sake. For David and Henry, the subject or overarching idea of their drawings of Happy is appropriately expressed by their symmetrically balanced compositions. David's bold, smiling figure is balanced in every quadrant with, for example, an eye for an eye and winged shapes on either side of the central form. This secure and comfortably balanced whole is resonant with the joyful interpretation of the emotion it represents. Similarly, Henry's equally curving blissful lines are everywhere balanced across the page. The stable symmetrical spread of open lines is resonant with the artist's understanding of the emotion of Happy.

Carol's interpretation of Alone relies entirely on the composition of the drawing for the conveyance of its meaning. A small darkly inked square (the only mark in the aesthetic space) is balanced by the vastness of space that surrounds it. The careful placement of that square in meaningful relationship to the other empty parts of the whole enables the drawing to be perceived all at once: "Yes, of course. Alone." There is no "yes, but" about the resonance of the overarching interpretation achieved by the purposefully adapted application of a compositional schema.

Linda's drawing of Sad demonstrates asymmetrical balance in which the shapes at the top of the page are balanced by the absence of shape in the remaining two-thirds of the aesthetic space. Linda's intent was not to create asymmetrical balance, but to aptly embody the resonance of sadness in a carefully composed and unified representation. Like artists, portraitists can benefit from schemata such as the generic outline—but they can never be ruled by them. Portraitists must follow the rules that ensure empirical rigor in their portrayals, but they must be ready to rewrite or adapt the standards of aesthetic schemata so as to authentically recreate the gestalts of their interpretations.

The four drawings presented here all satisfy the portraitist's mandates for resonance, coherence, and necessity. Arnheim rewrites Aristotle's criterion of necessity as follows: "Any part of a whole must remain incomplete in its meaning and form. It must be in need of the whole. Otherwise it will be self-sufficient and closed—a foreign body, which can do without its environment and therefore cannot endure it, since art must exclude everything that is not necessary" (1962, p. 44).

Consider artist Carol's portrayal of Alone. Cover the small square with your hand. Does the drawing still resonate with the gestalt of alone? Imagine Henry's all-over spread of happy lines without the lines in the lower left quadrant of the aesthetic space. Would the drawing still aptly convey the emotion of Happy? Reversing the test for necessity as Arnheim suggests, isolate the eyes of young David's figure as forms on their own. Do those dotted circles sufficiently express the overarching theme of the drawing? No. The circles say little on their own and instead rely for meaning on their rakish placement within the context of the other carefully selected shapes. It is only in concert with one another that the separate parts of all these drawings achieve their resonant expression of meaning as coherent and unified aesthetic wholes.

Like artists who apply or break rules intentionally and five-year-olds who may do either with less deliberation, portraitists need to carefully reflect on the reasons for the inclusion of each separate part of their portrayals as well as the relationship among all parts and the overall whole. Beyond the careful consideration of parts and whole that may be facilitated by a thoughtful schema, portraitists need to understand and embrace their own interpretations both all at once and in relation to the subjects or sites they represent.

The overarching vision must be commensurate with the gestalt of the subject or site and with the particular composition of the overall portrayal. It is only when the portraitist has achieved such unity of interpretation that the reader will find and comprehend the work as an aesthetic whole. As Arnheim explains, "Thinking requires more than the formation and assignment of concepts. It calls for the unraveling of relations, for the disclosure of elusive structure. Image making serves to make sense of the world" (1969, p. 257).

It is in the sense of the world that the portrait makes for general readers and for actors at a site that the methodology of portraiture draws its real strength and allows the portraitist to reciprocate the kindness of welcomed study with the gift of the final portrait.

REFERENCES

Aristotle. (1951 ed.). *Theory of poetry and fine art* (S. H. Butcher, Trans.). New York: Dover.

Arnheim, R. (1962). *The genesis of a painting: Picasso's Guernica.* Berkeley: University of California Press.

Arnheim, R. (1966). *Toward a psychology of art.* Berkeley: University of California Press.

Arnheim, R. (1969). *Visual thinking.* London: Faber & Faber.

Arnheim, R. (1974). *Art and visual perception: A psychology of the creative eye.* Berkeley: University of California Press.

Arnheim, R. (1988). *The power of the center: A study of composition in the visual arts.* Berkeley: University of California Press.

Belenky, M., Clinchy, B., Goldberger, N., & Tarule, J. (1986). *Women's ways of knowing: The development of self, voice, and mind.* New York: Basic Books.

Bernstein, R. J. (1992). *The new constellation: The ethical-political horizons of modernity/postmodernity.* Cambridge, MA: MIT Press.

Bogdan, R., & Biklen, S. K. (1992). *Qualitative research for education: An introduction to theory and methods* (2nd ed.). Needham Heights, MA: Allyn & Bacon.

Britzman, D. (1991). *Practice makes perfect: A critical study of learning to teach.* Albany: State University of New York Press.

Brown, L., et al. (1987). *A guide to reading narratives of moral conflict and choice for self and moral voice* (Monograph No. 2). Cambridge, MA: Center for the Study of Gender, Education, and Human Development, Harvard University.

Buber, M. (1958). *I and thou* (2nd ed.). New York: Scribner.

Carter, K. (1993). The place of story in the study of teaching and teacher education. *Educational Researcher, 22*(1), 5–12, 18.

Davis, J. (1991). "Sketch of the Children's Art Carnival." Unpublished manuscript. Cambridge, MA: Project Co-Arts data.

Davis, J. (1993a). *The Co-Arts assessment handbook.* Cambridge, MA: Harvard Project Zero, Harvard University.

Davis, J. (1993b). Why Sally can draw. In E. Eisner (Ed.), *Educational horizons, visual learning: In the mind's eye.* Bloomington, IN: Pi Lambda Theta.

Davis, J. (1996). Drawing demise: U-shaped development in graphic symbolization. In *Studies in art education.* Gainesville, FL: University of Florida Press.

Davis, J., Soep, E., Maira, S., Remba, N., & Putnoi, D. (1993). *Safe havens: Portraits of educational effectiveness in community art centers that focus on education in economically disadvantaged communities.* Cambridge, MA: Harvard Project Zero, Harvard University.

Davis, J., Solomon, B., Eppel, M., & Dameshek, W. (1996). *The wheel in motion: The Co-Arts assessment plan from theory to practice.* Cambridge, MA: Harvard Project Zero, Harvard University.

Davis, J., et al. (1996). *Another safe haven: Portraits of Boulevard Arts Center: Then and now.* Cambridge, MA: Harvard Project Zero, Harvard University.

Dewey, J. (1958). *Art as experience.* New York: Capricorn. (Original work published 1934)

Dewey, J. (1980). *The quest for certainty: A study of the relation of knowledge and action.* New York: Penguin Books.

Eisner, E. W. (1985). *The educational imagination: On the design and evaluation of school programs* (2nd ed.). New York: Macmillan.

Eliot, T. S. (1920). *The sacred wood: Essays on poetry and criticism.* London: Methuen.

Featherstone, J. (1989). To make the wounded whole. *Harvard Educational Review, 59,* 367–378.

Freedman, S., Jackson, J., & Boles, K. (1983). Teaching: An imperiled "profession." In L. Shulman & G. Sykes (Eds.), *Handbook of teaching and policy* (pp. 261–299). White Plains, NY: Longman.

Freeman, D. (1996). "To take them at their word": Language data in the study of teachers' knowledge. *Harvard Educational Review, 66,* 732–761.

Gardner, H. (1980). *Artful scribbles.* New York: Basic Books.

Geertz, C. (1973). *The interpretation of cultures.* New York: Basic Books.

Gilligan, C. (1982). *In a different voice: Psychological theory and women's development.* Cambridge, MA: Harvard University Press.

Gilligan, C., Brown, L. M., & Rogers, A. G. (1989). Psyche embedded: A place for body, relationships, and culture in personality theory. In A. Rubin, R. Zucker, R. Emmons, & S. Frank (Eds.), *Studying persons and lives* (pp. 86–147). New York: Springer.

Glaser, B. G., & Straus, A. S. (1967). *The discovery of grounded theory: Strategies for qualitative research.* New York: Aldine De Gruyter.

Glesne, C., & Peshkin, A. (1992). *Becoming qualitative researchers: An introduction.* White Plains, NY: Longman.

Goetz, J. P., & LeCompte, M. D. (1984). *Ethnography and qualitative design in educational research.* Orlando: Academic Press.

Gombrich, E. H. (1969). *Art and illusion: A study in the psychology of pictorial representation.* The A. W. Mellon Lectures in the Fine Arts, 1956. Princeton, NJ: Princeton University Press.

Gombrich, E. H. (1984). *The story of art.* Englewood, NJ: Phaidon Press.

Goodman, N. (1976). *Languages of art.* Indianapolis, IN: Hackett.

Goodman, N. (1978). *Ways of worldmaking.* Indianapolis, IN: Hackett.

Guba, E. G. (1978). *Toward a methodology of naturalistic inquiry in educational evaluation.* Los Angeles: Center for the Study of Evaluation, Graduate School of Education, University of California.

Jackson, M. (1989). *Paths toward a clearing: Radical empiricism and ethnographic inquiry.* Bloomington, IN: University of Indiana Press.

James, W. (1904). Humanism and Truth. *Mind,* xiii, n.s., 52.

James, W. (1978). *Pragmatism: A new name for some old ways of thinking.* Cambridge, MA: Harvard University Press.

Kaiser, J., Davis, J., & Dameshek, W. (1995). *Partners in portraiture: An account of the collaborative work of projects PRISM and Co-Arts.* Paper prepared for the National Association of Bilingual Education 1995 Conference, presented in Phoenix, Arizona, February.

Kidder, T. (1982). Face validity from multiple perspectives. In D. Brinberg & L. Kidder (Eds.), *Forms of validity in research.* New Directions for Methodology of Social and Behavioral Science, no. 12, pp. 41–57. San Francisco: Jossey-Bass.

Lather, P. (1991). *Getting smart: Feminist research and pedagogy with/in the postmodern.* New York: Routledge.

Lawrence-Lightfoot, S. (1983). *The good high school: Portraits of character and culture.* New York: Basic Books.

Lawrence-Lightfoot, S. (1994). *I've known rivers: Lives of loss and liberation.* Reading, MA: Addison-Wesley.

Lodge, D. (1992). *The art of fiction.* Hammondsworth, England: Penguin Books.

Madden, D. (1980). *A primer of the novel for readers and writers.* Metuchen, NJ: Scarecrow Press.

Malinowski, B. (1938). The problem of meaning in primitive languages. In C. U. Ogden & I. A. Richards (Eds.), *The meaning of meaning* (pp. 296–336). Orlando: Harcourt, Brace.

Marshall, C., & Rossman, G. (1989). *Designing qualitative research.* Thousand Oaks, CA: Sage.

Maxwell, J. A. (1996). *Qualitative research design: An interactive approach.* Thousand Oaks, CA: Sage.

May, R. (1939). *The art of counseling.* Nashville, TN: Abingdon.

Miles, M. B., & Huberman, A. M. (1994). *Qualitative data analysis: An expanded sourcebook* (2nd ed.). Thousand Oaks, CA: Sage.

Mishler, E. G. (1979). Meaning in context: Is there any other kind? *Harvard Educational Review, 49,* 1–19.

Moss, P. A. (1996). Enlarging the dialogue in educational measurement: Voices from interpretive research traditions. *Educational Researcher,* January/February, pp. 20–28, 43.

Nicolaides, K. (1941). *The natural way to draw.* Boston: Houghton Mifflin.

Nielsen, J. M. (Ed.). (1990). *Feminist research methods: Exemplary reading in the social sciences.* Boulder, CO: Westview Press.

Oakley, A. (1981). Interviewing women: A contradiction in terms. In H. Roberts (Ed.), *Doing feminist research,* pp. 30–61. New York: Routledge.

Parsons, M. J. (1992). Cognition as interpretation in art education. In B. Reimer & R. S. Smith (Eds.), *The arts, education and aesthetic knowing, ninety-first yearbook of the National Society for the Study of Education. Part II.* Chicago: University of Chicago Press.

Powell, K. (1995). *Musicianship at the Community Music Center of Boston: Nurturing artistic identity in adolescents in class collection.* Student papers for H–126: Perspectives on the Development and Education of the Child as Artist, Jessica Davis, Instructor, Harvard Graduate School of Education, Spring.

Rampersod, A. (1976). *The art and imagination of W.E.B. DuBois.* Cambridge, MA: Harvard University Press.

Rogers, C. (1942). *Counseling and psychotherapy.* Cambridge, MA: Riverside Press.

Rorty, R. (1979). *Philosophy and the mirror of nature.* Princeton, NJ: Princeton University Press.

Rorty, R. (1982). *Consequences of pragmatism: Essays, 1972–1980.* Minneapolis: University of Minnesota Press.

Sacks, O. (1985). *The man who mistook his wife for a hat and other clinical tales.* New York: Summit Books.

Seidman, I. E. (1991). *Interviewing as qualitative research.* New York: Teachers College Press.

Taylor, J. C. (1981). *Learning to look: A handbook for the visual arts.* Chicago: University of Chicago Press.

Terkel, S. (1976). *Naturalistic approaches to the study of human experience* (videotaped interview). WFMT Radio, Chicago.

Trilling, L. (1965). *Beyond culture.* New York: Viking.

Welty, E. (1983). *One writer's beginnings.* Cambridge, MA: Harvard University Press.

Whitehead, A. N. (1947). *Essays in science and philosophy.* New York: Philosophical Library.

Wilde, O. (1890). *The picture of Dorian Gray.* Philadelphia: Lippincott.

Williams, I. (Ed.). (1970). *Novel and romance, 1700–1800: A documentary record.* New York: Barnes and Noble.

INDEX